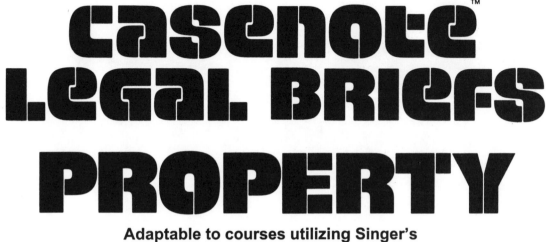

PROPERTY

Adaptable to courses utilizing Singer's
casebook on Property Law

NORMAN S. GOLDENBERG, SENIOR EDITOR
PETER TENEN, MANAGING EDITOR

STAFF WRITERS

INGE VAN HERLE
PATRICIA P. LAIACONA
DAVID J. GYEPES
DAVID KNOBLOCK

PUBLISHED BY CASENOTES PUBLISHING CO., INC. 1640 5th ST., SUITE 208 SANTA MONICA, CA 90401

ISBN 0-87457-221-5

FORMAT OF THE CASENOTE LEGAL BRIEF

CASE CAPSULE: This bold-faced section (first three paragraphs) highlights the procedural nature of the case, a short summary of the facts, and the rule of law. This is an invaluable quick-review device designed to refresh the student's memory for classroom discussion and exam preparation.

NATURE OF CASE: This section identifies the form of action (e.g., breach of contract, negligence, battery), the type of proceeding (e.g., demurrer, appeal from trial court's jury instructions) and the relief sought (e.g., damages, injunction, criminal sanctions).

FACT SUMMARY: The fact summary is included to refresh the student's memory. It can be used as a quick reminder of the facts when the student is chosen by an instructor to brief a case.

CONCISE RULE OF LAW: This portion of the brief summarizes the general principle of law that the case illustrates. Like the fact summary, it is included to refresh the student's memory. It may be used for instant recall of the court's holding and for classroom discussion or home review.

FACTS: This section contains all relevant facts of the case, including the contentions of the parties and the lower court holdings. It is written in a logical order to give the student a clear understanding of the case. The plaintiff and defendant are identified by their proper names throughout and are always labeled with a (P) or (D).

ISSUE: The issue is a concise question that brings out the essence of the opinion as it relates to the section of the casebook in which the case appears. Both substantive and procedural issues are included if relevant to the decision.

HOLDING AND DECISION: This section offers a clear and in-depth discussion of the rule of the case and the court's rationale. It is written in easy-to-understand language. When relevant, it includes a thorough discussion of the exceptions listed by the court, the concurring and dissenting opinions, and the names of the judges.

CONCURRENCE / DISSENT: All concurrences and dissents are briefed whenever they are included by the casebook editor.

EDITOR'S ANALYSIS: This last paragraph gives the student a broad understanding of where the case "fits in" with other cases in the section of the book and with the entire course. It is a hornbook-style discussion indicating whether the case is a majority or minority opinion and comparing the principal case with other cases in the casebook. It may also provide analysis from restatements, uniform codes, and law review articles. The editor's analysis will prove to be invaluable to classroom discussion.

CROSS-REFERENCE TO OUTLINE: Wherever possible, following each case is a cross-reference linking the subject matter of the issue to the appropriate place in the *Casenote Law Outline*, which provides further information on the subject.

WINTER v. G.P. PUTNAM'S SONS
938 F.2d 1033 (1991).

NATURE OF CASE: Appeal from summary judgment in a products liability action.

FACT SUMMARY: Winter (P) relied on a book on mushrooms published by Putnam (D) and became critically ill after eating a poisonous mushroom.

CONCISE RULE OF LAW: Strict products liability is not applicable to the expressions contained within a book.

FACTS: Winter (P) purchased The Encyclopedia of Mushrooms, a book published by Putnam (D), to help in collecting and eating wild mushrooms. In 1988, Winter (P), relying on descriptions in the book, ate some wild mushrooms which turned out to be poisonous. Winter (P) became so ill he required a liver transplant. He brought a strict products liability action against Putnam (D), alleging that the book contained erroneous and misleading information that caused his injury. Putnam (D) responded that the information in the book was not a product for purposes of strict products liability, and the trial court granted its motion for summary judgment. The trial court also rejected Winter's (P) actions for negligence and misrepresentation. Winter (P) appealed.

ISSUE: Is strict products liability applicable to the expressions contained within a book?

HOLDING AND DECISION: (Sneed, J.) No. Strict products liability is not applicable to the expressions contained within a book. Products liability is geared toward tangible objects. The expression of ideas is governed by copyright, libel, and misrepresentation laws. The Restatement (Second) of Torts lists examples of the items that are covered by §402A strict liability. All are tangible items, such as tires or automobiles. There is no indication that the doctrine should be expanded beyond this area. Furthermore, there is a strong public interest in the unfettered exchange of ideas. The threat of liability without fault could seriously inhibit persons who wish to share thoughts and ideas with others. Although some courts have held that aeronautical charts are products for purposes of strict liability, these charts are highly technical tools which resemble compasses. The Encyclopedia of Mushrooms, published by Putnam (D), is a book of pure thought and expression and therefore does not constitute a product for purposes of strict liability. Additionally, publishers do not owe a duty to investigate the contents of books that they distribute. Therefore, a negligence action may not be maintained by Winter (P) against Putnam (D). Affirmed.

EDITOR'S ANALYSIS: This decision is in accord with the rulings in most jurisdictions. See Alm v. Nostrand Reinhold Co., Inc., 480 N.E. 2d 1263 (Ill. 1985). The court also stated that since the publisher is not a guarantor of the accuracy of an author's statements, an action for negligent misrepresentation could not be maintained. The elements of negligent misrepresentation are stated in § 311 of the Restatement (Second) of Torts.

[For more information on misrepresentation, see Casenote Law Outline on Torts, Chapter 12, § III, Negligent Misrepresentation.]

NOTE TO THE STUDENT

OUR GOAL. It is the goal of Casenotes Publishing Company, Inc. to create and distribute the finest, clearest and most accurate legal briefs available. To this end, we are constantly seeking new ideas, comments and constructive criticism. As a user of *Casenote Legal Briefs,* your suggestions will be highly valued. With all correspondence, please include your complete name, address, and telephone number, including area code and zip code.

THE TOTAL STUDY SYSTEM. Casenote Legal Briefs are just one part of the Casenotes TOTAL STUDY SYSTEM. Most briefs are (wherever possible) cross-referenced to the appropriate *Casenote Law Outline,* which will elaborate on the issue at hand. By purchasing a Law Outline together with your Legal Brief, you will have both parts of the Casenotes TOTAL STUDY SYSTEM. (See the advertising in the front of this book for a list of Law Outlines currently available.)

A NOTE ABOUT LANGUAGE. Please note that the language used in *Casenote Legal Briefs* in reference to minority groups and women reflects terminology used within the historical context of the time in which the respective courts wrote the opinions. We at Casenotes Publishing Co., Inc. are well aware of and very sensitive to the desires of all people to be treated with dignity and to be referred to as they prefer. Because such preferences change from time to time, and because the language of the courts reflects the time period in which opinions were written, our case briefs will not necessarily reflect contemporary references. We appreciate your understanding and invite your comments.

A NOTE REGARDING NEW EDITIONS. As of our press date, this Casenote Legal Brief is current and includes briefs of all cases in the current version of the casebook, divided into chapters that correspond to that edition of the casebook. However, occasionally a new edition of the casebook comes out in the interim, and sometimes the casebook author will make changes in the sequence of the cases in the chapters, add or delete cases, or change the chapter titles. Should you be using this Legal Brief in conjuction with a casebook that was issued later than this book, you can receive all of the newer cases, which are available free from us, by sending in the "Supplement Request Form" in this section of the book (please follow all instructions on that form). The Supplement(s) will contain all the missing cases, and will bring your Casenote Legal Brief up to date.

EDITOR'S NOTE. Casenote Legal Briefs are intended to supplement the student's casebook, not replace it. There is no substitute for the student's own mastery of this important learning and study technique. If used properly, *Casenote Legal Briefs* are an effective law study aid that will serve to reinforce the student's understanding of the cases.

SUPPLEMENT REQUEST FORM

At the time this book was printed, a brief was included for every major case in the casebook and for every existing supplement to the casebook. However, if a new supplement to the casebook (or a new edition of the casebook) has been published since this publication was printed and if that casebook supplement (or new edition of the casebook) was available for sale at the time you purchased this Casenote Legal Briefs book, we will be pleased to provide you the new cases contained therein AT NO CHARGE when you send us a stamped, self-addressed envelope.

TO OBTAIN YOUR FREE SUPPLEMENT MATERIAL, **YOU MUST FOLLOW THE INSTRUCTIONS BELOW PRECISELY** OR YOUR REQUEST WILL NOT BE ACKNOWLEDGED!

1. Please check if there is in fact an existing supplement and, if so, that the cases are not already included in your Casenote Legal Briefs. Check the main table of cases as well as the supplement table of cases, if any.

2. **REMOVE THIS ENTIRE PAGE FROM THE BOOK.** You MUST send this ORIGINAL page to receive your supplement. This page acts as your proof of purchase and contains the reference number necessary to fill your supplement request properly. No photocopy of this page or written request will be honored or answered. Any request from which the reference number has been removed, altered or obliterated will not be honored.

3. Prepare a STAMPED self-addressed envelope for return mailing. Be sure to use a FULL SIZE (9 X 12) ENVELOPE (MANILA TYPE) so that the supplement will fit and AFFIX ENOUGH POSTAGE TO COVER 3 OZ. **ANY SUPPLEMENT REQUEST NOT ACCOMPANIED BY A STAMPED SELF-ADDRESSED ENVELOPE WILL ABSOLUTELY NOT BE FILLED OR ACKNOWLEDGED.**

4. MULTIPLE SUPPLEMENT REQUESTS: If you are ordering more than one supplement, we suggest that you enclose a stamped, self-addressed envelope for each supplement requested. If you enclose only one envelope for a multiple request, your order may not be filled immediately should any supplement which you requested still be in production. In other words, your order will be held by us until it can be filled completely.

5. Casenotes prints two kinds of supplements. A "New Edition" supplement is issued when a new edition of your casebook is published. A "New Edition" supplement gives you all major cases found in the new edition of the casebook which did not appear in the previous edition. A regular "supplement" is issued when a paperback supplement to your casebook is published. If the box at the lower right is stamped, then the "New Edition" supplement was provided to your bookstore and is *not* available from Casenotes; however, Casenotes will still send you any regular "supplements" which have been printed either before or after the new edition of your casebook appeared and which, according to the reference number at the top of this page, have not been included in this book. If the box is not stamped, Casenotes will send you any supplements, "New Edition" and/or regular, needed to completely update your Casenote Legal Briefs.

NOTE: REQUESTS FOR SUPPLEMENTS WILL NOT BE FILLED UNLESS THESE INSTRUCTIONS ARE COMPLIED WITH!

6. Fill in the following information:

    Full title of CASEBOOK _____ **PROPERTY** _____

    _____

    CASEBOOK author's name _____ **Singer** _____

    _____

    Date of new supplement you are requesting _____

    _____

    Name and location of bookstore where this Casenote Legal Brief

    was purchased _____

    _____

    Name and location of law school you attend _____

    _____

    Any comments regarding Casenote Legal Briefs _____

    _____

NOTE: IF THIS BOX IS STAMPED, NO NEW EDITION SUPPLEMENT CAN BE OBTAINED BY MAIL.

PUBLISHED BY CASENOTES PUBLISHING CO., INC. 1640 5th ST, SUITE 208 SANTA MONICA, CA 90401

PLEASE PRINT

NAME _____ PHONE _____ DATE _____

ADDRESS/CITY/STATE/ZIP _____

Announcing the First *Totally Integrated* Law Study System

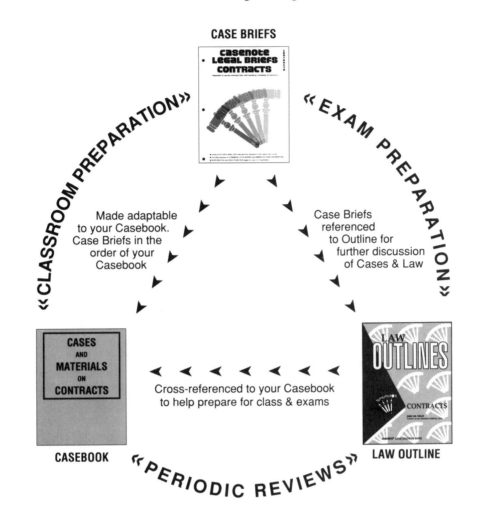

CASE BRIEFS

casenote LeGaL Briefs contracts

«CLASSROOM PREPARATION»

«EXAM PREPARATION»

Made adaptable to your Casebook. Case Briefs in the order of your Casebook

Case Briefs referenced to Outline for further discussion of Cases & Law

CASES AND MATERIALS ON CONTRACTS

Cross-referenced to your Casebook to help prepare for class & exams

LAW OUTLINES CONTRACTS

CASEBOOK

«PERIODIC REVIEWS»

LAW OUTLINE

Casenotes Integrated Study System Makes Studying Easier and More Effective Than Ever!

Casenotes has just made studying easier and more effective than ever before, because we've done the work for you! Through our exclusive integrated study system, most briefs found in this volume of Casenote Legal Briefs are cross-referenced to the corresponding area of law in the Casenote Law Outline series. The cross-reference immediately follows the Editor's Analysis at the end of the brief, and it will direct you to the corresponding chapter and section number in the Casenote Law Outline for further information on the case or the area of law.

This cross-referencing feature will enable you to make the most effective use of your time. While each Casenote Law

Outline focuses on a particular subject area of the law, each legal briefs volume is adapted to a specific casebook. Now, with cross-referencing of Casenote Legal Briefs to Casenote Law Outlines, you can have the best of both worlds – briefs for all major cases in your casebooks and easy-to-find, easy-to-read explanations of the law in our Law Outline series. Casenote Law Outlines are authored exclusively by law professors who are nationally recognized authorities in their field. So using Casenote Law Outlines is like studying with the top law professors.

Try Casenotes new totally integrated study system and see just how easy and effective studying can be.

Casenotes Integrated Study System Does The Work For You!

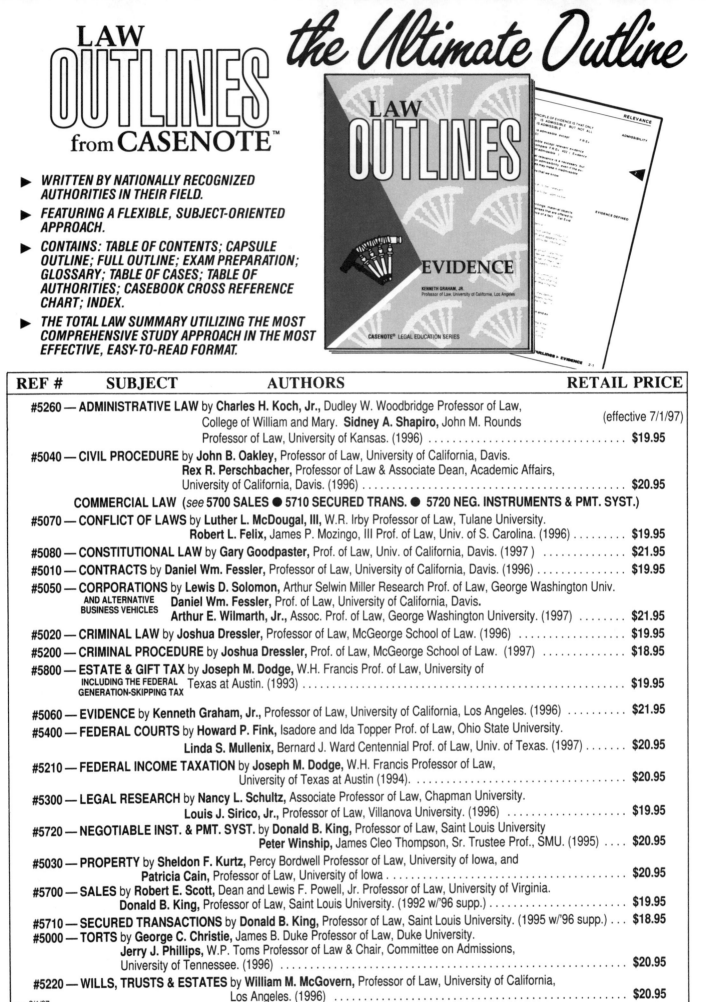

CASENOTE™ LEGAL BRIEFS

PRICE LIST — EFFECTIVE JULY 1, 1997 • PRICES SUBJECT TO CHANGE WITHOUT NOTICE

Ref. No.	Course	Adaptable to Courses Utilizing	Retail Price
1265	ADMINISTRATIVE LAW	BONFIELD & ASIMOV	17.00
1263	ADMINISTRATIVE LAW	BREYER, STEWART & SUNSTEIN	19.00
1266	ADMINISTRATIVE LAW	CASS, DIVER & BEERMAN	17.00
1260	ADMINISTRATIVE LAW	GELLHORN, B., S., R., S. & F.	17.00
1264	ADMINISTRATIVE LAW	MASHAW, MERRILL & SHANE	18.50
1267	ADMINISTRATIVE LAW	REESE	17.00
1262	ADMINISTRATIVE LAW	SCHWARTZ	18.00
1290	ADMIRALTY	HEALY & SHARPE	21.00
1350	AGENCY & PARTNERSHIP (ENT.ORG)	CONARD, KNAUSS & SIEGEL	21.00
1351	AGENCY & PARTNERSHIP	HYNES	20.00
1281	ANTITRUST (TRADE REGULATION)	HANDLER, P., G., & W.	17.50
1283	ANTITRUST	SULLIVAN & HOVENKAMP	18.00
1611	BANKING LAW	MACEY & MILLER	17.00
1303	BANKRUPTCY (DEBTOR-CREDITOR)	EISENBERG	19.00
1040	CIVIL PROCEDURE	COUND, F., M. & S	20.00
1043	CIVIL PROCEDURE	FIELD, KAPLAN & CLERMONT	20.00
1041	CIVIL PROCEDURE	HAZARD, TAIT & FLETCHER	19.00
1047	CIVIL PROCEDURE	MARCUS, REDISH & SHERMAN	19.00
1044	CIVIL PROCEDURE	ROSENBERG, S. & D.	20.00
1046	CIVIL PROCEDURE	YEAZELL	17.00
1311	COMM'L LAW	FARNSWORTH, H., R., H. & M.	19.00
1312	COMM'L LAW	JORDAN & WARREN	19.00
1310	COMM'L LAW (SALES/SEC.TR./PAY.LAW [Sys.])	SPEIDEL, SUMMERS & WHITE	22.00
1313	COMM'L LAW (SALES/SEC.TR./PAY.LAW)	WHALEY	19.00
1320	COMMUNITY PROPERTY	BIRD	17.50
1630	COMPARATIVE LAW	SCHLESINGER, B., D., & H.	16.00
1048	COMPLEX LITIGATION	MARCUS & SHERMAN	17.00
1072	CONFLICTS	BRILMAYER	17.00
1071	CONFLICTS	CRAMTON, C. K., & K.	17.00
1070	CONFLICTS	ROSENBERG, HAY & W.	20.00
1086	CONSTITUTIONAL LAW	BREST & LEVINSON	18.00
1082	CONSTITUTIONAL LAW	COHEN & VARAT	21.00
1088	CONSTITUTIONAL LAW	FARBER, ESKRIDGE & FRICKEY	18.00
1080	CONSTITUTIONAL LAW	GUNTHER & SULLIVAN	20.00
1081	CONSTITUTIONAL LAW	LOCKHART, K., C., S. & F.	18.00
1085	CONSTITUTIONAL LAW	ROTUNDA	20.00
1087	CONSTITUTIONAL LAW	STONE, S., S. & T.	19.00
1102	CONTRACTS	BURTON	20.00
1017	CONTRACTS	CALAMARI, PERILLO & BENDER	23.00
1101	CONTRACTS	CRANDALL & WHALEY	20.00
1014	CONTRACTS	DAWSON, HARVEY & H.	19.00
1010	CONTRACTS	FARNSWORTH & YOUNG	18.00
1011	CONTRACTS	FULLER & EISENBERG	20.00
1100	CONTRACTS	HAMILTON, RAU & WEINTRAUB	19.00
1013	CONTRACTS	KESSLER, GILMORE & KRONMAN	23.00
1016	CONTRACTS	KNAPP & CRYSTAL	20.50
1012	CONTRACTS	MURPHY & SPEIDEL	22.00
1018	CONTRACTS	MURRAY	22.00
1015	CONTRACTS	ROSETT	21.00
1019	CONTRACTS	VERNON	20.00
1502	COPYRIGHT	GOLDSTEIN	18.00
1501	COPYRIGHT	NIMMER, M., M., & N.	19.50
1218	CORPORATE TAXATION	LIND, S. L. & R	14.00
1050	CORPORATIONS	CARY & EISENBERG	19.00
1054	CORPORATIONS	CHOPER, COFFEE, & GILSON	21.50
1350	CORPORATIONS (ENTERPRISE ORG.)	CONARD, KNAUSS & SIEGEL	21.00
1053	CORPORATIONS	HAMILTON	19.00
1057	CORPORATIONS	O'KELLEY & THOMPSON	18.00
1056	CORPORATIONS	SOLOMON, S., B., & W.	19.00
1052	CORPORATIONS	VAGTS	17.00
1300	CREDITOR'S RIGHTS (DEBTOR-CREDITOR)	RIESENFELD	21.00
1550	CRIMINAL JUSTICE	WEINREB	18.00
1029	CRIMINAL LAW	BONNIE, C., J., & L.	17.00
1020	CRIMINAL LAW	BOYCE & PERKINS	22.00
1028	CRIMINAL LAW	DRESSLER	21.00
1027	CRIMINAL LAW	JOHNSON	20.00
1021	CRIMINAL LAW	KADISH & SCHULHOFER	19.00
1026	CRIMINAL LAW	KAPLAN, WEISBERG & BINDER	18.00
1023	CRIMINAL LAW	LAFAVE	19.00
1205	CRIMINAL PROCEDURE	ALLEN, KUHNS & STUNTZ	17.00
1202	CRIMINAL PROCEDURE	HADDAD, Z., S. & B.	20.00
1200	CRIMINAL PROCEDURE	KAMISAR, LAFAVE & ISRAEL	19.00
1204	CRIMINAL PROCEDURE	SALTZBURG & CAPRA	17.00
1203	CRIMINAL PROCEDURE (PROCESS)	WEINREB	18.50
1303	DEBTOR-CREDITOR	EISENBERG	19.00
1300	DEBTOR-CREDITOR (CRED. RTS.)	RIESENFELD	21.00
1304	DEBTOR-CREDITOR	WARREN & WESTBROOK	19.00
1224	DECEDENTS ESTATES	RITCHIE, ALFORD, EFFLAND & D.	21.00
1222	DECEDENTS ESTATES	SCOLES & HALBACH	21.50
1231	DECEDENTS ESTATES (TRUSTS)	WAGGONER, A. & F.	20.00
	DOMESTIC RELATIONS (see FAMILY LAW)		
3000	EDUCATION LAW (COURSE OUTLINE)	AQUILA & PETZKE	25.50
1670	EMPLOYMENT DISCRIMINATION	FRIEDMAN & STRICKLER	17.00
1671	EMPLOYMENT DISCRIMINATION	ZIMMER, SULLIVAN, R. & C.	18.00
1660	EMPLOYMENT LAW	ROTHSTEIN, KNAPP & LIEBMAN	19.50
1350	ENTERPRISE ORGANIZATION	CONARD, KNAUSS & SIEGEL	21.00
1342	ENVIRONMENTAL LAW	ANDERSON, MANDELKER & T.	16.00
1341	ENVIRONMENTAL LAW	FINDLEY & FARBER	18.00
1345	ENVIRONMENTAL LAW	MENELL & STEWART	17.00
1344	ENVIRONMENTAL LAW	PERCIVAL, MILLER, S. & L.	18.00
1343	ENVIRONMENTAL LAW	PLATER, ABRAMS & GOLDFARB	17.00
	EQUITY (see REMEDIES)		
1217	ESTATE & GIFT TAXATION	BITTKER, CLARK & McCOUCH	15.00
	ETHICS (see PROFESSIONAL RESPONSIBILITY)		
1065	EVIDENCE	GREEN & NESSON	20.00

Ref. No.	Course	Adaptable to Courses Utilizing	Retail Price
1066	EVIDENCE	MUELLER & KIRKPATRICK	17.00
1064	EVIDENCE	STRONG, BROUN & M.	22.50
1062	EVIDENCE	SUTTON & WELLBORN	22.00
1061	EVIDENCE	WALTZ & PARK	20.00
1060	EVIDENCE	WEINSTEIN, M., A. & B.	22.50
1244	FAMILY LAW (DOMESTIC RELATIONS)	AREEN	22.00
1242	FAMILY LAW (DOMESTIC RELATIONS)	CLARK & GLOWINSKY	19.00
1245	FAMILY LAW (DOMESTIC RELATIONS)	ELLMAN, KURTZ & BARTLETT	20.00
1243	FAMILY LAW (DOMESTIC RELATIONS)	KRAUSE	24.00
1240	FAMILY LAW (DOMESTIC RELATIONS)	WADLINGTON	20.00
1231	FAMILY PROPERTY LAW (WILLS/TRUSTS)	WAGGONER, A. & F.	20.00
1362	FEDERAL COURTS	CURRIE	17.00
1360	FEDERAL COURTS	FALLON, M. & S. (HART & W.)	19.00
1360	FEDERAL COURTS	HART & WECHSLER (FALLON)	19.00
1363	FEDERAL COURTS	LOW & JEFFRIES	16.00
1361	FEDERAL COURTS	McCORMICK, C. & W.	20.00
1364	FEDERAL COURTS	REDISH & NICHOL	17.00
1510	GRATUITOUS TRANSFERS	CLARK, LUSKY & MURPHY	18.00
1650	HEALTH LAW	FURROW, J., J., & S.	17.50
1640	IMMIGRATION LAW	ALEINIKOFF, MARTIN & M.	16.00
1641	IMMIGRATION LAW	LEGOMSKY	18.00
1371	INSURANCE LAW	KEETON	21.00
1372	INSURANCE LAW	YORK, WHELAN & MARTINEZ	19.00
1370	INSURANCE LAW	YOUNG & HOLMES	17.00
1394	INTERNATIONAL BUSINESS TRANSACTIONS	FOLSOM, GORDON & SPANOGLE	15.00
1393	INTERNATIONAL LAW	CARTER & TRIMBLE	16.00
1392	INTERNATIONAL LAW	HENKIN, P., S. & S.	17.00
1390	INTERNATIONAL LAW	OLIVER, F., B., S., & W.	22.00
1331	LABOR LAW	COX, BOK, GORMAN & FINKIN	19.00
1332	LABOR LAW	HARPER & ESTREICHER	20.00
1333	LABOR LAW	LESLIE	18.50
1330	LABOR LAW	MERRIFIELD, S. & C.	19.00
1471	LAND FINANCE (REAL ESTATE TRANS)	BERGER & JOHNSTONE	18.00
1620	LAND FINANCE (REAL ESTATE TRANS)	NELSON & WHITMAN	19.00
1452	LAND USE	CALLIES, FREILICH & ROBERTS	17.00
1450	LAND USE	WRIGHT & GITELMAN	23.00
1421	LEGISLATION	ESKRIDGE & FRICKEY	15.00
1480	MASS MEDIA	FRANKLIN & ANDERSON	15.00
1312	NEGOTIABLE INSTRUMENTS (COMM. LAW)	JORDAN & WARREN	19.00
1313	NEGOTIABLE INSTRUMENTS (COMM. LAW)	WHALEY	18.00
1541	OIL & GAS	KUNTZ, L., A. & S.	18.00
1540	OIL & GAS	MAXWELL, WILLIAMS, M. & K.	18.00
1560	PATENT LAW	FRANCIS & COLLINS	23.00
1310	PAYMENT LAW [SYST.][COMM. LAW]	SPEIDEL, SUMMERS & WHITE	22.00
1313	PAYMENT LAW (COMM.LAW / NEG. INST.)	WHALEY	19.00
1431	PRODUCTS LIABILITY	OWEN, MONTGOMERY & K.	20.00
1091	PROF. RESPONSIBILITY (ETHICS)	GILLERS	13.00
1093	PROF. RESPONSIBILITY (ETHICS)	HAZARD, KONIAK, & CRAMTON	18.00
1092	PROF. RESPONSIBILITY (ETHICS)	MORGAN & ROTUNDA	13.00
1030	PROPERTY	CASNER & LEACH	21.00
1031	PROPERTY	CRIBBET, J., F. & S.	21.50
1037	PROPERTY	DONAHUE, KAUPER & MARTIN	18.00
1035	PROPERTY	DUKEMINIER & KRIER	18.00
1034	PROPERTY	HAAR & LIEBMAN	20.50
1036	PROPERTY	KURTZ & HOVENKAMP	19.00
1033	PROPERTY	NELSON, STOEBUCK, & W.	20.50
1032	PROPERTY	RABIN & KWALL	20.00
1038	PROPERTY	SINGER	18.50
1621	REAL ESTATE TRANSACTIONS	GOLDSTEIN & KORNGOLD	18.00
1471	REAL ESTATE TRANS. & FIN. (LAND FINANCE)	BERGER & JOHNSTONE	18.00
1620	REAL ESTATE TRANSFER & FINANCE	NELSON & WHITMAN	18.00
1254	REMEDIES (EQUITY)	LAYCOCK	20.00
1253	REMEDIES (EQUITY)	LEAVELL, L., N. & K/F.	21.00
1252	REMEDIES (EQUITY)	RE & RE	23.00
1255	REMEDIES (EQUITY)	SHOBEN & TABB	22.50
1250	REMEDIES (EQUITY)	YORK, BAUMAN & RENDLEMAN	25.00
1312	SALES (COMM. LAW)	JORDAN & WARREN	19.00
1310	SALES (COMM. LAW)	SPEIDEL, SUMMERS & WHITE	22.00
1313	SALES (COMM. LAW)	WHALEY	19.00
1312	SECURED TRANS. (COMM. LAW)	JORDAN & WARREN	19.00
1310	SECURED TRANS.	SPEIDEL, SUMMERS & WHITE	22.00
1313	SECURED TRANS. (COMM. LAW)	WHALEY	19.00
1272	SECURITIES REGULATION	COX, HILLMAN, LANGEVOORT	18.00
1270	SECURITIES REGULATION	JENNINGS, MARSH & COFFEE	18.00
1680	SPORTS LAW	WEILER & ROBERTS	17.50
1217	TAXATION (ESTATE & GIFT)	BITTKER, CLARK & McCOUCH	15.00
1219	TAXATION (INDIV. INC.)	BURKE & FRIEL	19.00
1212	TAXATION (FED. INC.)	FREELAND, LIND & STEPHENS	18.00
1211	TAXATION (FED. INC.)	GRAETZ & SCHENK	17.00
1210	TAXATION (FED. INC.)	KLEIN & BANKMAN	18.00
1218	TAXATION (CORPORATE)	LIND, S., L. & R.	14.00
1006	TORTS	DOBBS	19.00
1003	TORTS	EPSTEIN	20.50
1004	TORTS	FRANKLIN & RABIN	17.50
1001	TORTS	HENDERSON, P. & S.	20.50
1000	TORTS	PROSSER, W., S., K., & P.	24.00
1005	TORTS	SHULMAN, JAMES & GRAY	22.00
1281	TRADE REGULATION (ANTITRUST)	HANDLER, P., G., & W.	17.50
1230	TRUSTS	BOGERT, O., H., & H.	20.50
1231	TRUSTS/WILLS (FAMILY PROPERTY LAW)	WAGGONER, A. & F.	20.00
1410	U.C.C.	EPSTEIN, MARTIN, H. & N.	15.00
1223	WILLS, TRUSTS & ESTATES	DUKEMINIER & JOHANSON	19.00
1220	WILLS	MECHEM & ATKINSON	20.00
1231	WILLS/TRUSTS (FAMILY PROPERTY LAW)	WAGGONER, A. & F.	20.00

(SERIES XL)

CASENOTES PUBLISHING CO. INC. ● 1640 FIFTH STREET, SUITE 208 ● SANTA MONICA, CA 90401 ● (310) 395-6500

E-Mail Address- casenote@westworld.com
Website-http://www.casenotes.com

PLEASE PURCHASE FROM YOUR LOCAL BOOKSTORE. IF UNAVAILABLE, YOU MAY ORDER DIRECT.*
4TH CLASS POSTAGE (ALLOW TWO WEEKS) $1.00 PER ORDER; 1ST CLASS POSTAGE $3.00 (ONE BOOK), $2.00 EACH (TWO OR MORE BOOKS)
*CALIF. RESIDENTS PLEASE ADD 8¼% SALES TAX

A GLOSSARY OF COMMON LATIN WORDS AND PHRASES
ENCOUNTERED IN THE LAW

A FORTIORI: Because one fact exists or has been proven, therefore a second fact that is related to the first fact must also exist.

A PRIORI: From the cause to the effect. A term of logic used to denote that when one generally accepted truth is shown to be a cause, another particular effect must necessarily follow.

AB INITIO: From the beginning; a condition which has existed throughout, as in a marriage which was void ab initio.

ACTUS REUS: The wrongful act; in criminal law, such action sufficient to trigger criminal liability.

AD VALOREM: According to value; an ad valorem tax is imposed upon an item located within the taxing jurisdiction calculated by the value of such item.

AMICUS CURIAE: Friend of the court. Its most common usage takes the form of an amicus curiae brief, filed by a person who is not a party to an action but is nonetheless allowed to offer an argument supporting his legal interests.

ARGUENDO: In arguing. A statement, possibly hypothetical, made for the purpose of argument, is one made arguendo.

BILL QUIA TIMET: A bill to quiet title (establish ownership) to real property.

BONA FIDE: True, honest, or genuine. May refer to a person's legal position based on good faith or lacking notice of fraud (such as a bona fide purchaser for value) or to the authenticity of a particular document (such as a bona fide last will and testament).

CAUSA MORTIS: With approaching death in mind. A gift causa mortis is a gift given by a party who feels certain that death is imminent.

CAVEAT EMPTOR: Let the buyer beware. This maxim is reflected in the rule of law that a buyer purchases at his own risk because it is his responsibility to examine, judge, test, and otherwise inspect what he is buying.

CERTIORARI: A writ of review. Petitions for review of a case by the United States Supreme Court are most often done by means of a writ of certiorari.

CONTRA: On the other hand. Opposite. Contrary to.

CORAM NOBIS: Before us; writs of error directed to the court that originally rendered the judgment.

CORAM VOBIS: Before you; writs of error directed by an appellate court to a lower court to correct a factual error.

CORPUS DELICTI: The body of the crime; the requisite elements of a crime amounting to objective proof that a crime has been committed.

CUM TESTAMENTO ANNEXO, ADMINISTRATOR (ADMINISTRATOR C.T.A.): With will annexed; an administrator c.t.a. settles an estate pursuant to a will in which he is not appointed.

DE BONIS NON, ADMINISTRATOR (ADMINISTRATOR D.B.N.): Of goods not administered; an administrator d.b.n. settles a partially settled estate.

DE FACTO: In fact; in reality; actually. Existing in fact but not officially approved or engendered.

DE JURE: By right; lawful. Describes a condition that is legitimate "as a matter of law," in contrast to the term "de facto," which connotes something existing in fact but not legally sanctioned or authorized. For example, de facto segregation refers to segregation brought about by housing patterns, etc., whereas de jure segregation refers to segregation created by law.

DE MINIMUS: Of minimal importance; insignificant; a trifle; not worth bothering about.

DE NOVO: Anew; a second time; afresh. A trial de novo is a new trial held at the appellate level as if the case originated there and the trial at a lower level had not taken place.

DICTA: Generally used as an abbreviated form of obiter dicta, a term describing those portions of a judicial opinion incidental or not necessary to resolution of the specific question before the court. Such nonessential statements and remarks are not considered to be binding precedent.

DUCES TECUM: Refers to a particular type of writ or subpoena requesting a party or organization to produce certain documents in their possession.

EN BANC: Full bench. Where a court sits with all justices present rather than the usual quorum.

EX PARTE: For one side or one party only. An ex parte proceeding is one undertaken for the benefit of only one party, without notice to, or an appearance by, an adverse party.

EX POST FACTO: After the fact. An ex post facto law is a law that retroactively changes the consequences of a prior act.

EX REL.: Abbreviated form of the term ex relatione, meaning, upon relation or information. When the state brings an action in which it has no interest against an individual at the instigation of one who has a private interest in the matter.

FORUM NON CONVENIENS: Inconvenient forum. Although a court may have jurisdiction over the case, the action should be tried in a more conveniently located court, one to which parties and witnesses may more easily travel, for example.

GUARDIAN AD LITEM: A guardian of an infant as to litigation, appointed to represent the infant and pursue his/her rights.

HABEAS CORPUS: You have the body. The modern writ of habeas corpus is a writ directing that a person (body) being detained (such as a prisoner) be brought before the court so that the legality of his detention can be judicially ascertained.

IN CAMERA: In private, in chambers. When a hearing is held before a judge in his chambers or when all spectators are excluded from the courtroom.

IN FORMA PAUPERIS: In the manner of a pauper. A party who proceeds in forma pauperis because of his poverty is one who is allowed to bring suit without liability for costs.

INFRA: Below, under. A word referring the reader to a later part of a book. (The opposite of supra.)

IN LOCO PARENTIS: In the place of a parent.

IN PARI DELICTO: Equally wrong; a court of equity will not grant requested relief to an applicant who is in pari delicto, or as much at fault in the transactions giving rise to the controversy as is the opponent of the applicant.

IN PARI MATERIA: On like subject matter or upon the same matter. Statutes relating to the same person or things are said to be in pari materia. It is a general rule of statutory construction that such statutes should be construed together, i.e., looked at as if they together constituted one law.

IN PERSONAM: Against the person. Jurisdiction over the person of an individual.

IN RE: In the matter of. Used to designate a proceeding involving an estate or other property.

IN REM: A term that signifies an action against the res, or thing. An action in rem is basically one that is taken directly against property, as distinguished from an action in personam, i.e., against the person.

INTER ALIA: Among other things. Used to show that the whole of a statement, pleading, list, statute, etc., has not been set forth in its entirety.

INTER PARTES: Between the parties. May refer to contracts, conveyances or other transactions having legal significance.

INTER VIVOS: Between the living. An inter vivos gift is a gift made by a living grantor, as distinguished from bequests contained in a will, which pass upon the death of the testator.

IPSO FACTO: By the mere fact itself.

JUS: Law or the entire body of law.

LEX LOCI: The law of the place; the notion that the rights of parties to a legal proceeding are governed by the law of the place where those rights arose.

MALUM IN SE: Evil or wrong in and of itself; inherently wrong. This term describes an act that is wrong by its very nature, as opposed to one which would not be wrong but for the fact that there is a specific legal prohibition against it (malum prohibitum).

MALUM PROHIBITUM: Wrong because prohibited, but not inherently evil. Used to describe something that is wrong because it is expressly forbidden by law but that is not in and of itself evil, e.g., speeding.

MANDAMUS: We command. A writ directing an official to take a certain action.

MENS REA: A guilty mind; a criminal intent. A term used to signify the mental state that accompanies a crime or other prohibited act. Some crimes require only a general mens rea (general intent to do the prohibited act), but others, like assault with intent to murder, require the existence of a specific mens rea.

MODUS OPERANDI: Method of operating; generally refers to the manner or style of a criminal in committing crimes, admissible in appropriate cases as evidence of the identity of a defendant.

NEXUS: A connection to.

NISI PRIUS: A court of first impression. A nisi prius court is one where issues of fact are tried before a judge or jury.

N.O.V. (NON OBSTANTE VEREDICTO): Notwithstanding the verdict. A judgment n.o.v. is a judgment given in favor of one party despite the fact that a verdict was returned in favor of the other party, the justification being that the verdict either had no reasonable support in fact or was contrary to law.

NUNC PRO TUNC: Now for then. This phrase refers to actions that may be taken and will then have full retroactive effect.

PENDENTE LITE: Pending the suit; pending litigation underway.

PER CAPITA: By head; beneficiaries of an estate, if they take in equal shares, take per capita.

PER CURIAM: By the court; signifies an opinion ostensibly written "by the whole court" and with no identified author.

PER SE: By itself, in itself; inherently.

PER STIRPES: By representation. Used primarily in the law of wills to describe the method of distribution where a person, generally because of death, is unable to take that which is left to him by the will of another, and therefore his heirs divide such property between them rather than take under the will individually.

PRIMA FACIE: On its face, at first sight. A prima facie case is one that is sufficient on its face, meaning that the evidence supporting it is adequate to establish the case until contradicted or overcome by other evidence.

PRO TANTO: For so much; as far as it goes. Often used in eminent domain cases when a property owner receives partial payment for his land without prejudice to his right to bring suit for the full amount he claims his land to be worth.

QUANTUM MERUIT: As much as he deserves. Refers to recovery based on the doctrine of unjust enrichment in those cases in which a party has rendered valuable services or furnished materials that were accepted and enjoyed by another under circumstances that would reasonably notify the recipient that the rendering party expected to be paid. In essence, the law implies a contract to pay the reasonable value of the services or materials furnished.

QUASI: Almost like; as if; nearly. This term is essentially used to signify that one subject or thing is almost analogous to another but that material differences between them do exist. For example, a quasi-criminal proceeding is one that is not strictly criminal but shares enough of the same characteristics to require some of the same safeguards (e.g., procedural due process must be followed in a parol hearing).

QUID PRO QUO: Something for something. In contract law, the consideration, something of value, passed between the parties to render the contract binding.

RES GESTAE: Things done; in evidence law, this principle justifies the admission of a statement that would otherwise be hearsay when it is made so closely to the event in question as to be said to be a part of it, or with such spontaneity as not to have the possibility of falsehood.

RES IPSA LOQUITUR: The thing speaks for itself. This doctrine gives rise to a rebuttable presumption of negligence when the instrumentality causing the injury was within the exclusive control of the defendant, and the injury was one that does not normally occur unless a person has been negligent.

RES JUDICATA: A matter adjudged. Doctrine which provides that once a court of competent jurisdiction has rendered a final judgment or decree on the merits, that judgment or decree is conclusive upon the parties to the case and prevents them from engaging in any other litigation on the points and issues determined therein.

RESPONDEAT SUPERIOR: Let the master reply. This doctrine holds the master liable for the wrongful acts of his servant (or the principal for his agent) in those cases in which the servant (or agent) was acting within the scope of his authority at the time of the injury.

STARE DECISIS: To stand by or adhere to that which has been decided. The common law doctrine of stare decisis attempts to give security and certainty to the law by following the policy that once a principle of law as applicable to a certain set of facts has been set forth in a decision, it forms a precedent which will subsequently be followed, even though a different decision might be made were it the first time the question had arisen. Of course, stare decisis is not an inviolable principle and is departed from in instances where there is good cause (e.g., considerations of public policy led the Supreme Court to disregard prior decisions sanctioning segregation).

SUPRA: Above. A word referring a reader to an earlier part of a book.

ULTRA VIRES: Beyond the power. This phrase is most commonly used to refer to actions taken by a corporation that are beyond the power or legal authority of the corporation.

ADDENDUM OF FRENCH DERIVATIVES

IN PAIS: Not pursuant to legal proceedings.

CHATTEL: Tangible personal property.

CY PRES: Doctrine permitting courts to apply trust funds to purposes not expressed in the trust but necessary to carry out the settlor's intent.

PER AUTRE VIE: For another's life; in property law, an estate may be granted that will terminate upon the death of someone other than the grantee.

PROFIT A PRENDRE: A license to remove minerals or other produce from land.

VOIR DIRE: Process of questioning jurors as to their predispositions about the case or parties to a proceeding in order to identify those jurors displaying bias or prejudice.

HOW TO BRIEF A CASE

A. DECIDE ON A FORMAT AND STICK TO IT

Structure is essential to a good brief. It enables you to arrange systematically the related parts that are scattered throughout most cases, thus making manageable and understandable what might otherwise seem to be an endless and unfathomable sea of information. There are, of course, an unlimited number of formats that can be utilized. However, it is best to find one that suits your needs and stick to it. Consistency breeds both efficiency and the security that when called upon you will know where to look in your brief for the information you are asked to give.

Any format, as long as it presents the essential elements of a case in an organized fashion, can be used. Experience, however, has led *Casenotes* to develop and utilize the following format because of its logical flow and universal applicability.

NATURE OF CASE: This is a brief statement of the legal character and procedural status of the case (e.g., "Appeal of a burglary conviction").

There are many different alternatives open to a litigant dissatisfied with a court ruling. The key to determining which one has been used is to discover *who is asking this court for what.*

This first entry in the brief should be kept as *short as possible.* The student should use the court's terminology if the student understands it. But since jurisdictions vary as to the titles of pleadings, the best entry is the one that apprises the student of who wants what in this proceeding, not the one that sounds most like the court's language.

CONCISE RULE OF LAW: A statement of the general principle of law that the case illustrates (e.g., "An acceptance that varies any term of the offer is considered a rejection and counteroffer").

Determining the rule of law of a case is a procedure similar to determining the issue of the case. Avoid being fooled by red herrings; there may be a few rules of law mentioned in the case excerpt, but usually only one is *the* rule with which the casebook editor is concerned. The techniques used to locate the issue, described below, may also be utilized to find the rule of law. Generally, your best guide is simply the chapter heading. It is a clue to the point the casebook editor seeks to make and should be kept in mind when reading every case in the respective section.

FACTS: A synopsis of only the essential facts of the case, i.e., those bearing upon or leading up to the issue.

The facts entry should be a short statement of the events and transactions that led one party to initiate legal proceedings against another in the first place. While some cases conveniently state the salient facts at the beginning of the decision, in other instances they will have to be culled from hiding places throughout the text, even from concurring and dissenting opinions. Some of the "facts" will often be in dispute and should be so noted. Conflicting evidence may be briefly pointed up. "Hard" facts must be included. Both must be *relevant* in order to be listed in the facts entry. It is impossible to tell what is relevant until the entire case is read, as the ultimate determination of the rights and liabilities of the parties may turn on something buried deep in the opinion.

The facts entry should never be longer than one to three *short* sentences.

It is often helpful to identify the role played by a party in a given context. For example, in a construction contract case the identification of a party as the "contractor" or "builder" alleviates the need to tell that that party was the one who was supposed to have built the house.

It is always helpful, and a good general practice, to identify the "plaintiff" and the "defendant." This may seem elementary and uncomplicated, but, especially in view of the creative editing practiced by some casebook editors, it is sometimes a difficult or even impossible task. Bear in mind that the *party presently* seeking something from this court may not be the plaintiff, and that sometimes only the cross-claim of a defendant is treated in the excerpt. Confusing or misaligning the parties can ruin your analysis and understanding of the case.

ISSUE: A statement of the general legal question answered by or illustrated in the case. For clarity, the issue is best put in the form of a question capable of a "yes" or "no" answer. In reality, the issue is simply the Concise Rule of Law put in the form of a question (e.g., "May an offer be accepted by performance?").

The major problem presented in discerning what is *the* issue in the case is that an opinion usually purports to raise and answer several questions. However, except for rare cases, only one such question is really the issue in the case. Collateral issues not necessary to the resolution of the matter in controversy are handled by the court by language known as *"obiter dictum"* or merely *"dictum."* While dicta may be included later in the brief, it has no place under the issue heading.

To find the issue, the student again asks *who wants what* and then goes on to ask *why did that party succeed or fail in getting it.* Once this is determined, the "why" should be turned into a question.

The complexity of the issues in the cases will vary, but in all cases a single-sentence question should sum up the issue. *In a few cases,* there will be two, or even more rarely, three issues of equal importance to the resolution of the case. Each should be expressed in a single-sentence question.

Since many issues are resolved by a court in coming to a final disposition of a case, the casebook editor will reproduce the portion of the opinion containing the issue or issues most relevant to the area of law under scrutiny. A noted law professor gave this advice: "Close the book; look at the title on the cover." Chances are, if it is Property, the student need not concern himself with whether, for example, the federal government's treatment of the plaintiff's land really raises a federal question sufficient to support jurisdiction on this ground in federal court.

The same rule applies to chapter headings designating sub-areas within the subjects. They tip the student off as to what the text is designed to teach. The cases are arranged in a casebook to show a progression or development of the law, so that the preceding cases may also help.

It is also most important to remember to *read the notes and questions* at the end of a case to determine what the editors wanted the student to have gleaned from it.

HOLDING AND DECISION: This section should succinctly explain the rationale of the court in arriving at its decision. In capsulizing the "reasoning" of the court, it should always include an application of the general rule or rules of law to the specific facts of the case. Hidden justifications come to light in this entry; the reasons for the state of the law, the public policies, the biases and prejudices, those considerations that influence the justices' thinking and, ultimately, the outcome of the case. At the end, there should be a short indication of the disposition or procedural resolution of the case (e.g., "Decision of the trial court for Mr. Smith (P) reversed").

The foregoing format is designed to help you "digest" the reams of case material with which you will be faced in your law school career. Once mastered by practice, it will place at your fingertips the information the authors of your casebooks have sought to impart to you in case-by-case illustration and analysis.

B. BE AS ECONOMICAL AS POSSIBLE IN BRIEFING CASES

Once armed with a format that encourages succinctness, it is as important to be economical with regard to the time spent on the actual reading of the case as it is to be economical in the writing of the brief itself. This does not mean "skimming" a case. Rather, it means reading the case with an "eye" trained to recognize into which "section" of your brief a particular passage or line fits and having a system for quickly and precisely marking the case so that the passages fitting any one particular part of the brief can be easily identified and brought together in a concise and accurate manner when the brief is actually written.

It is of no use to simply repeat everything in the opinion of the court; the student should only record enough information to trigger his or her recollection of what the court said. Nevertheless, an accurate statement of the "law of the case," i.e., the legal principle applied to the facts, is absolutely essential to class preparation and to learning the law under the case method.

To that end, it is important to develop a "shorthand" that you can use to make margin notations. These notations will tell you at a glance in which section of the brief you will be placing that particular passage or portion of the opinion.

Some students prefer to underline all the salient portions of the opinion (with a pencil or colored underliner marker), making marginal notations as they go along. Others prefer the color-coded method of underlining, utilizing different colors of markers to underline the salient portions of the case, each separate color being used to represent a different section of the brief. For example, blue underlining could be used for passages relating to the concise rule of law, yellow for those relating to the issue, and green for those relating to the holding and decision, etc. While it has its advocates, the color-coded method can be confusing and time-consuming (all that time spent on changing colored markers). Furthermore, it can interfere with the continuity and concentration many students deem essential to the reading of a case for maximum comprehension. In the end, however, it is a matter of personal preference and style. Just remember, whatever method you use, underlining must be used sparingly or its value is lost.

For those who take the marginal notation route, an efficient and easy method is to go along underlining the key portions of the case and placing in the margin alongside them the following "markers" to indicate where a particular passage or line "belongs" in the brief you will write:

N   (NATURE OF CASE)
CR   (CONCISE RULE OF LAW)
I   (ISSUE)
HC   (HOLDING AND DECISION, relates to the CONCISE RULE OF LAW behind the decision)
HR   (HOLDING AND DECISION, gives the RATIONALE or reasoning behind the decision)
HA   (HOLDING AND DECISION, APPLIES the general principle(s) of law to the facts of the case
        to arrive at the decision)

Remember that a particular passage may well contain information necessary to more than one part of your brief, in which case you simply note that in the margin. If you are using the color-coded underlining method instead of margin notation, simply make asterisks or checks in the margin next to the passage in question in the colors that indicate the additional sections of the brief where it might be utilized.

The economy of utilizing "shorthand" in marking cases for briefing can be maintained in the actual brief writing process itself by utilizing "law student shorthand" within the brief. There are many commonly used words and phrases for which abbreviations can be substituted in your briefs (and in your class notes also). You can develop abbreviations that are personal to you and which will save you a lot of time. A reference list of briefing abbreviations will be found elsewhere in this book.

C.   USE BOTH THE BRIEFING PROCESS AND THE BRIEF AS A LEARNING TOOL

Now that you have a format and the tools for briefing cases efficiently, the most important thing is to make the time spent in briefing profitable to you and to make the most advantageous use of the briefs you create. Of course, the briefs are invaluable for classroom reference when you are called upon to explain or analyze a particular case. However, they are also useful in reviewing for exams. A quick glance at the fact summary should bring the case to mind, and a rereading of the concise rule of law should enable you to go over the underlying legal concept in your mind, how it was applied in that particular case, and how it might apply in other factual settings.

As to the value to be derived from engaging in the briefing process itself, there is an immediate benefit that arises from being forced to sift through the essential facts and reasoning from the court's opinion and to succinctly express them in your own words in your brief. The process ensures that you understand the case and the point that it illustrates, and that means you will be ready to absorb further analysis and information brought forth in class. It also ensures you will have something to say when called upon in class. The briefing process helps develop a mental agility for getting to the *gist* of a case and for identifying, expounding on, and applying the legal concepts and issues found there. Of most immediate concern, that is the mental process on which you must rely in taking law school examinations. Of more lasting concern, it is also the mental process upon which a lawyer relies in serving his clients and in making his living.

TABLE OF CASES

Continued on next page

TABLE OF CASES (Continued)

CHAPTER 1
COMPETING CLAIMS TO ORIGINAL ACQUISITION AND
ALLOCATION OF PROPERTY RIGHTS

QUICK REFERENCE RULES OF LAW

1. **Property Rights Derived from Competing Sovereigns.** The act of discovery gives the discovering sovereign the power to extinguish the native title of occupancy. (Johnson v. M'Intosh)

    [For more information on possession and title, see Casenote Law Outline on Property, Chapter 3, § III, The Conflict between Possession and the Ability to Convey Good Title.]

2. **Forced Seizures of Property from American Indian Nations.** Mere possession does not constitute ownership for the purposes of the Fifth Amendment. (Tee-Hit-Ton Indians v. United States)

    [For more information on possession and ownership, see Casenote Law Outline on Property, Chapter 3, § III, The Conflict between Possession and the Ability to Convey Good Title.]

3. **Wild Animals.** Property in wild animals is only acquired by occupancy, and pursuit alone does not constitute occupancy or vest any right in the pursuer. (Pierson v. Post)

    [For more information on property rights in wild animals, see Casenote Law Outline on Property, Chapter 2, § I, Acquisition of Property Rights in Animals.]

4. **Oil and Gas.** The law of capture does not insulate a landowner from damages caused by the wrongful drainage of gas and distillate from beneath the land of another. (Elliff v. Texon Drilling Co.)

    [For more information on the application of capture to oil and gas, see Casenote Law Outline on Property, Chapter 2, § I, Acquisition of Property Rights in Animals.]

5. **News.** Publication for profit of news obtained from other news-gathering enterprises is a misappropriation of a property right. (International News Service v. Associated Press)

6. **Human Genes.** A person does not have a property interest in his cell tissue. (Moore v. Regents of the University of California)

    [For more information on property rights in body parts, see Casenote Law Outline on Property, Chapter 2, § IV, Property Right in Human Body Parts and Fetus.]

7. **Distribution of the House on Divorce.** A division of a marital estate that favors one party over the other may be acceptable if there is reason for it. (In re Marriage of King)

8. **American Indian Cultural Objects: Tribal Property or "Finders Keepers?"** Ownership in burial artifacts cannot be transferred to another under the theory of abandonment. (Charrier v. Bell)

    [For more information on abandoned property, see Casenote Law Outline on Property, Chapter 2, § II, Lost, Mislaid, and Abandoned Property.]

9. **Relativity of Title.** One in possession of land has title superior to all others except the actual, rightful titleholder. (Tapscott v. Lessee of Cobbs)

    [For more information on prior possession of real property, see Casenote Law Outline on Property, Chapter 3, § II, Application of Principle Protecting Prior Possession to Real Property.]

10. Unjust Enrichment versus Forced Sale. An improver who mistakenly improves the land of another is entitled to the value of the improvement which the landowner has benefited from. (Somerville v. Jacobs)

[For more information on title by adverse possession, see Casenote Law Outline on Property, Chapter 4, § II, Five Criteria to Acquire Title by Adverse Possession.]

11. Vacant Land. Whether a claimant's physical acts upon the land of another are sufficiently continuous, notorious and exclusive does not necessarily depend on the existence of significant improvements, substantial activity, or absolute exclusivity. (Nome 2000 v. Fagerstrom)

[For more information on acquisition of title by adverse possession, see Casenote Law Outline on Property, Chapter 4, § II, Five Criteria to Acquire Title by Adverse Possession.]

12. Border Disputes. The doctrine of tacking allows parties claiming adverse possession to use their predecessors' conduct on the property to meet the time requirements of adverse possession. (Brown v. Gobble)

[For more information on the doctrine of tacking, see Casenote Law Outline on Property, Chapter 4, § II, Five Criteria to Acquire Title by Adverse Possession.]

13. Prescriptive Easements. A general outline of consistent use is sufficient to establish a prescriptive easement. (Community Feed Store, Inc. v. Northeastern Culvert Corp.)

[For more information on prescriptive easements, see Casenote Law Outline on Property, Chapter 8, § II, Easements.]

JOHNSON v. M'INTOSH

Yes

21 U.S. (8 Wheat.) 543 (1823).

NATURE OF CASE: Appeal from action of ejectment.

FACT SUMMARY: Johnson (P) claimed title to a parcel of land through a grant from Native Americans, while M'Intosh (D) claimed the land based on a grant from the newly formed United States government.

CONCISE RULE OF LAW: The act of discovery gives the discovering sovereign the power to extinguish the native title of occupancy.

FACTS: In 1763 the King of Britain proclaimed that no British subject could purchase or acquire the land reserved to Native Americans. In 1775, the Tabac Indians conveyed a tract of land in Virginia to Louis Vivant. Thomas Jefferson succeeded to a portion of the lands acquired by Louis Vivant and willed it to his heir Johnson (P) upon his death. In 1776, the colony of Virginia declared its independence from British rule and subsequently acceded to the United States. Fourteen years later, the United States government sold the land in question to M'Intosh (D), who then took possession of the land. Johnson (P) brought an action for ejectment against M'Intosh (D) based on his prior claim. The trial court ruled against Johnson (P), and he appealed.

ISSUE: Does the act of discovery give the discovering sovereign the power to extinguish the native title of occupancy?

HOLDING AND DECISION: (Marshall, C.J.) Yes. The act of discovery gives the discovering sovereign the power to extinguish the native title of occupancy. Although the British government acknowledged Indian possession of the land by the act of discovery they retained the right to terminate that possession at any time. The Tabac Indians, at most, had the right to convey possession. The discovering country held title to the land. The United States took over Great Britain's claim to title by treaty and, thus, was the party with the authority to transfer the title. Therefore, Johnson (P) was not granted valid title. Affirmed.

EDITOR'S ANALYSIS: The Court claims to be applying a kinder rule than that of conquest because it is admitting the existence of an Indian right to occupy the land. However, the Court then states that right to possession is only valid so long as the Indians were peaceful inhabitants, thereby immediately negating their rights. Moreover, since absolute title cannot exist at the same time in different governments over the same land, the Court reasons that it would be inconsistent to vest absolute title in the Indians as a distinct nation and country.

[For more information on possession and title, see Casenote Law Outline on Property, Chapter 3, § III, The Conflict between Possession and the Ability to Convey Good Title.]

TEE-HIT-TON INDIANS v. UNITED STATES

Yes

348 U.S. 272 (1955).

NATURE OF CASE: Appeal from claim of a taking under the Fifth Amendment.

FACT SUMMARY: The Tee-Hit-Tons (P) claimed that the United States government's contract to sell Alaskan timber constituted a taking of their property.

CONCISE RULE OF LAW: Mere possession does not constitute ownership for the purposes of the Fifth Amendment.

FACTS: The Tee-Hit-Ton Indians (P) claimed that they had exercised property rights in the Alaskan territories since time immemorial. Since before the Russian came to Alaska the Tee-Hit-Tons (P) communally owned the land, occupied its expanse, and passed ownership rights thorough the female line. When the Russians came to Alaska, they occupied the same land with the Tee-Hit-Ton's (P) permission. In 1951, the federal government (D) began selling timber in the Alaskan territories to private entities. The Tee-Hit-Tons (P) brought suit under the Takings Clause of the Fifth Amendment of the U.S. Constitution. The Court of Claims found no ownership rights. The Tee-Hit Tons (P) appealed, and the Supreme Court granted certiorari.

ISSUE: Does mere possession constitute ownership for the purposes of the Fifth Amendment?

HOLDING AND DECISION: (Reed, J.) No. Mere possession does not constitute ownership for the purposes of the Fifth Amendment. The Tee-Hit-Tons (P) claimed that their use of the land differed from other native Americans because they claimed tribal ownership, and this constitutes ownership requiring compensation. The Alaskan Indians' use of land might be more substantial than that of other North American Indian tribes, but it only gives rise to the level of sovereignty, not ownership. The U.S. Constitution does not require compensation without a showing of a property right. The Tee-Hit-Tons (P) do not make out ownership. Thus their claim must be denied. Affirmed.

EDITOR'S ANALYSIS: In 1971 Congress passed the Alaska Native Claims Settlement Act, which compensated Alaskan natives for the taking of their lands without recognizing any actual property rights on their part. Congress ultimately reimbursed the tribes $962.5 million in order to extinguish 335 million land claims. It also transferred forty million acres of federal land as part of the settlement.

[For more information on possession and ownership, see Casenote Law Outline on Property, Chapter 3, § III, The Conflict between Possession and the Ability to Convey Good Title.]

PIERSON v. POST *yes*

N.Y. Sup. Ct., 3 Caines 175 (1805).

NATURE OF CASE: Action of trespass on the case.

FACT SUMMARY: Post (P) was hunting a fox. Pierson (D), knowing this, killed the fox and carried it off.

CONCISE RULE OF LAW: Property in wild animals is only acquired by occupancy, and pursuit alone does not constitute occupancy or vest any right in the pursuer.

FACTS: Post (P) found a fox upon certain wild, uninhabited, unpossessed wasteland. He and his dogs began hunting and pursuing the fox. Knowing that the fox was being hunted by Post (P) and within Post's (P) view, Pierson (D) killed the fox and carried it off.

ISSUE: Has a person in pursuit of a wild animal acquired such a right to or property in the wild animal as to sustain an action against a person who kills and carries away the animal, knowing of the former's pursuit?

HOLDING AND DECISION: (Per curiam) No. Property in wild animals is acquired by occupancy only. Mere pursuit vests no right in the pursuer. One authority holds that actual bodily seizure is not always necessary to constitute possession of wild animals. The mortal wounding of an animal or the trapping or intercepting of animals so as to deprive them of their natural liberty will constitute occupancy. However, here, Post (P) only showed pursuit. Hence, there was no occupancy or legal right vested in Post (P), and the fox became Pierson's (D) property when he killed and carried it off. The purpose of this rule is that if the pursuit of animals without wounding them or restricting their liberty were held to constitute a basis for an action against others for intercepting and killing the animals, "it would prove a fertile source of quarrels and litigation."

DISSENT: (Livingston, J.) A new rule should be adopted — that property in wild animals may be acquired without bodily touch, provided the pursuer be in reach or have a reasonable prospect of taking the animals.

EDITOR'S ANALYSIS: The ownership of wild animals is in the state for the benefit of all its people. A private person cannot acquire exclusive rights to a wild animal except by taking and reducing it to actual possession in a lawful manner or by a grant from the government. After the animal has been lawfully subjected to control, the ownership becomes absolute as long as the restraint lasts. Mere ownership of the land that an animal happens to be on does not constitute such a reduction of possession as to give the landowner a property right in the animal, except as against a mere trespasser who goes on such land for the purpose of taking the animal.

[For more information on property rights in wild animals, see Casenote Law Outline on Property, Chapter 2, § I, Acquisition of Property Rights in Animals.]

NOTES:

ELLIFF v. TEXON DRILLING CO. ✓es
210 S.W.2d 558 (Tex. 1948).

NATURE OF CASE: Appeal from reversal of award of damages in negligence action.

FACT SUMMARY: Texon (D) argued that it should not be liable to the Elliffs (D) after it caused severe damage to the Elliff's oil drilling operations.

CONCISE RULE OF LAW: The law of capture does not insulate a landowner from damages caused by the wrongful drainage of gas and distillate from beneath the land of another.

FACTS: Texon (D) was drilling for oil on land adjacent to the Elliffs' (P) land. The Elliffs (P) owned the surface of their land, as well as an interest in the oil and gas underlying it. They too were involved in drilling on their own land. Texon's (D) well blew out, cratered and caught fire. The Elliffs' (P) well was destroyed as a result of this blowout, as was the surface of their land, some of their cattle, and a great portion of the underlying mineral reservoir. The Elliffs (P) brought suit for damages, claiming that the blowout was caused by Texon's (D) negligent failure to use the proper drilling mud. The trial court awarded damages. The Court of appeals reversed and remanded, stating that the Elliffs (P) could not receive damages for the loss of the mineral estate based on the law of capture since they had no rights in the gas once it migrated from their land. The Elliffs (P) appealed.

ISSUE: Does the law of capture insulate a landowner from damages caused by the wrongful drainage of gas and distillate from beneath the land of another?

HOLDING AND DECISION: (Folley, J.) No. The law of capture does not insulate an adjacent land owner from damages caused by the wrongful drainage of gas and distillate from beneath the land of another. The law of capture states that minerals belong to the party that actually produces them, although part of the minerals, if they are oil or gas, may have migrated from adjoining lands. In other words, there is no liability for reasonable and legitimate drainage from the common pool. However, this does not give any owner the right to waste the gas. In this case, the waste and destruction of the Elliff's (P) gas was not a legitimate drainage or a lawful appropriation of it. Therefore the Elliffs (P) did not lose their right or title to the gas under the law of capture. Moreover, Texon (D) had a common law duty to exercise due care to avoid injury to the property of others. Since it breached this duty, it should be held liable. Reversed.

EDITOR'S ANALYSIS: The court's holding takes into account that advancing technology permits the determination of the approximate amount of oil and gas located in a common pool. However, the rule of capture no longer comes into play vis-a-vis " fugitive" minerals. Instead, oil and natural gas mining is highly regulated by state and federal law.

[For more information on the application of capture to oil and gas, see Casenote Law Outline on Property, Chapter 2, § I, Acquisition of Property Rights in Animals.]

NOTES:

5

INTERNATIONAL NEWS SERVICE v. ASSOCIATED PRESS
248 U.S. 215 (1918).

NATURE OF CASE: Appeal from denial of injunctive relief.

FACT SUMMARY: Associated Press (AP) (P) sued to enjoin International News Service (INS) (D) from publishing as its own news stories obtained from early editions of AP (P) publications.

CONCISE RULE OF LAW: Publication for profit of news obtained from other news-gathering enterprises is a misappropriation of a property right.

FACTS: AP (P) sued INS (D) for the latter's admitted use of AP (P) news stories in INS (D) publications. INS (D) would obtain advance publication of AP (P) news and would then use such in its newspapers. AP (P) contended it had a proprietary right to all news it gathered through the efforts of its contributors. INS (D) contended any such right terminated upon its first publication. The court of appeals issued AP (P) an injunction, and the Supreme Court granted a hearing.

ISSUE: Is the publication for profit of news obtained from other news-gathering enterprises a misappropriation of a property right?

HOLDING AND DECISION: (Pitney, J.) Yes. Publication for profit of news obtained from other news-gathering enterprises is a misappropriation of a property right. News itself is a collection of observable facts which obviously cannot be owned vis-a-vis the public at large. The nonprofit communication of news, regardless of source, is endemic in a free society and involves no property right. However, when two competing news organizations are involved, each gaining their livelihood from beating the other's deadline, the use of such news, for profit, is a misappropriation of the other's product. As a result, injunctive relief is properly issued. Affirmed.

DISSENT: (Brandeis, J.) News, like all products of the mind, loses economic exclusivity upon communication to others. Only where through public property policy determinations does the proprietary right continue.

EDITOR'S ANALYSIS: Some commentators suggest this case as a prime example of the first in time-first in right principle of ownership. Some go so far as to argue it provides authority for the proposition that all things created, either tangible or intangible, belong to the creator. This expands the reach of this case beyond news-gathering and into any area wherein exclusivity of design or idea is important. This would include everything from clothing design to computer programming.

NOTES:

6

MOORE v. REGENTS OF THE UNIVERSITY OF CALIFORNIA

Yes

793 P.2d 479 (Cal. 1990).

NATURE OF CASE: Appeal from action for conversion.

FACT SUMMARY: Moore (P) claimed that Dr. Golde (D) wrongfully used cells from Moore's (P) diseased spleen and other organs for pecuniary advantage.

CONCISE RULE OF LAW: A person does not have a property interest in his cell tissue.

FACTS: John Moore (P) went to UCLA Medical Center where he was diagnosed with hairy-cell leukemia. His treating physician, Dr. Golde (D) recommended that he have his spleen removed. Golde (D) was aware that the cells of the diseased spleen were valuable for research and commercial purpose; however, he secured Moore's (P) consent for the operation without disclosing this information. Dr. Golde (D) and his colleagues (D) arranged to preserve the removed cells and through their own efforts, developed the cells into a lucrative cell line. After the surgery, Moore (P) was required to return to UCLA from his home in Seattle for additional samples of genetic materials. The materials were used for further research on the cell line again without Moore's knowledge or consent. Dr. Golde (D) patented the cell line and received several hundred thousand dollars from pharmaceutical companies for products derived from the cell line. Moore (P) brought suit for conversion.

ISSUE: Does a person have a property interest in his cell tissue?

HOLDING AND DECISION: (Panelli, J.) No. A person does not have a property interest in his cell tissue. Although a person does have a right to his own likeness, the products produced from cells are based on genetic material that is common to all human beings. Thus, Moore (P) had no unique personality interest in the materials taken. California law dictates specifically how removed human tissue must be disposed of. Dr. Golde's (D) use of the tissue was in accordance with statutory requirements. If Moore (P) had desired to dispose of the cells on his own, he would have been barred by law from doing so. Once the cells were removed, he no longer had the right to possess them. Moore (P) cannot be held to have a property interest in the cells. Furthermore, public policy mitigates against a finding that would chill beneficial research. Moore (P) may sue for breach of fiduciary duty or lack of informed consent, but not for conversion.

CONCURRENCE AND DISSENT: (Arabian, J.) Moore (P) asks us to recognize and enforce a right to sell one's own body tissue for profit. Golde's (D) conduct was outrageous, but the legislature is the proper forum for resolution of this problem.

DISSENT: (Broussard, J.) The court's holding is anomalous; it prevents Moore (P) from selling his body for profit but allows Golde (D) and the Regents (D) to profit from cells wrongfully acquired.

DISSENT: (Mosk, J.) Moore (P) had at least as much right to dispose of his own cells as Golde (D) did.

EDITOR'S ANALYSIS: Justice Mosk makes two compelling policy arguments in his dissent — one based on equity and the other on ethics. Because, he argues, Moore (P) made a crucial contribution to the cell line developed by Golde (D), he should be permitted to share in the profits. Mosk contends that when research treats the human body as a mere commodity, the dignity and respect due the human body are sacrificed. For more on this debate, see Danforth, Cells, Sales, and Royalties, 6 Yale L. and Pol'y Rev. 179 (1988).

[For more information on property rights in body parts, see Casenote Law Outline on Property, Chapter 2, § IV, Property Right in Human Body Parts and Fetus.]

NOTES:

IN RE MARRIAGE OF KING

Mont. Sup. Ct., 700 P.2d 591 (Mont. 1985).

NATURE OF CASE: Appeal from division of assets in divorce.

FACT SUMMARY: A district court awarded Pamela King (D) the family home rather than child support in the division of assets pursuant to her divorce.

CONCISE RULE OF LAW: A division of a marital estate that favors one party over the other may be acceptable if there is reason for it.

FACTS: Jack and Pamela King were married in 1971 and had two children. Jack was a professional gambler. After ten years they filed for divorce. The district court found that the sale of the family home would not adequately provide for the support of the children, particularly due to the reduction in its value that would be caused by the expense of the sale. The court also found it would be an undue hardship on the children to require them to move from the family home. Based on these findings, the court awarded the home to Pamela in lieu of child support payments which, due to Jack's occupation, would be an unreliable source of support. Jack appealed, claiming that the court's distribution of assets constituted an abuse of discretion.

ISSUE: May a division of a marital estate that favors one party over the other be acceptable if there is reason for it?

HOLDING AND DECISION: (Hunt, J.) Yes. A division of a marital estate that favors one party over the other may be acceptable if there is reason for it. It is not an abuse of discretion for a court to award the family home to the custodial house in lieu of a support order. A district court, in making determinations of division of assets and awards of support, must take all factors into consideration. In this case, the likelihood that Jack would not meet his child support obligations because of his occupation was adequate cause to justify the district court's findings. Affirmed.

EDITOR'S ANALYSIS: Jack's contention was that property issues and family issues should be dealt with separately. However, where there are children and a family home it would seem that the two become inextricably linked. But not all courts are in accord with this view. In Ramsey v. Ramsey, 546 N.E.2d. 1280 (Ind. Ct. App. 1989), the court ordered the sale of the marital home notwithstanding the couple's desire to retain it so as not to be forced to uproot their five children.

NOTES:

CHARRIER v. BELL
469 So.2d 601 (La. Ct. App. 1986).

NATURE OF CASE: Appeal from denial of compensatory and declaratory relief confirming ownership.

FACT SUMMARY: After Charrier (P) uncovered Tunica Indian artifacts while excavating property without the property owner's (D) permission, descendants of the Tunica tribe claimed ownership of the artifacts.

CONCISE RULE OF LAW: Ownership in burial artifacts cannot be transferred to another under the theory of abandonment.

FACTS: Charrier (P), an amateur archeologist, located a Tunica Indian burial site on a privately held plantation. Charrier (P) received permission to excavate from the caretaker but not from the owner. He spent three years uncovering a great number of Tunica artifacts. When he tried to sell the artifacts to a museum he found he could not do so without proving ownership. Charrier (P) brought suit against Bell (D) and the other landowners to quiet title to the artifacts. The State (D) bought the plantation and took over defense of the suit in favor of the descendants of the Tunica Indians. The trial court found the Tunica-Biloxi Indians to be the owners of the artifacts, and Charrier (P) appealed.

ISSUE: Can ownership in burial artifacts be transferred to another under the theory of abandonment?

HOLDING AND DECISION: (Ponder, J.) No. Ownership in burial artifacts cannot be transferred to another under the theory of abandonment. Charrier's (P) claim to the artifact is based on the theory that the Tunica Indians abandoned them, and he became the owner by finding them. Abandonment requires intent to abandon. Traditionally burial goods do not fall under the classification of treasures to be found. Otherwise burial grounds would be subject to despoilment. When a society buries goods with the deceased person, it is for religious, spiritual or moral reasons, not with the intent that the next person to come along should uncover them. The artifacts were buried with the intent that they would remain there for all eternity. There is thus no intent to abandon connected with burial goods, and finding them cannot transfer them away from the rightful owners. Affirmed.

EDITOR'S ANALYSIS: Lost property is personal property that has been parted from its rightful owner involuntarily or unintentionally left somewhere and forgotten. Abandoned property has been intentionally relinquished. As a practical matter, however, most states do not make these common law distinctions any longer; by law, the finder is permitted to claim ownership after depositing the property with the police for a certain amount of time.

[For more information on abandoned property, see Casenote Law Outline on Property, Chapter 2, § II, Lost, Mislaid, and Abandoned Property.]

NOTES:

TAPSCOTT v. LESSEE OF COBBS
Va. Ct. App., 52 Va. (11 Gratt.) 172 (1854).

NATURE OF CASE: Action of ejectment to regain possession of real property.

FACT SUMMARY: Lewis, who never had title to the land of which she was in possession until her death, bequeathed that land to Cobbs (P). Without any pretense of title, Tapscott (D) took possession of the land. Cobbs (P) sued to eject Tapscott (D).

CONCISE RULE OF LAW: One in possession of land has title superior to all others except the actual, rightful titleholder.

FACTS: Anderson, the original owner of the land in question, devised it to his executors to sell after his death. The executors contracted to sell to Mrs. Lewis in about 1820, but it appeared that she never paid the purchase price or received a deed to the land. Despite this, Mrs. Lewis entered the land, took possession, built upon it, and remained in possession until her death in 1835. Mrs. Cobbs (P), Mrs. Lewis' lessor and heir, brought this action to eject Tapscott (D) who entered and took possession of the land without pretense of title.

ISSUE: Can one in mere possession of land without title maintain an action against another also without title who attempts to take possession away?

HOLDING AND DECISION: (Daniel, J.) Yes. Cobbs (P), as prior possessor, had the right to possession "against all except him who has the actual right to the possession." The defendant, who without title or authority to enter and who attempts to oust the prior possessor, cannot defend his action on the ground that title is outstanding in another. Instead, to successfully defend, Tapscott (D) had to show he had either title or authority to enter under the title. Being heir to Lewis' possessory interest, Cobbs (P) was presumed to be in rightful possession at the time she was ousted by Tapscott (D) even though there was no evidence of Lewis (P) being in possession.

EDITOR'S ANALYSIS: The court states that the general rule is that the right of the plaintiff in ejectment "rests on the strength of his own title," and that the defendant may defend by simply showing that title is not in the plaintiff, but in another. But this case is an exception. After reviewing the English and American cases, prior possession was found to be good against the whole world except the rightful owner. In ejectment, the question is the right to possession and prior peaceful possession in a protected interest. Mrs. Cobbs (P) was in adverse possession of the land. In most jurisdictions, one who is in uninterrupted adverse possession, usually for a period of twenty years, acquires title to the land. While the time of possession was not clear here, the issue was not argued.

[For more information on prior possession of real property, see Casenote Law Outline on Property, Chapter 3, § II, The Conflict between Possession and the Ability to Convey Good Title.]

SOMERVILLE v. JACOBS
W. Va. Sup. Ct., 170 S.E.2d 805 (1969).

NATURE OF CASE: Appeal from claim for equitable relief.

FACT SUMMARY: The Somervilles (P) built a warehouse on property that they mistakenly believed to be their own.

CONCISE RULE OF LAW: An improver who mistakenly improves the land of another is entitled to the value of the improvement which the landowner has benefited from.

FACTS: The Somervilles (P) owned three plots of land. Based on a surveyor's report, they constructed a warehouse on what they believed to be their own land. Jacobs and other owners (D) discovered that the warehouse was in fact built upon their land only after it was completed. The Somervilles (P) brought suit for equitable relief either in the form of sale of the land to them or reimbursement of the value of the improvements.

ISSUE: Is an improver who mistakenly improves the land of another entitled to the value of the improvement which the landowner has benefited from?

HOLDING AND DECISION: (Haymond, Pres.) Yes. An improver who mistakenly improves the land of another is entitled to the value of the improvement that the landowner has benefited from. The Somervilles (P) made a reasonable good-faith mistake of fact in building on Jacobs' (D) land. If Jacobs (D) keeps the improvements to the land without compensating the Somervilles (P), he will be unjustly enriched. Equity allows the type of relief the Somervilles (P) are requesting. Jacobs (D) must either pay for the improvement he received or sell the land back to Somerville (P) in order to avoid unjust enrichment.

DISSENT: (Caplan, J.) Having been entirely without fault, Jacobs (D) should not be forced to purchase the building. That is nothing less than condemnation of private property, a power reserved to government only. He who made the mistake should suffer the hardship.

EDITOR'S ANALYSIS: Other jurisdictions hold that a trespasser, no matter how innocent, cannot be compensated for any improvements. However, all courts agree that under the doctrine of annexation, intentional improvements by one who knows he is trespassing belong to the owner of the real estate. In that case, the bad faith of the improver negates the injustice of the enrichment.

[For more information on title by adverse possession, see Casenote Law Outline on Property, Chapter 4, § II, Five Criteria to Acquire Title by Adverse Possession.]

NOME 2000 v. FAGERSTROM
Alaska Sup. Ct., 799 P.2d 304 (1990).

NATURE OF CASE: Suit for ejectment and counterclaim to acquire title by adverse possession.

FACT SUMMARY: Charles and Peggy Fagerstrom (D) used a parcel of land owned by Nome 2000 (P) for various purposes from 1944 to 1987 but did not build a house on it until 1978, thereby defeating their adverse possession claim, according to Nome (P).

CONCISE RULE OF LAW: Whether a claimant's physical acts upon the land of another are sufficiently continuous, notorious and exclusive does not necessarily depend on the existence of significant improvements, substantial activity, or absolute exclusivity.

FACTS: Fagerstrom (D) used a rural parcel of land owned by Nome 2000 (P) for recreational purposes beginning in 1944. In the 1970s, Fagerstrom's (D) family began to make more substantial use of the land, adding improvements and spending more time there each year. In 1977 they built a reindeer shelter that occasionally housed reindeer. They also excluded trailers from the land and spent weekends there. In 1987 the Fagerstroms (D) built a cabin on the land and continued to use the land on weekends and vacations for recreational purposes. In 1987 Nome 2000 (P) brought suit to quiet title. The Fagerstroms (D) counterclaimed for title by adverse possession.

ISSUE: Does a claim of adverse possession depend on the existence of significant improvements, substantial activity, or absolute exclusivity?

HOLDING AND DECISION: (Matthews, J.) No. Whether a claimant's physical acts upon the land of another are sufficiently continuous, notorious and exclusive does not necessarily depend on the existence of significant improvements, substantial activity, or absolute exclusivity. Use consistent with the use by any similarly situated owner is sufficient to establish claim by adverse possession. The statute requires continuous, notorious, hostile and exclusive use of a property for ten years in order to succeed in a claim for adverse possession. Nome (P) claimed that the Fagerstroms' (D) possession only became adverse when they built the cabin in 1978, and thus they did not meet the statutory ten-year period. But the statute does not require actual improvements to the land, only sufficient use based on the type of property occupied. The land in question is rural and thus has a lower requirement of use. The Fagerstroms (D) occupied the land sufficiently that their occupation was visible in 1977. The various structures erected and the feeling of the community that the Fagerstroms were the owners of the property meets the statutory requirement of continuous, notorious exclusive and hostile possession.

EDITOR'S ANALYSIS: The court found that what the Fagerstroms (D), as Native Alaskans, believed or intended vis-a-vis the property had nothing to do with whether their possession was hostile. The hostility requirement merely means that the adverse possessor acted toward the land as if he were the owner. But the Fagerstroms (D) claim title to a large portion of the land was only partially granted by the court. The Fagerstroms' (D) use of certain trails for hiking did not constitute dominion and control over the south portion of the land sufficient to demonstrate adverse possession.

_____

[For more information on acquisition of title by adverse possession, see Casenote Law Outline on Property, Chapter 4, § II, Five Criteria to Acquire Title by Adverse Possession.]

NOTES:

BROWN v. GOBBLE

1996 WL 264808 (W. Va. 1996).

NATURE OF CASE: Appeal from judgment in an action to enjoin interference with use of real property.

FACT SUMMARY: Brown (P) and Gobble (D) disputed ownership of a two-foot-wide tract of property on the boundary of their properties.

CONCISE RULE OF LAW: The doctrine of tacking allows parties claiming adverse possession to use their predecessors' conduct on the property to meet the time requirements of adverse possession.

FACTS: Gobble (D) purchased real property in 1985. At the time, a fence ran along the rear boundary of the property which adjoined property purchased by Brown (P) in 1989. Brown (P) discovered, prior to buying, that this fence actually extended two feet past the true boundary. However, Brown (P) did not claim ownership of this two-foot-wide tract until 1994, when he decided to build a road along that property. Gobble (D) sought to prevent the building of the road, and Brown (P) filed suit to enjoin this interference. Gobble (D) counterclaimed that he owned the two-foot-wide tract through adverse possession. Gobble (D) presented evidence that both Blevins and Fletcher, who owned the Gobble (D) property from 1937 through 1985, believed they owned the boundary tract and treated the property as their own. However, the trial court ruled that adverse possession had not been proved and entered judgment for Brown (P). Gobble (D) appealed.

ISSUE: Does the doctrine of tacking allow parties claiming adverse possession to use their predecessors' conduct on the property to meet the time requirements of adverse possession?

HOLDING AND DECISION: (Cleckley, J.) Yes. The doctrine of tacking allows parties claiming adverse possession to use their predecessors' conduct on the property to meet the time requirements of adverse possession. In order to prove adverse possession, a party must prove the following elements: (1) the property has been held adversely; (2) there has been actual possession; (3) possession has been open and notorious; (4) possession has been exclusive; (5) possession has been continuous; and (6) the property has been held under claim or color of title. In the case at hand, the requisite period of time for adverse possession is ten years. The principle of tacking has long been recognized in adverse possession cases. This principle allows different adverse possessions to make up the requisite time for holding such possessions, so long as they are connected by privity of title or claim. Thus, although Gobble (D) had personally adversely held the property for only nine years, the adverse possession by the prior owners of the property, who are connected to him through the title to his property, helps to satisfy the elements of adverse possession long before the ten-year period. Accordingly, if their adverse possession was tacked onto his own adverse possession, Gobble (D) would meet the time requirement. The trial court apparently misunderstood the relationship between tacking and adverse possession. Reversed and remanded.

EDITOR'S ANALYSIS: This decision also established the standard of proof for adverse possession claims. The court held that adverse possession must be proved by clear and convincing evidence. Although some jurisdictions require only a preponderance standard, the majority view is in accord with this decision.

[For more information on the doctrine of tacking, see Casenote Law Outline on Property, Chapter 4, § II, Five Criteria to Acquire Title by Adverse Possession.]

NOTES:

COMMUNITY FEED STORE INC. v. NORTHEASTERN CULVERT CORP.

Yes

Vt. Sup. Ct., 559 A.2d 1068 (Vt. 1989).

NATURE OF CASE: Appeal from rejection of claim of prescriptive easement and judgement for defense of counterclaim of ejectment.

FACT SUMMARY: Community Feed Store (P) claimed a prescriptive easement over a portion of a gravel area used by its vehicles but owned by Northeastern Culvert Corp.(D).

CONCISE RULE OF LAW: A general outline of consistent use is sufficient to establish a prescriptive easement.

FACTS: Community (P) used a parcel of land lying between their building and that of Northeastern's building as a turning and backing up area for trucks making deliveries to the store. The use was continuous from 1956 to 1984. A survey in 1984 showed that the majority of this area was owned by Northeastern (D). Upon this finding, Northeastern (D) erected a wall to discontinue Community's (P) use. Community (P) brought suit, claiming a prescriptive easement. The trial court found for Northeastern (D) on the basis that the use was not stated with enough specificity to establish a prescriptive easement and that the use was consensual. Community (P) appealed.

ISSUE: Is a general outline of consistent use sufficient to establish a prescriptive easement?

HOLDING AND DECISION: (Gibson, J.) Yes. A general outline of consistent use is sufficient to establish a prescriptive easement. A prescriptive easement acquires a non-fee interest in land by adverse possession. The trial court found that Community (P) had not been able to define the easement acquired with enough specificity. The extent of the use need not be absolute. Instead, Community (P) need only show the general outline of consistent pattern of use with certainty. Community (P) introduced more than sufficient evidence of a pattern of use. Reversed.

EDITOR'S ANALYSIS: The second basis on which the lower court rejected the claim was that use of the area was made by Community (P) with the permission of Northeastern (D). The Supreme Court applied the general presumption that open and notorious use is adverse to ownership and rejected the consent defense. There is a "public use" exception to the general presumption of adversity, whereby an owner "throws open" his land to general passage, but that exception did not apply in the instant case because Northeastern (D) could not show a generalized public use of the loading area.

[For more information on prescriptive easements, see Casenote Law Outline on Property, Chapter 8, § II, Easements.]

NOTES:

NOTES

CHAPTER 2
PUBLIC RIGHTS OF ACCESS TO PROPERTY:
RULES LIMITING THE RIGHT TO EXCLUDE NONOWNERS

QUICK REFERENCE RULES OF LAW

1. **Public Policy Limits on the Right to Exclude.** Real property rights are not absolute; and, "necessity, private or public, may justify entry upon the lands of another." (State v. Shack)

2. **Right of Reasonable Access to Property Open to the Public.** Owners of property open to the public do not have the right to unreasonably exclude particular members of the public. (Uston v. Resorts International Hotel, Inc.)

3. **Race and Sex Discrimination.** An association that solicits unlimited membership and membership dues is a place of public accommodation under the Minnesota statute prohibiting discrimination. (United States Jaycees v. McClure)

4. **Race and Sex Discrimination.** Where a place of public accommodation and a private club share a close and mutually beneficial and necessary relationship, the private club also becomes a place of public accommodation. (Frank v. Ivy Club)

5. **The First Amendment.** A privately held shopping center is not so dedicated to public use as to allow private parties the right to exercise their First Amendment rights on its premises. (Lloyd Corp., Ltd. v. Tanner)

6. **State Constitutions: The Right to Speak Freely.** The extent of free speech rights on private property depend on the nature of the use of the property, the extent of the public invitation to use that property, and the purpose of the speech activity in relation to the use of the property. (New Jersey Coalition Against War in the Middle East v. J.M.B. Realty Corp.)

7. **Beach Access and the Public Trust.** The public's right to enjoy tidal lands includes a right of access over privately held dry sand lands. (Matthews v. Bay Head Improvement Association)

STATE v. SHACK

N.J. Sup. Ct., 58 N.J. 297, 277 A.2d 369 (1971).

NATURE OF CASE: Appeal from a conviction of trespassing.

FACT SUMMARY: Tejeras (D) and Shack (D) entered upon private property against the orders of the owner of that property, to aid migrant farmworkers employed and housed there.

CONCISE RULE OF LAW: Real property rights are not absolute; and, "necessity, private or public, may justify entry upon the lands of another."

FACTS: Tejeras (D) and Shack (D) worked with migrant farmworkers. Tejeras (D) was a field worker for the Farm Workers Division of the Southwest Citizens Organization for Poverty Elimination (known as SCOPE), a nonprofit corporation funded by the Office of Economic Opportunity which provided for the "health services of the migrant farmworker." Shack (D) was a staff attorney with the Farm Workers Division of Camden Regional Legal Services, Inc. (known as CRLS), also a nonprofit corporation funded by the Office of Economic Opportunity which provided (along with other services) legal advice for, and representation of, migrant farmworkers. Tejeras (D) and Shack (D), pursuant to their roles in SCOPE and CRLS, entered upon private property to aid migrant workers employed and housed there. When both Tejeras (D) and Shack (D) refused to leave the property at the owner's request, they were charged with trespassing under a New Jersey statute which provides that "any person who trespasses on any lands . . . after being forbidden so to trespass by the owner . . . is a disorderly person and shall be punished by a fine of not more than $50." After conviction for trespassing, Tejeras (D) and Shack (D) brought this appeal.

ISSUE: Does an owner of real property have the absolute right to exclude all others from that property?

HOLDING AND DECISION: (Weintraub, C.J.) No. Real property rights are not absolute; and, "necessity, private or public, may justify entry upon the lands of another." This rule is based upon the basic rationale that "property rights serve human values. They are recognized to that end and are limited by it." Here, a central concern is the welfare of the migrant farmworkers — a highly disadvantaged segment of society. Migrant farmworkers, in general, are "outside of the mainstream of the communities in which they are housed and are unaware of their rights and opportunities, and of the services available to them." As such, here, the "necessity" of effective communication of legal rights and of providing medical services for the migrant farmworkers justifies entry upon the private property. Of course, the owner of such property has the right to pursue his farming activities without interference, but, here, there is no legitimate need for the owner to exclude those attempting to assist the migrant farmworkers. Furthermore, the migrant farmworker must be allowed to receive visitors of his choice, so long as there is no behavior harmful to others, and members of the press may not be denied access to any farmworker who wishes to see them. In any of these situations, since

no possessory right of the farmer-employer-landowner has been invaded (i.e., since he has no right to exclude such persons), there can be no trespassing. Reversed.

EDITOR'S ANALYSIS: Generally, the right to exclusive possession is considered "the oldest, most widely recognized right of private property in land." This case, though, illustrates the central limitation on the right to possession or use of private property — i.e., it may not be used to harm others. Here, the exclusion of Tejeras (D) and Shack (D) was, therefore, invalid because it would harm a very disadvantaged segment of society (the farmworkers). Note, that under this principle, an owner of property, also, has no right to maintain a nuisance, to violate a building code, or to violate any "police power" laws (i.e., laws for the general public welfare).

NOTES:

USTON v. RESORTS INTERNATIONAL HOTEL, INC. (yes)

N.J. Sup. Ct., 445 A.2d 370 (1982).

NATURE OF CASE: Action for denial of access to a public place.

FACT SUMMARY: Because Uston (P) was well known for his ability to count cards, he was excluded from Resorts International Hotel's (D) casino.

CONCISE RULE OF LAW: Owners of property open to the public do not have the right to unreasonably exclude particular members of the public.

FACTS: Uston (P) developed a system of counting cards that allowed him to win at blackjack. Uston (P) was well known for this practice and for teaching the system to others. Because of his ability to increase the chances of his winning, under the Gambling Commissions rules Resorts International (D) excluded Uston (P) from its casino. Uston (P) brought suit for access.

ISSUE: Do owners of property open to the public have the right to unreasonably exclude particular members of the public?

HOLDING AND DECISION: (Pashman, J.) No. Owners of property open to the public do not have the right to unreasonably exclude particular members of the public. The old common law rule gave owners of private property the absolute right to exclude members of the public from the property regardless of the nature of their use of the property. The civil rights amendments and statutes subsequently prevented owners of public facilities from excluding others based on race. To the extent that a property caters to the public, it must also take into account the rights of that public. Uston (P) did not come to the casino to disrupt the activities going on there, nor was he a security risk. Resorts (D) had no legitimate interest in excluding Uston (P) from a place to which the public was invited.

EDITOR'S ANALYSIS: The current majority American rule disregards the right of reasonable access applied in the above case. Instead it grants to proprietors of amusement places an absolute right to arbitrarily eject or exclude any person consistent with state and federal civil rights laws. The majority rule may have originated in response to anti-segregation measures taken by the federal government.

NOTES:

UNITED STATES JAYCEES v. McCLURE (no)
Minn. Sup. Ct., 305 N.W.2d 764 (Minn. 1981).

NATURE OF CASE: Review of certified question in U.S. District Court.

FACT SUMMARY: The Jaycees (P) a national organization, refused to grant full memberships to women, resulting in charges of sexual discrimination.

CONCISE RULE OF LAW: An association that solicits unlimited membership and membership dues is a place of public accommodation under the Minnesota statute prohibiting discrimination.

FACTS: The Jaycees (D) were a national association that actively sought memberships and carried out various internal and external activities. The Jaycees (D) claimed to give a social and business advantage to its members. It allowed women to join, but only on an associate level. The dues for associate memberships were only slightly less than for full membership, but associate members were not allowed to run for office, vote in elections, participate in many programs, or receive awards. Two local affiliates of the national organizations (P) allowed women full membership. The national organization (D) threatened to revoke their charter if they did not revoke their policy of offering women full membership. The two affiliates (D) brought suit, claiming that the national Jaycees' (D) policy violated state sexual discrimination laws. The district court certified to the state supreme court the question of whether the Jaycees (D) were "a place of public accommodation" and thus subject to the state antidiscrimination statute.

ISSUE: Is an association that solicits unlimited memberships and membership dues a place of public accommodation under the Minnesota statute prohibiting discrimination? in public business facilities?

HOLDING AND DECISION: (Otis, J.) Yes. An association which solicits unlimited membership and memberships dues is a place of public accommodation under the Minnesota statute prohibiting discrimination. The Jaycees (D) are a business that sells the commodity of memberships. There are two factors in determining whether a business is private or public: the selection process and whether it sets limits on the size of the membership. The Jaycees (D) actively seek to expand their membership and seek increase in membership without regard to screening criteria. It is not selective; all young men are invited to join. Furthermore, the Jaycees (D) have no limit on the number of members they are willing to accept. Thus, the Jaycees (D) are not a private club and may not discriminate on the basis of gender.

DISSENT: (Sheran, J.) The legislature did not intend a service organization to be considered a place of public accommodation.

EDITOR'S ANALYSIS: The majority's holding hinges on the belief that a public accommodation does not need a particular statute to qualify as such. The dissent would limit the reach of the statute to exclusion from a particular premise. The majority, however, uses a good example — a little league organization may not be located in any one particular area, yet there is an interest in assuring that such organizations do not discriminate.

NOTES:

FRANK v. IVY CLUB (*no*)

N.J. Sup. Ct., 576 A.2d 241 (N.J. 1990).

NATURE OF CASE: Appeal from finding of gender discrimination.

FACT SUMMARY: Three dining clubs, including the Ivy Club (D), catered solely to Princeton students and excluded women from membership.

CONCISE RULE OF LAW: Where a place of public accommodation and a private club share a close and mutually beneficial and necessary relationship, the private club also becomes a place of public accommodation.

FACTS: Princeton University relied on a dining club system to provide dining service to its large student body. These clubs were privately owned and run independent of the university. The membership was almost exclusively made up of Princeton students, and the clubs were involved in university activities and were to some degree subject to university regulation. Two of the clubs, the Tiger Club (D) and the Ivy Club (D), excluded women from their membership. Frank (P), a Princeton student, was denied membership to these clubs because of her gender. Frank (P) filed a complaint with the New Jersey Division of Civil Rights. The Division found probable cause for gender discrimination and further found that the Clubs (D), through their association with Princeton, were places of public accommodation. The Ivy and Tiger Clubs (D) appealed.

ISSUE: Where a place of public accommodation and a private club share a close and mutually beneficial and necessary relationship, does the private club also becomes a place of public accommodation?

HOLDING AND DECISION: (Garibaldi, J.) Yes. Where a place of public accommodation and a private club share a close and mutually beneficial and necessary relationship, the private club also becomes a place of public accommodation. Princeton University was clearly a place of public accommodation. Despite the fact that these clubs were financially and legally distinct from the University, the two entities' functions were so closely intertwined that the clubs lost their private character. As places of public accommodation, they must not discriminate on the basis of gender. Affirmed.

EDITOR'S ANALYSIS: Places of public accommodation are regulated under Title II of the Civil Rights Act as well as individually by the states. Federal law sets the minimum standard above which states are allowed to legislate. Any state law inconsistent with the Act is preempted by the Act pursuant to the Supremacy Clause of the U.S. Constitution.

LLOYD CORP., LTD. v. TANNER (*yes*)

407 U.S. 551 (1972).

NATURE OF CASE: Appeal from grant of permanent injunction.

FACT SUMMARY: Tanner (D) distributed political handbills in the interior of a privately owned mall.

CONCISE RULE OF LAW: A privately held shopping center is not so dedicated to public use as to allow private parties the right to exercise their First Amendment rights on its premises.

FACTS: Lloyd Corp. (P) owned a large in-door shopping mall. The mall allowed organizations to use the auditorium for various public activities, but upon invitation only. Tanner (D) handed out flyers protesting the Vietnam war within the interior of the mall in an orderly and nondisruptive manner. Tanner (D) was asked by mall security to leave to avoid arrest. Tanner (D) did leave and later filed suit seeking declaratory and injunctive relief. The district court issued an injunction against the mall, and the court of appeal affirmed. Lloyd (P) petitioned for certiorari.

ISSUE: Is a privately held shopping center so dedicated to public use to allow private parties the right to exercise their First Amendment rights on its premises?

HOLDING AND DECISION: (Powell, J.) No. A privately held shopping center is not so dedicated to public use as to allow private parties the right to exercise their first amendment rights on its premises. The First Amendment is a prohibition on state action only. Dedication to public use is not the equivalent of state action. The mall is not the functional equivalent of a municipal use because its services are not so broad to simulate the function of a city government. Since the mall is not a state actor, Lloyd (P) is entitled to exclude handbillers from its private property. Reversed.

DISSENT: (Marshall, J.) The balance between free speech and the right to control private property must be struck in favor of free speech.

EDITOR'S ANALYSIS: The lower court issued its injunctions based on an analogy between the mall and the company town. The Supreme Court found this analogy unpersuasive. However, malls do function in modern society as a great deal more than just a place to shop — they are gathering places, entertainment centers, and to some degree public forums.

NEW JERSEY COALITION AGAINST WAR IN THE MIDDLE EAST v. J.M.B. REALTY CORP.
650 A.2d 757 (N.J. 1994).

(yes)

NATURE OF CASE: Action to enjoin private property owners from banning political leafleting.

FACT SUMMARY: J.M.B. Realty (D), which owns several private indoor malls, banned the Coalition (P) from passing out political leaflets in its malls.

CONCISE RULE OF LAW: The extent of free speech rights on private property depend on the nature of the use of the property, the extent of the public invitation to use that property, and the purpose of the speech activity in relation to the use of the property.

FACTS: The Coalition (P) sought to conduct a massive leafleting campaign in 1990 to seek support for their position that the U.S. should not be involved in the Gulf War. The Coalition (P) wanted to pass out their leaflets in ten large shopping center malls in New Jersey. Nine of the ten shopping centers had between 93 and 244 tenants, which included restaurants, department stores, banks, hair salons, theaters, doctor's offices, and many other specialty stores. In addition to these services, each of the malls also permitted and encouraged a variety of nonshopping, community activities. Most of these malls rejected the Coalition's (P) attempts to obtain permission to distribute leaflets at the malls. The Coalition (P) sought judicial relief, claiming that J.M.B.'s (D) denial of permission violated their free speech rights under the First Amendment and the New Jersey Constitution.

ISSUE: Does the extent of free speech rights on private property depend on the nature of the use of the property, the extent of the public invitation to use that property, and the purpose of the speech activity in relation to the use of the property?

HOLDING AND DECISION: (Wilentz, J.) Yes. The extent of free speech rights on private property depend on the nature of the use of the property, the extent of the public invitation to use that property, and the purpose of the speech activity in relation to the use of the property. According to Supreme Court precedent, the First Amendment does not afford a general right to free speech in privately owned shopping centers. However, the New Jersey right to free speech has been held to confer some rights against interference from private property owners. The holding in State v. Schmid, 423 A.2d 615 (1980), determined that there are some free speech rights on private property provided that the use of the property and the nature of the speech meets certain criteria. The predominant characteristic of the use of large shopping center malls is their all-inclusiveness. People engage in all of the activities that previously took place in the public areas of towns and cities. Additionally, malls make an all-embracing invitation to the public and have significant nonretail uses. Given this invitation and wide range of use, J.M.B. (D) cannot deny all free speech rights. Historical records show that leafleting has not been a burden on retail locations. The speech interest at stake here goes to the central

reason for free speech commentary regarding government actions. Therefore, J.M.B.'s (D) shopping centers must accommodate speech of this type, although they remain free to set reasonable time, place, and manner restrictions.

DISSENT: (Garibaldi, J.) The majority ignores the fact that the primary users of malls are shoppers and that mall owners are in business to sell goods. Under the majority's analysis, any time the public is invited onto large, privately owned property, it becomes a place to congregate and the functional equivalent of a downtown.

EDITOR'S ANALYSIS: This case represents the minority view. Only about five other states have maintained similar rights based upon their state constitutions. The majority went to great lengths to demonstrate that today's shopping malls are the equivalent of the town square and downtown business district of years ago. They seemed to feel that political groups would not be able to reach large amounts of people any other way.

NOTES:

MATTHEWS v. BAY HEAD IMPROVEMENT ASSOCIATION   Yes
N.J. Sup. Ct., 471 A.2d 355 (1984).

NATURE OF CASE: Action under the public trust doctrine.

NOTES:

FACT SUMMARY: Bay Head Improvement Association (D) permitted only members to use its beach area between 10:00 A.M. and 5:30 P.M. in the summer.

CONCISE RULE OF LAW: The public's right to enjoy tidal lands includes a right of access over privately held dry sand lands.

FACTS: Bay Head Improvement Association (D) was incorporated as a nonprofit organization to regulate and protect the privately held beaches of the Borough of Bay Head. The Association (D) owned title to six of the seventy-six beachfront lots of land and leased other properties from residents. It operated these lots as a private beach for the benefit of the community, providing lifeguards, beach cleaners, and membership police. The Association (D) limited public access to the dry sand area during certain hours of the day and times of the year. The public could access the foreshore area during low tide from the adjacent boroughs. Matthews (P) brought suit claiming that the public had the right to gain access to the tidal land across the property owned by the Association (D).

ISSUE: Does the public's right to enjoy tidal lands include a right of access over privately held dry sand lands?

HOLDING AND DECISION: (Schreiber, J.) Yes. The public's right to enjoy tidal lands includes a right of access over privately held dry sand lands. Tidal areas and the foreshore are held in the public trust to insure the public's right to use and enjoy such areas. The right to enjoy such areas is meaningless without proper access. The doctrine of public trust also requires that the public has use of the dry sand area so they may fully enjoy their right in the tidal area. Because the Association (D) is a quasi-public institution, it cannot deny the public membership to its beaches. Furthermore, the public right to enjoyment is severely limited by the fact that there are no public beaches in the borough. The public must be given access to the Association's (D) land.

EDITOR'S ANALYSIS: The court refrained from stating that the public's interest amounted to a prescriptive easement over privately held beach land. Public use does not readily lend itself to prescription due to the difficulties involved in proving continuous use and taking. In the alternatives, courts have relied on custom and implied dedication to confer access rights.

NOTES

3

CHAPTER 3
RULES GOVERNING RELATIONS AMONG NEIGHBORS
IN THE ABSENCE OF AGREEMENT

QUICK REFERENCE RULES OF LAW

1. **Water Rights.** A possessor of land is not privileged to discharge upon adjoining land, by artificial means, large quantities of surface water in a concentrated flow otherwise than through natural drainways, regardless of the means by which the surface water is collected and discharged. (Armstrong v. Francis Corp.)

   [For more information on nuisance claims — reasonable use, see Casenote Law Outline on Property, Chapter 9, § I, The Law of Private Nuisance.]

2. **Support Easements: Lateral Support.** An adjacent landowner is strictly liable for acts of omission and commission which withdraw lateral support of his neighbor's land sufficient to support it in its natural state; however, if as a result of the additional weight of a building so much strain is placed on the lateral support that it will not hold, then in the absence of negligence the adjacent landowner is not liable for any resulting damages. (Noone v. Price)

3. **Right to Dig versus Right to Support.** A person is liable for damages caused by drawing water from his own land only to the extent that his activity was negligent. (Friendswood Development Co. v. Smith-Southwest Industries, Inc.)

   [For more information on nuisance and negligence, see Casenote Law Outline on Property, Chapter 9, § I, The Law of Private Nuisance.]

4. **Radiation: Defining Unreasonable Land Use.** Lawful activity constitutes a nuisance if it unreasonably interferes with another's enjoyment of his or her property. (Page County Appliance Center, Inc. v. Honeywell, Inc.)

   [For more information on nuisance and unreasonable use, see Casenote Law Outline on Property, Chapter 9, § I, The Law of Private Nuisance.]

5. **Light and Air.** There is no legal right to the free flow of light or air from an adjoining parcel of land. (Fontainebleau Hotel Corp. v. Forty-Five Twenty-Five, Inc.)

   [For more information on easements for light and air, see Casenote Law Outline on Property, Chapter 9, § I, The Law of Private Nuisance.]

6. **Nuisance Doctrine Applied to Light.** The doctrine of prior appropriation applies to the use of sunlight as a protectable resource. (Prah v. Maretti)

   [For more information on easements for light and air, see Casenote Law Outline on Property, Chapter 9, § I, The Law of Private Nuisance.]

ARMSTRONG v. FRANCIS CORPORATION
Sup. Ct. of N.J., 20 N.J. 320, 120 A.2d 4 (1956).

NOTES:

NATURE OF CASE: Action in equity to enjoin landowner from artificially discharging waste waters from his land.

FACT SUMMARY: Francis (D) drained off excess water from its land by means of culverts and pipes, thereby causing severe injury to its neighbor's (P) property.

CONCISE RULE OF LAW: A possessor of land is not privileged to discharge upon adjoining land, by artificial means, large quantities of surface water in a concentrated flow otherwise than through natural drainways, regardless of the means by which the surface water is collected and discharged.

FACTS: Francis (D) wanted to develop a tract of land for residential subdivision. To drain off excess water, Francis (D) constructed a series of underground pipes and culverts. Water from this system emptied into a natural stream which ran across the lands of Armstrong (P) and Klemp (P). Because of the increased flow of water, the stream often flooded and caused considerable erosion or silting on surrounding banks. In addition, the stream, being polluted by Francis' (D) pipes, became discolored and evil-smelling and lost all fish. Armstrong (P) and Klemp (P) sued to have Francis (D), on its own cost, pipe the rest of its water discharge.

ISSUE: Does a landowner have an absolute right to rid his property of excess surface waters as he will?

HOLDING AND DECISION: (Brennan, J.) No. Most states adopt the rule that, since surface water is the "common enemy" of necessary development, the landowner has an absolute right to discharge it upon adjoining land regardless of the harm caused his neighbors by the means he employs. However, no state applies this harsh rule literally. Courts will read in a "reasonable use" approach which has the particular virtue of flexibility. The issue of reasonableness includes such factors as the amount of harm caused, the foreseeability of the harm which results, the purpose or motive with which the possessor acted, and other relevant matter. Accordingly, Frances (D) is liable to fix its drainage system.

EDITOR'S ANALYSIS: The competing approach with the "common enemy" rule is the civil law rule, which holds that a possessor has no privilege, under any circumstances, to interfere with the surface water on his land so as to cause it to flow upon adjoining land in a manner or quantity substantially different from its natural flow. Even here, however, courts will read in a "reasonable use" exception to permit minor alterations.

[For more information on reasonable use, see Casenote Law Outline on Property, Chapter 9, § I, The Law of Private Nuisance.]

NOONE v. PRICE

W.Va. Ct. of App., 298 N.E.2d 218 (1982).

NATURE OF CASE: Appeal from grant of summary judgment denying damages for eroding lateral support of land.

FACT SUMMARY: Noone (P) contended Price (D) breached her duty to supply lateral support for Noone's (P) hillside home by allowing a retaining will to fall into disrepair.

CONCISE RULE OF LAW: An adjacent landowner is strictly liable for acts of omission and commission which withdraw lateral support of his neighbor's land sufficient to support it in its natural state; however, if as a result of the additional weight of a building so much strain is placed on the lateral support that it will not hold, then in the absence of negligence the adjacent landowner is not liable for any resulting damages.

FACTS: In 1912, a house was built at the base of a hill, along with a stone and cement wall located at the base of the hillside. In 1928, Union Carbide built a house on the hillside, above the wall. After several years, the wall fell into disrepair. In 1955, Price (D) purchased the house at the base of the hill. She made no repairs to the wall. Noone (P) bought the house above on the hillside in 1960. Subsequently, Noone (P) discovered that his house was slipping down the hillside, and sued Price (D), contending the wall was constructed to supply lateral support to his property, and that its disrepair caused the slippage. Price (D) moved for summary judgment, contending Noone (P) was negligent in failing to protect his own property and estopped from suing because he had purchased his house with knowledge of the wall's deteriorating condition. The trial court agreed and granted summary judgment to Price (D). Noone appealed.

ISSUE: Is an adjacent landowner liable only for supplying lateral support to his neighbor's land in its natural state?

HOLDING AND DECISION: (Neely, J.) Yes. An adjacent landowner is strictly liable for acts of omission and commission which withdraw lateral support from his neighbor's land sufficient to support it in its natural state. However, if as a result of the additional weight of a building so much strain is placed on the lateral support that it will not hold, then in the absence of negligence, the adjacent landowner is not liable for any resulting damages. At the time the retaining wall was built, there were no structures on Noone's (P) land. Therefore, the wall needed only to support the land in its natural state. The builder was not required to supply support sufficient to withstand the erection of any building on the land. Therefore, Price (D), as the successor in interest, was not obligated to strengthen the wall to support Noone's (P) house. If Noone (P) is to recover, he must do so by proving that the disrepair of the wall would have inevitably led to the subsidence of his land in its natural condition, without the house upon it. Consequently, as this is a factual question, the entry of summary judgment was error. Reversed and remanded for trial.

EDITOR'S ANALYSIS: This case illustrates the scope of the duty to supply lateral support. The duty is absolute as to the land in its natural state, but to recover for damages to a building, negligence must be shown. A negligent withdrawal of support is actionable even if the land would not have slipped but for the presence of the added weight of a building. In determining whether negligence exists, the type of withdrawal, the nature of the soil, and whether notice of the proposed withdrawal was given are all relevant.

NOTES:

**FRIENDSWOOD DEVELOPMENT CO. v.
SMITH-SOUTHWEST INDUSTRIES, INC.**
Tex. Sup. Ct., 576 S.W.2d 21 (1978).

NATURE OF CASE: Appeal from summary judgment in class action in tort.

FACT SUMMARY: Friendswood Development (D) pumped a great deal of subsurface water from their land, causing subsidence in adjoining plots of land.

CONCISE RULE OF LAW: A person is liable for damages caused by drawing water from his own land only to the extent that his activity was negligent.

FACTS: Friendswood Development Co. (D) pumped water from their land for sale to industrial users. Friendswood (D) pumped vast quantities despite an engineer report stating that withdrawal of such quantities would cause subsidence in the area surrounding the pumping. Southwest Industries (P) filed suit, claiming that Friendswood's (D) negligent withdrawal of excessive quantities of ground water was the cause in fact of severe subsidence on their lands. The appellate court refused to grant Friendwood's (D) request for summary judgment. Friendswood (D) appealed.

ISSUE: Is a person liable for damages caused by drawing water from his own land limited to the extent that his activity was negligent?

HOLDING AND DECISION: (Price, J.) Yes. A person is liable for damages caused by drawing water from his own land only to the extent that his activity was negligent. Under the common law, a landowner had absolute right to withdraw the water lying beneath his land. Under this rule, a landowner could not be held liable for any damage to neighboring property which resulted from activity on his own land. However, modern lawmakers have moved away from this harsh rule to hold a landowner liable for the damage to the extent his activity was negligent. Nonetheless, the case law to date has upheld the common law. Thus it would be unjust to apply a new standard to Friendswood (D) at this time. From this day forward, however, landowners will be held liable for damages caused by the negligent, willfully wasteful, or malicious withdrawal of subterranean waters. Reversed.

DISSENT: (Pope, J.) This case should be decided based on the fact that Southwest Industries (P) had a right to subadjacent support, which Friendswood's (D) negligent activity deprived them of.

EDITOR'S ANALYSIS: Restatement (Second) of Torts, § 818 gives landowners absolute right to subadjacent support. This strict liability approach, however, is the rule in only a few states such as Washington. See Muskatell v. City of Seattle, 116 P.2d. 363 (1941).

[For more information on nuisance and negligence, see Casenote Law Outline on Property, Chapter 9, § I, The Law of Private Nuisance.]

PAGE COUNTY APPLIANCE CENTER, INC. v. HONEYWELL, INC.

Iowa Sup. Ct., 347 N.W.2d 171 (1984).

NATURE OF CASE: Appeal from jury award of damages for claim of nuisance and tortious interference with business relations.

FACT SUMMARY: Honeywell (D) placed a computer in a business adjoining Page County Appliance Center (P) that interfered with Page's (P) business of selling television sets.

CONCISE RULE OF LAW: Lawful activity constitutes a nuisance if it unreasonably interferes with another's enjoyment of his or her property.

FACTS: Since 1953, Page (P) had engaged in the sale of electrical appliances, including television sets, in a store located next to a travel agent. In 1980 Honeywell (D) placed a computer in the travel agency, and from that time forward, Page (P) experienced reception problems on his display televisions. The reception problem was traced to a radiation leak in the computer. It took Honeywell (D) over two years to completely resolve the reception problem. Page (P) brought suit for nuisance and tortious interference. The trial court awarded Page (P) compensatory and punitive damages. Honeywell (D) appealed.

ISSUE: Does lawful activity constitute a nuisance if it unreasonably interferes with another's enjoyment of his or her property?

HOLDING AND DECISION: (Reynoldson, J.) Yes. Lawful activity constitutes a nuisance if it unreasonably interferes with another's enjoyment of his or her property. A litigant need not show negligence in an action for nuisance; he only need show that the activity was unreasonable in the context in which it took place. Honeywell (D) contends that placement of the computer in a business area was reasonable and Page's (P) use of the property was unreasonably sensitive. However, it is unlikely that the presence of a television set constitutes a hypersensitive use. However, the trial court did not sufficiently instruct the jury on the standard of reasonableness. Reversed and remanded for a new trial consistent with the finding of this court.

EDITOR'S ANALYSIS: Courts often rely on the nuisance analysis stated in the Restatement (Second) of Torts. It balances the social utility of the harmful conduct against its effect on the plaintiff. If the gravity of the harm outweighs the utility of the actor's conduct, in view of all the surrounding circumstances, then the use will be held to be unreasonable.

_____

[For more information on nuisance and unreasonable use, see Casenote Law Outline on Property, Chapter 9, § I, The Law of Private Nuisance.]

FONTAINEBLEAU HOTEL CORP. v. FORTY-FIVE TWENTY-FIVE, INC.

Fla. Dist. Ct. App., 114 So.2d 357 (1959).

NATURE OF CASE: Interlocutory appeal from issuance of an injunction.

FACT SUMMARY: Forty-Five Twenty-Five (P) sought to enjoin the Fontainebleau Hotel's (D) construction of an addition that would block all sunshine from Forty-Five's (P) hotel.

CONCISE RULE OF LAW: There is no legal right to the free flow of light or air from an adjoining parcel of land.

FACTS: Forty-Five (P) owned the Eden Roc Hotel (P), which was subsequently built next to the Fontainebleau (D). Fontainebleau (D) commenced construction on an addition which, when completed, would be fourteen stories tall and completely block all light from Eden Roc's (P) swimming pool area. Forty-Five (P) sought an injunction to halt construction on the tower, claiming it would interfere with their pre-existing light and air easement. The lower court issued an injunction, and Fontainebleau (D) appealed.

ISSUE: Is there a legal right to the free flow of light or air from an adjoining parcel of land?

HOLDING AND DECISION: (Per curiam) No. There is no legal right to the free flow of light or air from an adjoining parcel of land. Forty-Five (P) claims the right to an injunction based on the law of nuisance. However, nuisance law states that one property holder cannot use his property right to harm the lawful rights of an adjacent landholder. No court has ever found that a property owner has a legal right to air or sunlight. Absent a legal right to the light, Forty-Five (P) has not made a claim in nuisance. Order granting injunction reversed.

EDITOR'S ANALYSIS: Should the fact that the Fontainebleau (D) apparently erected the addition where it did out of spite and malice have any effect on the court's decision? To enjoin the addition as a so-called "spite fence," Forty-Five (P) would have to prove that the addition's sole purpose was to irritate; in other words, that the addition had no social utility whatsoever. In mixed motive cases, however, courts will almost certainly deny the injunction.

_____

[For more information on easements for light and air, see Casenote Law Outline on Property, Chapter 9, § I, The Law of Private Nuisance.]

PRAH v. MARETTI

Wis. Sup. Ct., 108 Wis. 2d 223, 321 N.W.2d 182 (1982).

NATURE OF CASE: Appeal from summary judgment denying relief from a proposed obstruction of sunlight.

FACT SUMMARY: Prah (P) sued to enjoin Maretti (D) from building on his land so as to block the flow of sunlight to Prah's (P) solar heated house.

CONCISE RULE OF LAW: The doctrine of prior appropriation applies to the use of sunlight as a protectable resource.

FACTS: In 1978, Prah (P) built a house which was equipped to use solar energy. Subsequently, Maretti (D) proposed to build a house which would have obstructed the free flow of sunlight onto Prah's (P) land and therefore interfered with his solar energy system. He sued to enjoin the construction contending he had begun using sunlight as a resource prior to Maretti's (D) plans and therefore under the doctrine of prior appropriation he had a protectable right in the sunlight. He then asserted that Maretti's (D) construction constituted a private nuisance. The trial court granted Maretti's (D) motion for a summary judgment holding that prior appropriation doctrine did not apply and no easement in light and air could be recognized. Prah (P) appealed.

ISSUE: Does the doctrine of prior appropriation apply to the use of sunlight as a protectable resource?

HOLDING AND DECISION: (Abrahamson, J.) Yes. The doctrine of prior appropriation applies to the use of sunlight as a protectable resource. Because of the development of technology allowing the practical use of solar energy, sunlight has taken on an enhanced value. At early American common law, sunlight was valued for the aesthetic purposes only, and it was left that an adjacent landowner's ability to use his land as he wished outweighed this aesthetic value, and no easement of light and air was recognized. However, given this new technology, sunlight must be regarded as a valuable resource and the doctrine of prior appropriation applies to protect those who first exploit the resource. Consequently, Prah (P) could maintain an action for nuisance. A factual question is presented whether Prah's (P) use was reasonable, therefore summary judgment should not have been granted. Reversed.

DISSENT: (Callow, J.) The facts of the present case do not give rise to a cause of action for private nuisance. The majority has failed to establish the obsolescence of the policies behind the restrictions in protecting a landowner's access to sunlight in spite fence cases. The majority's policy arguments are more properly directed to a case involving a public, not a private nuisance. This court should not intrude on an area of legislative responsibility. A private nuisance involves an "invasion," and the obstruction involved in the present case does not appear to fall within the definition of invasion. Maretti's (D) actions were lawful and should not be considered intentional and unreasonable. The "sensitive use" of the property by Prah (P) should not convert this otherwise lawful use into a public private nuisance, especially where Prah (P) has taken no efforts to protect his investment. The prospective application of its decision is also troubling.

EDITOR'S ANALYSIS: Some states, such as New Mexico, have enacted statutes which create property rights in access to solar energy. Local governments are given the power under which statutes to enact zoning regulations concerning solar rights. The New Mexico statute provides regulations protecting access in the absence of local regulations. Also, in order to be protected, solar rights as other property rights must be recorded.

[For more information on easements for light and air, see Casenote Law Outline on Property, Chapter 9, § I, The Law of Private Nuisance.]

NOTES:

4

CHAPTER 4
PUBLIC REGULATION OF PRIVATE ARRANGEMENTS
RESTRICTING USE OR OWNERSHIP OF LAND

QUICK REFERENCE RULES OF LAW

1. **Easements by Estoppel (Irrevocable Licenses).** Where use of a roadway, improvements to and maintenance of a roadway all have occurred with the tacit approval of the landowner, the landowner is estopped
from barring access to the improving party. (Holbrook v. Taylor)

   *[For more information on easement by estoppel, see Casenote Law Outline on Property, Chapter 8,
   § II, Easements.]*

2. **Constructive Trusts.** Where a buyer takes title with knowledge of an occupant's expectation of long-term
occupancy and subject to seller's condition that the occupants license not be terminated, the buyer holds the
land in constructive trust for the occupants. (Rase v. Castle Mountain Ranch, Inc.)

   *[For more information on equitable servitudes, see Casenote Law Outline on Property, Chapter 8,
   § III, Real Covenants and Equitable Servitudes.]*

3. **Easements Implied from Prior Use.** A grant of land is subject to servitude for prior use if the property was
originally joined, obviously used jointly, and the servitude is beneficial to the use of the servient estate.
(Granite Properties Limited Partnership v. Manns)

   *[For more information on prescriptive easements, see Casenote Law Outline on Property, Chapter
   8, § II, Easements.]*

4. **Easements by Necessity.** Where an owner conveys a portion of his land which has no outlet except over the
land of the grantor, or of strangers, an easement by necessity exists over the retained land of the grantor.
(Finn v. Williams)

   *[For more information on easements by estoppel, see Casenote Law Outline on Property, Chapter
   8, § II, Easements.]*

5. **Running with the Land.** An easement is not personal if there is anything in the grant to suggest that it was
intended to be tied to the land retained or conveyed. (Green v. Lupo)

   *[For more information on creation of easements, see Casenote Law Outline on Property, Chapter 8,
   § II, Easements.]*

6. **Appurtenant Easements.** Where the grant is unclear, the extent of the easement must be construed as
broadly as necessary to carry out the purposes for which it was granted. (Cox v. Glenbrook Co.)

   *[For more information on easements appurtenant, see Casenote Law Outline on Property, Chapter
   8, § II, Easements.]*

7. **Easements in Gross.** Easements in gross are freely transferable. (Henley v. Continental Cablevision of St.
Louis County, Inc.)

   *[For more information on transfer of easements, see Casenote Law Outline on Property, Chapter 8,
   § II, Easements.]*

8. **Neighboring Parcels.** Reasonable covenants against competition may be considered to run with the land when they serve a purpose of facilitating orderly and harmonious development for commercial use. (Whitinsville Plaza v. Kotseas)

   [For more information on real covenants, see Casenote Law Outline on Property, Chapter 8, § III, Real Covenants and Equitable Servitudes.]

9. **Equitable Servitudes and the Common Plan.** A general plan of subdivision restriction need not apply to all tracts in a subdivision for the doctrine of implied reciprocal negative easements to apply. (Evans v. Pollack)

   [For more information on negative easements, see Casenote Law Outline on Property, Chapter 8, § II, Easements.]

10. **Equitable Servitudes and the Common Plan.** If the owner of two or more lots, which are situated so as to bear a relation to each other, sells one with restrictions which are of benefit the land retained, during the period of restraint, the owner of the lot or lots retained can do nothing forbidden to the owner of the lot said. This is the doctrine of reciprocal negative easements. (Sanborn v. McLean)

    [For more information on negative easements, see Casenote Law Outline on Property, Chapter 8, § II, Easements.]

11. **Equitable Servitudes and the Common Plan.** Restrictive covenants are only enforceable against subsequent grantees when the restriction is in the chain of title and the grantee has actual or constructive notice. (Riley v. Bear Creek Planning Committee)

    [For more information on restrictive covenants, see Casenote Law Outline on Property, Chapter 8, § III, Real Covenants and Equitable Servitudes.]

12. **Group Homes as "Single-Family Dwellings."** Ambiguous restrictive covenants should be read narrowly to allow the least restrictive use of the land. (Blevins v. Barry-Lawrence County Association for Retarded Citizens)

    [For more information on restrictive covenants, see Casenote Law Outline on Property, Chapter 8, § III, Real Covenants and Equitable Servitudes.]

13. **Common Law: Changed Conditions.** A restrictive covenant will not be enforced where a fundamental change in the nature of the neighborhood has made the purpose sought by the covenant unattainable. (El Di, Inc. v. Town of Bethany Beach)

    [For more information on abandonment or waiver of restrictive covenant, see Casenote Law Outline on Property, Chapter 8, § III, Real Covenants and Equitable Servitudes.]

14. **Statutory Regulation of Covenants.** Building restrictions may be denied specific enforcement where they would unreasonably impede the most feasible use of land and money damages would adequately compensate the party asserting the restriction. (Blakeley v. Gorin)

    [For more information on restrictive covenants and changed conditions, see Casenote Law Outline on Property, Chapter 8, § III, Real Covenants and Equitable Servitudes.]

15. **Presumption against Forfeitures and the Grantor's Intent.** A grant of fee simple determinable must clearly state that the estate will terminate if not used in accordance with the grant. (Wood v. Board of County Commissioners of Freemont County)

[For more information on fee simple determinable, see Casenote Law Outline on Property, Chapter 5, § II, Present Possessory Estates.]

16. **Presumption against Forfeitures and the Grantor's Intent.** Where the language of a deed clearly evinces the intent to create a fee simple subject to a condition subsequent, the absence of a provision for re-entry will not be fatal to the grantor's claim. (Forsgren v. Sollie)

[For more information on fee simple subject to condition subsequent, see Casenote Law Outline on Property, Chapter 5, § II, Present Possessory Estates.]

17. **Direct Restraints on Alienation.** A restrictive restraint on the sale of fee simple title is a violation of public policy. (Riste v. Eastern Washington Bible Camp, Inc.)

[For more information on fee simple defensible, see Casenote Law Outline on Property, Chapter 5, § II, Present Possessory Estates.]

18. **Direct Restraints on Alienation.** Where land is granted or devised in fee, a provision of any sort that the taker shall not alienate, or shall not have power to alienate, is void. (Hankins v. Mathews)

[For more information on forfeiture restraint of land, see Casenote Law Outline on Property, Chapter 5, § II, Present Possessory Estates.]

19. **Grantor Consent Clauses.** Covenants retraining a grantee's ability to sell property are inconsistent with a grant of fee simple and are thus invalid. (Northwest Real Estate Co. v. Serio)

[For more information on restraints on alienation, see Casenote Law Outline on Property, Chapter 5, § II, Present Possessory Estates.]

20. **Void Only if Unreasonable.** A restraint on alienation is valid only if it is reasonable in light of the justifiable interests of the parties. (Horse Pond Fish & Game Club, Inc. v. Cormier)

[For more information on restraints on alienation, see Casenote Law Outline on Property, Chapter 5, § II, Present Possessory Estates.]

21. **Equitable Reformation and Constructive Trust.** A constructive trust will be imposed on the holder of legal title acquired through conduct short of actual fraud where such retention would result in his unjust enrichment. (Roper v. Edwards)

[For more information on disabling restraint on alienation, see Casenote Law Outline on Property, Chapter 5, § II, Present Possessory Estates.]

22. **Anticompetitive Covenants.** A restrictive covenant preventing a landlord from leasing space to a competitor will not be deemed to violate the Antitrust Act absent a showing of substantial anticompetitive effect. (Dunafon v. Delaware McDonald's Corp.)

[For more information on enforcement of restrictive covenants, see Casenote Law Outline on Property, Chapter 8, § III, Real Covenants and Equitable Servitudes.]

23. **Options to Purchase.** A restrictive covenant in a deed allowing unlimited time for repurchase of property conveyed is a purchase option subject to the Rule Against Perpetuities. (Central Delaware County Authority v. Greyhound Corp.)

[For more information on restrictive covenants, see Casenote Law Outline on Property, Chapter 8, § III, Real Covenants and Equitable Servitudes.]

24. **Options to Purchase.** An option to purchase contained in a commercial lease, at least if the option must be exercised within the leasehold term, is valid without regard to the Rule Against Perpetuities. (Texaco Refining and Marketing, Inc. v. Samowitz)

[For more information on options to purchase, see Casenote Law Outline on Property, Chapter 5, § IV, The Rule Against Perpetuities.]

25. **Preemtive Rights.** The Rule Against Perpetuities will be applied to preemptive rights only where the purposes of the rule are served. (Cambridge Co. v. East Slope Investment Corp.)

[For more information on the rule against perpetuities, see Casenote Law Outline on Property, Chapter 5, § IV, The Rule Against Perpetuities.]

26. **Social Welfare and Intergenerational Equity: Waste.** Laches is an equitable defense and will not bar recovery for permissive waste from mere lapse of time nor where there is a reasonable excuse for nonaction of a party in making inquiry as to his rights and asserting them. (Moore v. Phillips)

[For more information on voluntary waste, see Casenote Law Outline on Property, Chapter 5, § II, Present Possessory Estates.]

27. **Protection of Equality: Racially Discriminatory Covenants and Conditions.** The Equal Protection Clause of the Fourteenth Amendment prohibits judicial enforcement by state courts of restrictive covenants based on race or color. (Shelley v. Kraemer)

[For more information on restrictions on use of land, see Casenote Law Outline on Property, Chapter 5, § II, Present Possessory Estates.]

28. **Protection of Equality: Racially Discriminatory Covenants and Conditions.** The cy pres doctrine is not applicable when the testator would presumably have preferred to have the whole trust fail if the particular purpose of the trust became impossible to accomplish. (Evans v. Abney)

[For more information on restrictions on use of land, see Casenote Law Outline on Property, Chapter 5, § II, Present Possessory Estates.]

29. **Protection of Equality and Liberty: Restraints on Marriage.** The law will hold all devises as being in fee simple if no intent is expressed to create a life estate only, and also no further devise is made to take effect after the death of the devisee. (Lewis v. Searles)

[For more information on creation of a life estate, see Casenote Law Outline on Property, Chapter 5, § II, Present Possessory Estates.]

HOLBROOK v. TAYLOR

Ky. Sup. Ct., 532 S.W.2d 763 (1976).

NATURE OF CASE: Appeal from claim of easement by estoppel.

FACT SUMMARY: The Taylors (P) claimed an easement to use a road on the Holbrook's (D) property that they contended they had been using without Holbrook's (D) permission.

CONCISE RULE OF LAW: Where use of a roadway, improvements to and maintenance of a roadway all have occurred with the tacit approval of the landowner, the landowner is estopped from barring access to the improving party.

FACTS: In 1944 Holbrook (D) gave permission for a haul road to be constructed on his property. The road was used by a nearby mine, by Holbrook (D), and Holbrook's (D) tenant. The Taylors (P) purchased the adjacent property in 1964 and used the road for access during the construction of their home. After the house was completed, the Taylors (P) continued to use the road for access to their home, making improvements and generally maintaining the roadway. A dispute arose after Holbrook attempted to have the Taylors acknowledge his ownership of the land. Holbrook (D) blocked the roadway, leaving the Taylors (P) without access to their land. The Taylors (P) brought suit claiming an easement by estoppel. The trial court ruled in their favor, and Holbrook (D) appealed.

ISSUE: Where use of a roadway, improvements to, and maintenance of a roadway all have occurred with the tacit approval of the landowner, is the landowner estopped from barring access to the improving party?

HOLDING AND DECISION: (Sternberg, J.) Yes. Where use of a roadway, improvements to, and maintenance of a roadway have all occurred with the tacit approval of the landowner, the landowner is estopped from barring access to the improving party. A person may obtain a license to use land by expending money and effort in connection with a roadway or its use with the knowledge of the owner. It would be unconscionable to allow an owner to revoke such a license after he has watched the licensee expend money and effort on reliance on the existence of such a license. Whether or not the Taylors' (P) use was with Holbrook's (D) permission, they expended a great deal of money on improvement with his knowledge and in reliance that they would continue to be allowed to use the road. Holbrook (D) is estopped from preventing their use of the road. Affirmed.

EDITOR'S ANALYSIS: The Taylors (P) claimed that the dispute arose when Holbrook (D) demanded they buy the road for $500. Would the court have granted the easement by estoppel if from the beginning the Taylors (P) had paid a royalty to Holbrook (D) for use of the road?

[For more information on easement by estoppel, see Casenote Law Outline on Property, Chapter 8, § II, Easements.]

NOTES:

RASE v. CASTLE MOUNTAIN RANCH, INC.
Mont. Sup. Ct., 631 P.2d 680 (1981).

NATURE OF CASE: Cross-appeal from imposition of a constructive trust.

FACT SUMMARY: Rase (P) represented owners of cabins built on Castle Mountain Ranch's (D) land, who were told they must vacate the land.

CONCISE RULE OF LAW: Where a buyer takes title with knowledge of an occupant's expectation of long-term occupancy and subject to seller's condition that the occupants license not be terminated, the buyer holds the land in constructive trust for the occupants.

FACTS: Travenor held a piece of land for over fifty years. During that time he invited Rase (P) and other friends to build cabins on the property and use the property. After several years, Travenor had cabin owners sign a standard license agreement that provided for a nominal license fee and a termination provision. For fifty years the cabins were bought, sold, and improved. Never once did Travenor terminate a license agreement. Travenor sold the property to Castle Mountain (D). Prior to the sale, Castle Mountain (D) asked Travenor to terminate all the license agreements. Travenor refused and went so far as to make the continued validity of these agreements a condition of sale. Upon the closing of the sale, Castle Mountain (D) terminated all license agreements. The cabin owners (P) brought suit to quiet title. The trial court imposed a constructive trust on the land in favor of the cabin owners for thirteen years. Both parties appealed.

ISSUE: Where a buyer takes title with knowledge of an occupant's expectation of long-term occupancy and subject to the seller's condition that the occupant's license not be terminated, does the buyer hold the land in constructive trust for the occupants?

HOLDING AND DECISION: (Sheehy, J.) Yes. Where a buyer takes title with knowledge of occupant's expectation of long-term occupancy and subject to the seller's condition that the occupants license not be terminated, the buyer holds the land in constructive trust for the occupants. Travenor's actions allowing cabin owners to continue to make improvements to the cabins gave the owners a reasonable expectation of long-term occupancy. Castle Mountain (D) accepted the cabin owners' expectations of occupancy as a condition of the contract. Castle Mountain (D) is barred by equity from denying these expectations. Castle Mountain (D) holds the land and the cabins in constructive trust for the cabin owners for a period of thirteen years. Affirmed.

DISSENT: (Shea, J.) The only term of occupancy presented into evidence was fifty years. Thus the constructive trust should be held for that term.

EDITOR'S ANALYSIS: Castle Mountain (D) also raised the parole evidence rule as a defense to the imposition of the trust. The parole evidence rule does not apply however, when the validity of the agreement is in question. The court found that to be the case with the existing license agreements.

[For more information on equitable servitudes, see Casenote Law Outline on Property, Chapter 8, § III, Real Covenants and Equitable Servitudes.]

NOTES:

GRANITE PROPERTIES LIMITED PARTNERSHIP v. MANNS
Ill. Sup. Ct., 512 N.E.2d 1230 (1987).

NATURE OF CASE: Appeal from grant of injunction preventing interference with use of easement.

FACT SUMMARY: Granite Properties (P) argued that it had acquired, by implied reservation, easements over two driveways providing access to its properties when it sold an adjoining parcel of land to Manns (D).

CONCISE RULE OF LAW: If a previous use is continuous and apparent, the degree of necessity required to create an implied easement is reduced.

FACTS: Granite Properties (P) held three contiguous parcels in common ownership from 1963 to 1982, when it sold the middle parcel to Manns (D). About five times a week, trucks servicing a shopping center located on Granite's (P) easternmost parcel used a driveway located partially on Manns' (D) property. Another driveway, also located on Manns' property, serviced an apartment building on Granite's (P) property to the west. Manns (D) saw the driveways, which had been used by Granite (P) since the sixties, before he bought the middle parcel. After his purchase, finding no recorded easements following a title search, Manns (D) notified Granite (P) to discontinue its use of the driveways. Granite (P) subsequently brought an action to enjoin Manns (D) from interfering with Granite's (P) use and enjoyment of the two driveways. The trial court denied injunctive relief as to the shopping center driveway, but found an implied easement for Granite (P) as to the apartment complex driveway. The appellate court found acquired easements for both driveways. Manns (D) appealed.

ISSUE: If a previous use is continuous and apparent, is the degree of necessity required to create an implied easement reduced?

HOLDING AND DECISION: (Ryan, J.) Yes. If a previous use is continuous and apparent, the degree of necessity required to create an implied easement is reduced. An easement implied from a prior existing use arises when an owner of two or more adjoining parcels sells part of the property without mentioning any incidental benefit one parcel may convey on another. This benefit must be obvious, continuous, and permanent, and the claimed easement must be necessary to the enjoyment of the parcel retained by the grantor. Proof of the prior use is evidence that the parties probably intended an easement. In this case, any alternatives to the two driveways would be expensive and impractical. Given the strong evidence of Granite's (P) prior use of the driveways and Manns' (D) knowledge thereof, the evidence was sufficient to fulfill the elastic necessity requirement. Affirmed.

EDITOR'S ANALYSIS: There is one other type of implied easement — the easement by necessity. The easement by necessity usually arises when an owner of land conveys to another an inner portion which is entirely surrounded by lands owned either by the grantor or the grantor plus strangers. Unless a contrary intent is manifested, the grantee is found to have a right-of-way across the retained land of the grantor for ingress and egress to the land-locked parcel.

[For more information on prescriptive easements, see Casenote Law Outline on Property, Chapter 8, § II, Easements.]

NOTES:

FINN v. WILLIAMS
376 Ill. 95, 33 N.E.2d 226, 133 A.L.R. 1390 (1941).

NATURE OF CASE: Appeal from judgment establishing an easement by necessity.

FACT SUMMARY: Finn's (P) land was entirely landlocked after its purchase from Williams (D).

CONCISE RULE OF LAW: Where an owner conveys a portion of his land which has no outlet except over the land of the grantor, or of strangers, an easement by necessity exists over the retained land of the grantor.

FACTS: Charles Williams owned 140 acres of land. In 1895, he conveyed 40 acres of his holdings to Bacon, and in 1937, Finn (P) acquired title to those 40 acres. Zelphia Williams (D) inherited the remaining 100 acres from Charles, who was her husband. The 40 acres acquired by Finn (P) were entirely landlocked, but for many years access was gained over private roads of strangers and a road over the Williams land. In 1939, Williams (D) refused Finn (P) any further access over her land. By that time all of the other private roads leading out had been closed. Finn (P) was unable to take his stock and produce to market and had to walk to the highway on a footpath carrying what produce he could.

ISSUE: Is an easement by necessity created when an owner conveys a portion of his land which has no outlet except over the retained land of the grantor or over the land of strangers?

HOLDING AND DECISION: (Wilson, J.) Yes. If at one time there had been unity of title, the easement by necessity will pass with each transfer as appurtenant to the dominant estate and may be exercised at any time by the holder. It makes no difference that the easement was not used earlier. The easement came into existence when the unity of title was split. Where an owner of land conveys a parcel which has no outlet except over the remaining lands of the grantor or over the land of strangers, a right of way by necessity exists over the remaining lands of the grantor. When permission to go over the land of strangers is denied, the subsequent grantees of the dominant estate may avail themselves of the dominant easement implied in the deed severing the dominant and servient estates.

EDITOR'S ANALYSIS: A landlocked parcel of land was about the only situation that the common-law courts would recognize as creating an easement by necessity. This was the strict necessity view of such easements. In recent years, some American courts have refused to create an easement by necessity even for landlocked parcels. Their reasoning was that to do so would be to sanction a form of private eminent domain. Since only a governmental unit holds the power of eminent domain, it was the obligation of the landlocked owner to prevail upon the appropriate governmental unit to condemn a right of way and build a public road.

[For more information on easements by estoppel, see Casenote Law Outline on Property, Chapter 8, § II, Easements.]

GREEN v. LUPO
647 P. 2d 51 (Wash Ct. App 1982).

NATURE OF CASE: Appeal from refusal to enforce an agreement to grant an easement.

FACT SUMMARY: Green (P) granted Lupo (D) a deed release upon the sale of his property on the condition that when Lupo (D) acquired title he would grant Green (P) an easement .

CONCISE RULE OF LAW: An easement is not personal if there is anything in the grant to suggest that it was intended to be tied to the land retained or conveyed.

FACTS: Green (P) originally owned an entire parcel of land. Later he transferred a portion of the land to Lupo (D). Lupo (D) asked Green (P) for a deed release he needed in order to obtain financing to build a home. Green (P) granted the release on the condition that Lupo (D) grant him an easement for ingress and egress when he acquired title. Lupo (D) agreed. Green (P) turned his parcel into a mobile home park, and the occupants used the part of the land designated as the easement as a runway for motorcycles. In protest of Green's (P) use, Lupo (D) refused to transfer the easement as promised when he acquired title. Green (P) brought suit to specifically enforce the grant of the easement. The trial court found that the easement was personal and enjoined the motorcycles' use of it. Green (P) appealed.

ISSUE: Is an easement personal if there is anything in the grant to suggest that it was intended to be tied to the land retained or conveyed?

HOLDING AND DECISION: (Petrich, J.) No. An easement is not personal if there is anything in the grant to suggest that it was intended to be tied to the land retained or conveyed. There is a presumption against personal easements. The written instrument granting Lupo (D) his easement states the easement would be granted to Green (P) for ingress and egress to their property. Thus the easement was granted to gain access to a particular piece of land and is thus appurtenant, not personal. The lower court erred in ordering the cycles banned. Reversed and remanded.

EDITOR'S ANALYSIS: The appeal was actually based on the admissibility of parol evidence. The court found that parol evidence is always admissible to demonstrate intent when the written instrument is unclear.

[For more information on creation of easements, see Casenote Law Outline on Property, Chapter 8, § II, Easements.]

COX v. GLENBROOK COMPANY
Nev. Sup. Ct., 371 P.2d 647 (1962).

NATURE OF CASE: Appeal from request for declaratory judgment.

FACT SUMMARY: Glenbrook (D) owned land subject to an easement for access from Cox's (P) land; the parties contested the extent of the easement.

CONCISE RULE OF LAW: Where the grant is unclear, the extent of the easement must be construed as broadly as necessary to carry out the purposes for which it was granted.

FACTS: The Quill property was surrounded on four sides by land owned by others. There was an easement granted through the Glenbrook (D) property to provide ingress and egress to the Quill property. The Quill property changed hands several times before it ended up in the hands of Cox (D). Cox (P) planned to develop the land as resort area. To achieve this goal, Cox (P) would have to expand the existing easement from a one-lane dirt road to a paved, two-way road. Both parties brought suit for declaratory judgment as to the extent of the easement. The trial court found that the easement was limited to those uses necessary for access by a single family. Cox (P) appealed.

ISSUE: Where the grant is unclear, must the extent of the easement be construed as broadly as necessary?

HOLDING AND DECISION: (Thompson, J.) Yes. Where the grant is unclear, the extent of the easement must be construed as broad as necessary to carry out the purposes for which it was granted. The trial court's construction of the limits on the easement erroneously makes the easement personal. As broadly as necessary for family use defines the easement by the person holding it rather than the land it benefits. The grant was intended to give ingress and egress to the land. This intent does not support doubling the size of the road and paving it. The easement is limited to the size and nature at the time of the grant.

EDITOR'S ANALYSIS: Another way appurtenant easements are limited is by the nature of the servient estate. An easement cannot cause unwarranted interference or burden on the servient estate. The court found that mere grading of the road in this case would not pole such a burden, but that widening the road would.

[For more information on easements appurtenant, see Casenote Law Outline on Property, Chapter 8, § II, Easements.]

HENLEY v. CONTINENTAL CABLEVISION OF ST. LOUIS COUNTY, INC.
Mo. Ct. App., 692 S.W. 2d 825 (1985).

NATURE OF CASE: Action for injunction and damages.

FACT SUMMARY: Henley (P) granted the telephone company the right to construct and maintain telephone and electrical systems that Continental Cable (D) licensed in order to install cable services.

CONCISE RULE OF LAW: Easements in gross are freely transferable.

FACTS: In 1922 Henley's (P) predecessors granted the telephone company an easement in gross to install and maintain electrical and telephone systems on the back five feet of all the properties in their subdivision. This easement was transferable to other parties to create such systems. In 1981 Continental Cable (D) acquired licenses from the phone company to install a cable system in the area. Henley (P) filed suit for injunction to prevent and compel removal of Continental's (D) cables, and for damages.

ISSUE: Are easements in gross freely transferable?

HOLDING AND DECISION: (Gaerntner, J.) Yes. Easements in gross are freely transferable. The easement granted by Henley (P) was not tied to a dominant estate and was thus in gross. The easement granted was exclusive to the telephone company, and thus the owners of the servient estate could not affect how the rights are exercised. Because the rights are exclusive they are also alienable, consistent with the use for which the easement was granted. When determining the purpose of the grant, technological advances must be considered. The addition of cable wire falls into the same electrical and telephone wiring and is no more burdensome on the servient estate. The easement should be broadly construed to allow the addition of cable wire. Judgment for Continental (D).

EDITOR'S ANALYSIS: A court looks at three factors in determining the scope of an easement: (1) the burden the use causes, (2) the type of use proposed, and (3) whether the easement is alienable. Even if the activities are contemplated by the grantor of the easement, it may be too burdensome if it puts too much stress on the easement. However, most courts will allow the subdivision of a dominant tenement even if the usage of the easement is increased thereby, unless the grantor has specifically forbidden subdivision.

[For more information on transfer of easements, see Casenote Law Outline on Property, Chapter 8, § II, Easements.]

WHITINSVILLE PLAZA, INC. v. KOTSEAS
Mass. Sup. Jud. Ct., 378 Mass. 85, 390 N.E.2d 243 (1979).

NATURE OF CASE: Action for injunction and breach of contract.

FACT SUMMARY: In selling land to the Plaza's (P) predecessor in interest, Kotseas (D) had agreed to a covenant not to have a competing business on his adjoining land.

CONCISE RULE OF LAW: Reasonable covenants against competition may be considered to run with the land when they serve a purpose of facilitating orderly and harmonious development for commercial use.

FACTS: Kotseas (D) had sold land to the Plaza's (P) predecessor in interest, the deed containing a covenant not to use the adjacent land Kotseas (D) retained in competition with the discount store to be built and to use it only for enumerated business purposes. The Plaza (P), as successor to the original covenantee, brought an action against Kotseas (D) and CVS (D), the party to whom Kotseas (D) had subsequently leased his retained land. The action was for declaratory, injunctive, and monetary relief and was based on violation of the covenant and breach of contract. The allegation was that Kotseas (D) had, with the full knowledge of CVS (D), leased his property to CVS (D) for purposes of carrying on a competitive business in violation of the aforementioned covenant. The superior court dismissed the complaint for failure to state a claim. The Plaza (P) appealed.

ISSUE: Can covenants against competition run with the land?

HOLDING AND DECISION: (Quirico, J.) Yes. Reasonable covenants against competition may run with the land when they serve a purpose of facilitating orderly and harmonious development for commercial use. Insofar as the Norcross case held that such covenants not to compete can never be considered to "touch and concern" the land and are, thus, always precluded from running with the land, it is overruled. Commentators have long opined that Massachusetts' continued observation of the Norcross rule is anachronistic and in need of change. Furthermore, this jurisdiction is practically alone in maintaining such a rigid rule. In adopting a more reasonable approach, parties such as the Plaza (P) now have the opportunity to prove their particular covenants meet the criteria for running with the land. The Plaza (P) was improperly foreclosed from making its case on both real property and contractual theories. Reversed and remanded.

EDITOR'S ANALYSIS: Those decisions holding all anticompetitive covenants unenforceable as not running with the land are generally considered to have been based on the courts' views toward the free enterprise system and not strictly on real property concepts. Such covenants were seen as effecting monopolies of trade or business and, thus, being undesirable.

[For more information on real covenants, see Casenote Law Outline on Property, Chapter 8, § III, Real Covenants and Equitable Servitudes.]

NOTES:

EVANS v. POLLACK
Tex. Sup. Ct., 796 S.W.2d 465 (1990).

NATURE OF CASE: Appeal from defense verdict in declaratory, equitable, and injunctive relief.

FACT SUMMARY: Evans (P) sought to enjoin the commercial use of unrestricted lots within a restricted subdivision under the implied reciprocal negative easement doctrine.

CONCISE RULE OF LAW: A general plan of subdivision restriction need not apply to all tracts in a subdivision for the doctrine of implied reciprocal negative easements to apply.

FACTS: Evans' (P) predecessors bought the subdivision in question, platted it, and then further subdivided the plats. The majority of the plats contained a restriction against commercial use and limited construction to single family homes. Many of these lots were sold. Pollack (D) sought to buy some of the unrestricted lots for use as a marina, a private club, and condominiums. Evans (P) sought to enjoin the sale of the land without imposition of the restrictions. He also sought a declaration that the restrictive covenants on his property were implied on the other properties by reciprocity. The trial court found that restrictions were intended to apply to all lots in the subdivision. The court of appeals reversed. Evans (P) appealed.

ISSUE: Must a general plan of subdivision restriction apply to all tracts in a subdivision for the doctrine of reciprocal negative easement to apply?

HOLDING AND DECISION: (Ray, J.) No. A general plan of subdivision restriction need not apply to all tracts in a subdivision for a general plan of subdivision restriction to apply. Evans (P) is asking that we imply a reciprocal negative easement on the land Pollack (D) seeks to buy. A court may imply such an easement on a showing that the subdivider had a general development scheme for the subdivision. Here, the restricted lots are all similarly situated. They need not encompass the whole subdivision, so long as the restrictions apply to well-defined lots. Since that is the case here, reciprocal negative easements may be implied. Reversed.

EDITOR'S ANALYSIS: Note that the doctrine of implied reciprocal negative servitudes binds the buyers even though the grantor omits to include the mutual restrictions in subsequent deeds. The state of California, for one, has refused to recognize the doctrine on the grounds that it fails to protect buyer expectations, fosters uncertainty, and circumvents the orderly development of subdivisions. Instead, state law requires that only restrictive covenants must be in writing or on the deed in order to be enforceable.

[For more information on negative easements, see Casenote Law Outline on Property, Chapter 8, § II, Easements.]

NOTES:

SANBORN v. McLEAN

Mich. Sup. Ct., 233 Mich. 227, 206 N.W. 496 (1925).

NATURE OF CASE: Action to enjoin erection of gasoline filling station.

FACT SUMMARY: Sanborn (P) and McLean (D) trace the titles to their adjoining lots to the proprietor of the subdivision. Residences are built on all the surrounding lots. Sanborn (P) objected to McLean's (D) erection of a gas station on her lot.

CONCISE RULE OF LAW: If the owner of two or more lots, which are situated so as to bear a relation to each other, sells one with restrictions which are of benefit the land retained, during the period of restraint, the owner of the lot or lots retained can do nothing forbidden to the owner of the lot said. This is the doctrine of reciprocal negative easements.

FACTS: On December 28, 1892, McLaughlin, who was then owner of the lots on Collingwood Avenue, deeded four of the lots with the restriction that only residences would be built on the lots. On July 24, 1893, McLaughlin conveyed several more lots with the same restriction. Sanborn (P) traces title to McLaughlin. McLean's (D) title runs back to a deed dated September 7, 1893, which does not contain the restrictions. No buildings other than residences have been erected on any of the lots of the subdivision.

ISSUE: (1) If the owner of two or more lots, which are situated so as to bear a relation to each other, sells one with restrictions which are of benefit to the land retained, during the period of restraint, can the owner of the lot or lots retained do anything forbidden to the owner of the lot sold? (2) Is a reciprocal negative easement personal to owners?

HOLDING AND DECISION: (Wiest, J.) (1) No. The doctrine of reciprocal negative easements makes restrictions which are of benefit to the land retained mutual so that the owner can do nothing upon the land he has retained that is forbidden to the owner of the lot sold. In this case McLaughlin deeded lots with the restriction that only residences be built on them. Such restrictions were imposed for the benefit of the lands retained by McLaughlin to carry out the scheme of a residential district, and a restrictive negative easement attached to the lots retained. Since his was one of the lots retained in the December 1892 and July 1893 deeds, a reciprocal negative easement attached to the lot which later became McLean's (D). (2) No. Reciprocal negative easements are not personal to owners but are operative upon use of the land by any owner having actual or constructive notice thereof. In this case the reciprocal negative easement attached to McLean's (D) lot may now be enforced by Sanborn (P) provided McLean (D) had constructive knowledge of the easement at the time of purchase. At the time of purchase, McLean (D) had an abstract of title showing the subdivision and that his lot had 97 companion lots. He could not avoid noticing the strictly uniform residential character of the companion lots, and the least inquiry would

have revealed the fact that his lot was subject to a reciprocal negative easement. The injunction is granted.

EDITOR'S ANALYSIS: Reciprocal negative easements must start with common owners. They cannot arise and fasten upon one lot by reason of other lot owners conforming to a general plan. Such easements are never retroactive, and as demonstrated here, they pass their benefits and carry their obligations to all purchasers of land provided the purchaser has constructive notice of the easement.

[For more information on negative easements, see Casenote Law Outline on Property, Chapter 8, § II, Easements.]

NOTES:

RILEY v. BEAR CREEK PLANNING COMMITTEE
551 P.2d 1213 (Cal. 1976).

NATURE OF CASE: Appeal of an action to quiet title.

FACT SUMMARY: Riley (P) purchased a lot in a subdivision; however, the deed did not include a restrictive covenant which was imposed on the surrounding lots.

CONCISE RULE OF LAW: Restrictive covenants are only enforceable against subsequent grantees when the restriction is in the chain of title and the grantee has actual or constructive notice.

FACTS: The Alpine Slopes Development Company conveyed a lot in a subdivision to Riley (P) in 1964. The deed contained no restrictions upon the use of the land. Nine months later, Alpine recorded a document which purported to place restrictions on all of the lots in the subdivision, including Riley's (P) property. The restrictions were also included in the other deeds. One of the restrictions limited additions and required approval from the Bear Creek Planning Committee (D). In 1972, after Riley (P) constructed a snow tunnel without prior approval, the Bear Creek Planning Committee (D) claimed the structure was a violation of the restrictive covenant. Riley (P) filed suit to quiet title on the property. The trial court ruled for Riley (P), the appellate court affirmed, and Bear Creek (D) appealed.

ISSUE: Are restrictive covenants enforceable against subsequent purchasers when the restriction is not contained in the original deed?

HOLDING AND DECISION: (Per curiam) No. Restrictive covenants are only enforceable against subsequent grantees when the restriction is in the chain of title and the grantee has actual or constructive notice. Parties not in privity may enforce restrictive covenants based upon mutually enforceable equitable servitudes which benefit the whole area. Equitable servitudes are enforceable if the language in the deed expresses a common plan of restrictions. The intent of the parties must be ascertained by looking at only the deed, which is the final expression of their understanding. If a restrictive covenant is placed in the deed by the original grantor, it is enforceable by the adjoining property owners who are part of the common plan against any subsequent purchasers. However, if the restriction is not included in the deed, it is not enforceable. The deed conveyed to Riley (P) did not contain any restrictions. Although Alpine had the intent to establish a common plan, it was not expressed in Riley's (P) deed. Therefore, the restrictions are not enforceable against Riley (P). Affirmed.

DISSENT: (Tobriner, J.) The majority's conclusion that a buyer of a subdivision lot who takes his deed with actual knowledge of a general plan of mutual restrictions for the entire subdivision thereafter may proceed to violate all such restrictions because they were inadvertently omitted from his deed is reasonable. This holding will permit future subdivision buyers to ignore similar restrictions designed to preserve natural beauty and property values. Common sense and substantive justice dictate that Riley (P) should not be permitted to violate such restrictions.

EDITOR'S ANALYSIS: The decision rested heavily on the precedent of Werner v. Graham, 181 Cal. 174 (1919), which barred extrinsic evidence regarding the intention of the parties based upon a rigid application of the parol evidence rule. However, the court did not completely rely on this aspect of Werner. They suggested that the Statute of Frauds also supplied reason for making the deed the sole source of restrictive covenants.

[For more information on restrictive covenants, see Casenote Law Outline on Property, Chapter 8, § III, Real Covenants and Equitable Servitudes.]

NOTES:

BLEVINS v. BARRY-LAWRENCE COUNTY ASSOCIATION FOR RETARDED CITIZENS

Mo. Sup. Ct., 707 S.W.2d 407 (1986).

NATURE OF CASE: Appeal from circuit court issuance of injunction preventing use of property as a group home.

FACT SUMMARY: Blevins (P) contended that a group home for retarded adults violated the restrictive covenant on the land.

CONCISE RULE OF LAW: Ambiguous restrictive covenants should be read narrowly to allow the least restrictive use of the land.

FACTS: Barry-Lawrence County Association for Retarded Citizens (Barry) (D) established group homes for retarded adults. Eight unrelated retarded persons lived in these homes supervised by couples who served as house parents. In all ways the individuals acted as a family — taking meals together, discussing problems, and sharing the chores of the household. The situations were permanent and meant to teach these adults socialization skills. The group homes were single-family residences. Blevins (P), who lived next to a prospective group home, brought suit claiming that this use violated the restrictive covenant limiting the use of the land "for residential purposes" only. The trial court agreed, and Barry (D) appealed.

ISSUE: Should ambiguous restrictive covenant be read narrowly to allow the least restrictive use of the land?

HOLDING AND DECISION: (Welliver, J.) Yes. Ambiguous restrictive covenants should be read narrowly to allow the least restrictive use of the land. Public policy opposes restrictions on the use of land. Thus, where a covenant is unclear, it should be read in the least restrictive manner possible. The plain meaning of residential purposes is a place where individuals live rather than work. Clearly the group homes are meant as permanent residences for retarded adults, not as a workplace. The second covenant, limiting use to a single family residence, refers to the type of structure allowed on the lot. The group home structure fits within this definition. Barry's (D) use of the lot does not violate the covenant. Reversed.

EDITOR'S ANALYSIS: Would the fact that Barry (D) is a for-profit organization make any difference to the court? Courts have differed on the definition of "family." Some have interpreted the term to encompass unrelated adults living together in emulation of a conventional family environment, thereby effectively removing group homes from the reach of restrictive covenants. See, e.g., Malcolm v, Shamie, 290 N.W. 2d. 101 (Mich,Ct. App. 1980). Other courts have been less generous. In Shaver v. Hunter, 626 S.W.2d. 574 (1981), the Texas Court of Appeals concluded that "family" required a blood or marital relationship.

NOTES:

[For more information on restrictive covenants, see Casenote Law Outline on Property, Chapter 8, § III, Real Covenants and Equitable Servitudes.]

EL DI, INC. v. TOWN OF BETHANY BEACH
Del. Sup. Ct., 477 A.2d 1066 (1984).

NATURE OF CASE: Appeal of injunction enforcing a restrictive covenant.

FACT SUMMARY: Bethany Beach (P) sought to enforce a restrictive covenant prohibiting the sale of alcoholic beverages, even though the nature of the neighborhood had changed greatly since the creation of the covenant.

CONCISE RULE OF LAW: A restrictive covenant will not be enforced where a fundamental change in the nature of the neighborhood has made the purpose sought by the covenant unattainable.

FACTS: The town of Bethany Beach (P) was originally established by a church and was intended to be a quiet, residential community. The property originally forming the town had a restrictive covenant placed on it preventing commercial use and the sale of alcoholic beverages. Over the years, the community grew. The covenant against non-residential use was ignored; in fact, the original center of town was zoned for commercial use. In 1981, El Di, Inc. (D), operator of a restaurant, applied for and received a license to sell alcohol, which it began to do. The town of Bethany Beach (P) obtained an injunction enforcing the restrictive covenant. El Di (D) appealed.

ISSUE: Will a restrictive covenant be enforced where a fundamental change in the nature of the neighborhood has made the purpose sought by the covenant unattainable?

HOLDING AND DECISION: (Herrmann, J.) No. A restrictive covenant will not be enforced where a fundamental change in the nature of the neighborhood has made the purpose sought by the covenant unattainable. Courts will not enforce a restrictive covenant to no purpose. Here, the purpose of the covenant was to ensure that Bethany Beach (P) remained a quiet, residential community. This has not occurred, however. Rather, commercial development has occurred, and the town is now a seaside resort. Therefore, the community is no longer that envisioned by its founders, and the covenant has outlived its purpose. Reversed.

DISSENT: (Christie, J.) Despite its growth, Bethany (P) still remains a quiet family-oriented community, justifying the continued enforcement of the restrictions. The tolerance of public consumption of alcohol does not negate the prohibition on its sale.

EDITOR'S ANALYSIS: "Changed conditions" is conceptually distinct from "abandonment," another rationale for extinguishment of a servitude. The former refers to changes in the community outside the restricted land. Abandonment occurs when the use of the dominant tenement is altered so as to make enforcement of the covenant unreasonable.

[For more information on abandonment or waiver of restrictive covenant, see Casenote Law Outline on Property, Chapter 8, § III, Real Covenants and Equitable Servitudes.]

NOTES:

BLAKELY v. GORIN
365 Mass. 590, 313 N.E.2d 903 (1974).

NATURE OF CASE: Action to remove building restrictions.

FACT SUMMARY: Blakely (P) wanted to build a hotel to be connected by a passageway over an alley with an existing structure owned by him.

CONCISE RULE OF LAW: Building restrictions may be denied specific enforcement where they would unreasonably impede the most feasible use of land and money damages would adequately compensate the party asserting the restriction.

FACTS: Massachusetts placed certain restrictions on land sold to private parties. Blakely (P) owned property subject to these restrictions. One parcel had a hotel built on it. Behind the property, separated by an alley, Blakely (P) owned a vacant lot. Blakely (P) wanted to build an addition to the hotel on this lot and to connect the two buildings by a walkway over the alley. Gorin (D), who owned an eight-story apartment building adjacent to the vacant lot, objected to the building of the walkway, alleging that it would infringe on light and air rights. Gorin (D) also alleged that the new construction would violate the no mercantile restriction and the 16-foot distance requirement between abutting buildings contained in the original deeds issued by Massachusetts. The court found that the restrictions were no longer valid and should not be enforced since they would unreasonably impede the most reasonable use of the property. The court found authority for its position under a state law which allowed the court to deny specific enforcement of outdated restrictions or that money damages could, where appropriate be awarded in lieu of enforcement. Gorin (D) appealed, alleging that the statute allowed for a taking of property rights without compensation, and he had been denied damages for loss of air and light rights.

ISSUE: May enforcement of building restrictions be denied where use is unreasonably denied?

HOLDING AND DECISION: (Hennessey, J.) Yes. The legislature may provide that outdated or unnecessary building restrictions may be denied specific enforcement by the court. If the person asserting the restrictions can establish damages, a money award in lieu of enforcement may be allowed, if appropriate. Any mercantile businesses established in the new structure are merely subsidiary to the primary business of operating a hotel. They will have no effect on any property owner. The passageway between buildings does constitute an infringement on Gorin's (D) property rights, but it is not so substantial as to require enforcement of the restriction. Rather than deprive Blakely (P) of the best and most reasonable use of his property, money damages were sufficient to compensate Gorin (D). Private building restrictions are not the equivalent of constitutionally protected rights. Reasonable government regulation and control are permissible if it serves a valid public purpose. It is sufficient to state that a new hotel would increase the city's tax base. Remanded for a determination of damages to be awarded.

DISSENT: (Quirico, J.) The statute allowing nonenforcement of private restrictions is unconstitutional as applied herein. It allows private parties to deprive others of valuable property rights for a very large number of reasons.

EDITOR'S ANALYSIS: Normally, if any of the following conditions exist, building restrictions/covenants may be avoided (depending on the jurisdiction): (1) change in the neighborhood's character rendering the restriction unfair/ unnecessary, (2) conduct of the party imposing the condition constituting waiver, (3) the party claiming enforcement owns no land in the parcel subdivision and the restrictions are not required to achieve a common plan, and/or (4) the restriction serves no public/private interest and would inhibit growth of the neighborhood and/or best use of the land.

[For more information on restrictive covenants and changed conditions, see Casenote Law Outline on Property, Chapter 8, § III, Real Covenants and Equitable Servitudes.]

NOTES:

WOOD v. BOARD OF COUNTY COMMISSIONERS OF FREMONT COUNTY
Wyo. Sup. Ct., 759 P.2d 1250 (1988).

NATURE OF CASE: Appeal from summary judgment for defense in action for reversion.

FACT SUMMARY: Wood (P) claimed that a grant of land to the Commissioner of Freemont County (D) was subject to a condition subsequent that the land be used as a hospital.

CONCISE RULE OF LAW: A grant of fee simple determinable must clearly state that the estate will terminate if not used in accordance with the grant.

FACTS: Wood (P) gave a parcel of land to the Freemont County Board of Commissioners (D). The transfer stated that the purpose of the grant was that it be used for a hospital, but it did not express what would happen to the estate if it were not so used. The County (D) operated a hospital on the land for nearly forty years before putting it up for sale. Wood (P) then brought suit, claiming a right to a reversion in the grant which became effective when the land ceased to be used for the intended purpose. The trial court granted summary judgment to the County (D). Wood (P) appealed.

ISSUE: Must a grant of fee simple determinable clearly state that the estate will terminate if not used in accordance with the grant?

HOLDING AND DECISION: (Brown, J.) Yes. A grant of fee simple determinable must clearly state that the estate will terminate if not used in accordance with the grant. A fee simple determinable is characterized by its expiration upon the happening of an uncertain event. However, the grant must clearly state that the estate will expire automatically upon the happening of the uncertain event. The grant from Wood clearly stated the condition but failed to state that the grant would not continue to be valid if the condition were not met. Nor did Wood (P) grant a fee simple subject to a condition subsequent, because the grant made no clear provision for termination. Wood (P) retained no interest in the property. The trial court is affirmed.

EDITOR'S ANALYSIS: There is a presumption against forfeiture in the law. Thus any grant purporting to cause such a forfeiture will be strictly construed against the grantor absent clear intent otherwise. Although the grantor's intent, if realizable, typically prevails, ambiguous grants give rise to public policy considerations — in the above case, the free alienability of property.

[For more information on fee simple determinable, see Casenote Law Outline on Property, Chapter 5, § II, Present Possessory Estates.]

FORSGREN v. SOLLIE
Utah Sup. Ct., 659 P.2d 1068 (1983).

NATURE OF CASE: Appeal from finding of fee simple in name of grantor.

FACT SUMMARY: Forsgren (P) granted land to Sollie (D) subject to several conditions subsequent. When Sollie (D) failed to meet these conditions, Forsgren (P) retook possession of the lands.

CONCISE RULE OF LAW: Where the language of a deed clearly evinces the intent to create a fee simple subject to a condition subsequent, the absence of a provision for re-entry will not be fatal to the grantor's claim.

FACTS: Forsgren (P) granted adjacent property to Sollie (D) on the condition that Sollie (D) build a fence, survey the property, and use the property for church or residence purposes only. Sollie (D) failed to meet any of the conditions nor did he pay property tax. The property was sold to LeFleur (D) for taxes owed. LeFleur (D) located Sollie (D) in another state and received a quitclaim deed for title. After LeFleur (D) destroyed improvements made by Forsgren (P), Forsgren (P) sued to quiet title. The trial court found in favor of Forsgren (P). LaFleur (D) appealed.

ISSUE: Where the language of a deed clearly evinces the intent to create a fee simple subject to a condition subsequent, will the absence of a provision for re-entry be fatal to the grantor's claim?

HOLDING AND DECISION: (Oaks, J.) No. Where the language of a deed clearly evinces the intent to create a fee simple subject to a condition subsequent, the absence of a provision for re-entry will not be fatal to the grantor's claim. A condition subsequent will be inferred when the condition has particular importance to the grantor and the condition is meant to benefit adjacent land. In this case the transfer was apparently caused by the desire to achieve the conditions that would clearly benefit the adjoining land. The court will apply a reasonable period of time during which the condition of use needed to be meet and was not. Forsgren's (P) re-entry freed the land of restriction. The trial court is affirmed.

DISSENT: (Howe, J.) There is no condition subsequent created without express language of re-entry. The condition on use did not require that use be made, but only if the land were to be used should it be used in a particular manner.

EDITOR'S ANALYSIS: Courts generally follow two rules when faced with an ambiguous grant. The court should first try to carry out the grantor's intent if they can figure it out. Only if they are unable to do so must they assume that the grantor gave away all rights he held.

[For more information on fee simple subject to condition subsequent, see Casenote Law Outline on Property, Chapter 5, § II, Present Possessory Estates.]

RISTE v. EASTERN WASHINGTON BIBLE CAMP, INC.
Wash. Ct. App., 605 P.2d 1294 (1980).

NATURE OF CASE: Suit for reformation of deed.

FACT SUMMARY: Riste (P) wanted to sell his property in a manner that violated the occupancy and resale restrictions in the deed.

CONCISE RULE OF LAW: A restrictive restraint on the sale of fee simple title is a violation of public policy.

FACTS: Eastern Washington Bible Camp (D) sold land in a subdivision with the restriction that the grantee could only sell the property to members of the Assembly of God Church. The deed Riste (P) held clearly stated the restriction. Riste (P) attempted to sell the land to someone who was not a member of the Assembly of God. Bible Camp (D) refused to remove the restriction, so Riste (P) sued to reform the deed and for a declaration that the restrictions were invalid.

ISSUE: Is a restrictive restraint on the sale of fee simple title a violation of public policy?

HOLDING AND DECISION: (Roe, J.) Yes. A restrictive restraint on the sale of fee simple title is a violation of public policy. Here, the restriction in the deed clearly prevented Riste (P) from selling land he purportedly received in fee simple. Under state law, any restriction on the transfer of property based on race, creed, color, or national origin violates public policy. The restriction in question bars alienation based on creed, i.e., religious belief, and is thus void.

EDITOR'S ANALYSIS: The court went on to suggest that it was the grant of fee simple that was fatal to the restriction. If the Bible Camp (D) chose to license the land to church members it could restrict its use as it saw fit.

_____

[For more information on fee simple defeasible, see Casenote Law Outline on Property, Chapter 5, § II, Present Possessory Estates.]

NOTES:

HANKINS v. MATHEWS

Tenn. Sup. Ct., 425 S.W.2d 608 (1968).

NATURE OF CASE: Appeal from judgment in an action to establish ownership of the reversionary interest in land devised in fee simple.

FACT SUMMARY: The holder of land bequeathed by an uncle transferred his interest in the property despite a ten-year restriction against such transfers, and the heirs at law of the deceased filed suit, contending that the property had reverted to them.

CONCISE RULE OF LAW: Where land is granted or devised in fee, a provision of any sort that the taker shall not alienate, or shall not have power to alienate, is void.

FACTS: When A.A. Hankins died, he bequeathed personal property and two large parcels of land to a nephew, Jim Grubb. One parcel was held jointly by A.A. and his wife, Sarah, who left all her property to the same nephew at her death. A.A.'s will stipulated that Grubb was not to sell, mortgage, or in any other manner incumber and dispose of the land until he had held the property for ten years. If he did so, the land would revert to A.A.'s heirs. After Sarah died, but within the ten year period, Grubb transferred both parcels of land to Mathews (D). James Hankins (P) and other heirs filed this complaint, contending that one parcel had reverted to them in its entirety and that they held an undivided one-half interest in the other parcel in accordance with A.A.'s will. Mathews (D) demurred on the ground that the restriction was void as an illegal attempt to restrain alienation of the property. This appeal followed the ruling by the trial court.

ISSUE: Where land is granted or devised in fee, is a provision of any sort that the taker shall not alienate, or shall not have power to alienate, void?

HOLDING AND DECISION: (Burnett, J.) Yes. Where land is granted or devised in fee, a provision of any sort that the taker shall not alienate, or shall not have power to alienate, is void. Even though the restriction at issue here is only to last for ten years, it is still a total restriction upon the right of alienation. As Mr. Justice Gailor stated in Keeling v. Keeling, 203 S.W.2d 601 (Tenn. 1947): "We can find no exception to the rule that conditions subsequent preventing alienation of an estate in fee, even for a limited time, are universally held void as inconsistent with the incidents and nature of the estate devised and contrary to public policy." Therefore, the demurrer should be sustained and the case dismissed.

EDITOR'S ANALYSIS: The reasoning behind the general rule is that such a restraint on a conveyance of a fee simple absolute is repugnant to the fee. The court pointed out, however, that a less than total restriction, such as that seen in Overton v. Lea, 68 S.W. 250 (Tenn. 1902), or a restriction attached to equitable estates not greater than life estates, as seen in Fowlkes v. Wagoner, S.W. 586 (Tenn. Ch. App. 1898), have been allowed. A grantor cannot convey a fee simple absolute estate and then deprive the owner of one of the rights of such ownership.

[For more information on forfeiture restraint of land, see Casenote Law Outline on Property, Chapter 5, § II, Present Possessory Estates.]

NOTES:

NORTHWEST REAL ESTATE CO. v. SERIO
Md. Sup. Ct., 144 A. 245 (1929).

NATURE OF CASE: Action for specific performance to compel the sale of real property.

FACT SUMMARY: Northwest Real Estate (D) prevented the sale of property to Serio (P) based on a covenant restricting the alienation of the property.

CONCISE RULE OF LAW: Covenants retraining a grantee's ability to sell property are inconsistent with a grant of fee simple and are thus invalid.

FACTS: Northwest Real Estate (D) included a covenant in a deed preventing its grantees from selling a property before a certain date without its consent. The grantees attempted to sell the property to Serio (P) before the required date, and Northwest (D) refused to consent. The Serios (P) sued Northwest (D) for specific performance of the contract for sale.

ISSUE: Are covenants restraining a grantee's ability to sell property inconsistent with a grant of fee simple and thus invalid?

HOLDING AND DECISION: (Urner, J.) Yes. Covenants restraining a grantee's ability to sell property is inconsistent with a grant of fee simple and thus invalid. Freedom to alienate is essential to a grant of title in fee simple. The restriction imposed on the deed by Northwest (D) was designed to temporarily deprive the grantees of the unrestrained power of alienation and was clearly repugnant to the fee simple title conveyed by the grants.

DISSENT: (Bond, C.J.) The court's holding would hinder a developer's plan to create a city as a single large enterprise and thus is contrary to public policy.

EDITOR'S ANALYSIS: The purpose of the covenant in question was to develop a high-class neighborhood. By retaining the right to approve of sales, developers can attempt to keep out undesirables.

[For more information on restraints on alienation, see Casenote Law Outline on Property, Chapter 5, § II, Present Possessory Estates.]

NOTES:

HORSE POND FISH & GAME CLUB, INC. v. CORMIER
N.H. Sup. Ct., 581 A. 2d 478 (1990).

NATURE OF CASE: Appeal from grant of summary judgment in action to void restraint against alienation.

FACT SUMMARY: Horse Pond (P) transferred an unrestricted property to a third party who then transferred the property back to Horse Pond with a restraint on alienation.

CONCISE RULE OF LAW: A restraint on alienation is valid only if it is reasonable in light of the justifiable interests of the parties.

FACTS: Horse Pond Fish & Game Club (P) acquired unrestricted title to land that it used for activities and on which it built a clubhouse. Horse Pond (P) transferred the title to two members who in turn transferred the title back with a restriction preventing alienation of the property without 100% approval of the membership. Due to the increasingly residential nature of the surrounding neighborhood, Horse Pond (P) structured a deal whereby they could swap the restricted property for property better suited to the activities of the club. When the members gather to vote, Cormier (D) was the sole member to vote against the proposal, thus preventing the transaction from occurring due to the restriction. Horse Pond (P) filed suit to declare the restriction void. The trial court found the restraint to be void. Cormier (D) appealed.

ISSUE: Is a restraint on alienation only valid if it is reasonable in light of the justifiable interests of the parties?

HOLDING AND DECISION: (Batchelder, J.) Yes. A restraint on alienation is valid only if it is reasonable in light of the justifiable interests of the parties. The trial court found that the restriction was unreasonable in this case because it meant in essence that the Club (P) had to be dissolved before the property could be sold. The rule of reasonable restraints does not apply to charitable grants because the policy of freedom of alienation does not apply to such grants. Thus the validity of the restriction depends on whether the Club (P) is a charitable entity. Reversed and remanded for that determination.

EDITOR'S ANALYSIS: Total restraints on alienation of fee simple interests are universally disfavored, although the rationale behind their unenforceability may differ from court to court. Dispersal of ownership of property is considered a social necessity; restraints on alienation would concentrate ownership in a few wealthy families. Autonomy is another consideration militating against restraints. And the need for efficient transactions counsels against monopolizing resources in the hands of a few owners.

[For more information on restraints on alienation, see Casenote Law Outline on Property, Chapter 5, § II, Present Possessory Estates.]

ROPER v. EDWARDS
N.C. Sup. Ct., 373 S.E.2d 423 (1988).

NATURE OF CASE: Appeal from a judgment in an action seeking to impose a constructive trust to enforce an agreement to convey a parcel of land.

FACT SUMMARY: Roper (P) brought this action to compel Edwards (D) to convey one acre of the land acquired by Edwards (D) from Roper's (P) grandmother in settlement of a civil suit, with the stipulation that the one acre be conveyed to Roper (P) as specified in the grandmother's will at her death.

CONCISE RULE OF LAW: A constructive trust will be imposed on the holder of legal title acquired through conduct short of actual fraud where such retention would result in his unjust enrichment.

FACTS: In a settlement agreement resulting from civil litigation, Roper's (P) grandmother conveyed title to Edwards (D) to a 136-acre parcel of land, stipulating that Edwards (D) was to convey a one-acre tract within that parcel to Roper (P) as the grandmother might specify in her will. Absent such specification, the one-acre tract was to remain Edwards' (D) property in fee simple absolute. At her death, the grandmother devised the one-acre tract to Roper (P). However, Edwards (D) refused to convey the land. Roper (P) brought this action, seeking to compel Edwards (D) to convey the land to Roper (P) free of any encumbrances. Roper (P) sought the remedy of a constructive trust. This appeal followed the lower court's decision.

ISSUE: Will a constructive trust be imposed on the holder of legal title acquired through conduct short of actual fraud where such retention would result in his unjust enrichment?

HOLDING AND DECISION: (Whichard, J.) Yes. A constructive trust will be imposed on the holder of legal title acquired through conduct short of actual fraud where such retention would result in his unjust enrichment. Although Edwards (D) has no legal duty to convey the property to Roper (P), the undisputed facts here present a compelling case for application of the constructive trust remedy. To permit Edwards (D) to retain the extensive benefits received in the bargained-for settlement while refusing to perform the apparently meager concession made in the process would result in his unjust enrichment, and would be manifestly against equity and good conscience. Complete justice clearly cannot be obtained if Edwards (D) is permitted, to Roper's (P) detriment, to retain title to the one-acre tract that was bargained away in exchange for uncontested title to the remaining 135 acres originally in dispute.

EDITOR'S ANALYSIS: A constructive trust is a duty imposed by courts of equity to prevent the unjust enrichment of the holder of title to property that the holder acquired through fraud, breach of duty or some other circumstance making it inequitable for him to retain it. Here, Edwards (D) argued that the absence of fraud defeated Roper's (P) request for a constructive trust. However, the court focused on the "some other circumstance" language enunciated in Wilson v. Development Co., 171 S.E.2d 873 (N.C. 1970).

[For more information on disabling restraint on alienation, see Casenote Law Outline on Property, Chapter 5, § II, Present Possessory Estates.]

NOTES:

DUNAFON v. DELAWARE MCDONALD'S CORP.

601 F. Supp. 1232 (W.D. Mo. 1988).

NATURE OF CASE: Action under the Sherman Antitrust Act.

FACT SUMMARY: Dunafon (P) brought suit against McDonald's (D) to prevent it from enforcing a restrictive covenant not to compete.

CONCISE RULE OF LAW: A restrictive covenant preventing a landlord from leasing space to a competitor will not be deemed to violate the Antitrust Act absent a showing of substantial anticompetitive effect.

FACTS: Dunafon (P), a Taco Bell franchisee, sought to lease space in the Biscayne Mall. McDonald's (D) currently had a lease in the Biscayne Mall that contained a covenant not to compete. If it were not for that covenant not to compete, the Mall would have been willing to lease space to Dunafon (P). There were several fast food restaurants in the general area of the Mall. The McDonald's (D) in the Mall had generally held prices below the amount recommended by the parent company in order to compete with other local fast food restaurants. There were several other potential locations for a restaurant that Dunafon (P) rejected as unacceptable. Dunafon (P) brought suit to enjoin McDonald's' (D) from enforcing the restrictive covenant.

ISSUE: Will a restrictive covenant preventing a landlord from leasing space to a competitor be deemed to violate the Antitrust Act absent a showing of substantial anticompetitive effect?

HOLDING AND DECISION: (Wright, J.) No. A restrictive covenant preventing a landlord from leasing space to a competitor will not be deemed to violate the Antitrust Act absent a showing of substantial anti-competitive effect. The restrictive covenant in this case is not anticompetitive since it is the method whereby McDonald's (D) expended a greater investment to enter an underdeveloped market. It should be given a benefit for being a pioneer. Dunafon (P) has not demonstrated that McDonald's (D) has gained any market advantage through the restrictive covenant. There are several other substitute sites available in the geographic area. The restrictive covenant does not have a significant anticompetitive effect, does not restrain, and does not violate the Sherman Act.

EDITOR'S ANALYSIS: The above court applied a rule of reason standard of review to the case, meaning that the burden was on Dunafon (P) to prove that the lease covenant had a substantial impact on competition in the relevant market, even though the Sherman Antitrust Act prohibits all contacts "in restraint of trade" in order to implicate the Act.

[For more information on enforcement of restrictive covenants, see Casenote Law Outline on Property, Chapter 8, § III, Real Covenants and Equitable Servitudes.]

NOTES:

CENTRAL DELAWARE COUNTY
AUTHORITY v. GREYHOUND CORP.
Pa. Sup. Ct., 588 A.2d 485 (1991).

NATURE OF CASE: Appeal from a judgment as to the validity of a restriction in a deed in an action seeking to quiet title to land.

FACT SUMMARY: The Central Delaware County Authority (P) brought this action to quiet title in land it had used for a sewage treatment plant, alleging that the restrictive covenants in the deeds for the land, allowing for repurchase of the properties were void as violative of the rule against perpetuities.

CONCISE RULE OF LAW: A restrictive covenant in a deed allowing unlimited time for repurchase of property conveyed is a purchase option subject to the rule against perpetuities.

FACTS: The Baldwin Locomotive Works conveyed two parcels of land to the Authority (P). The deeds for both parcels conveyed a fee simple interest subject to a restrictive covenant allowing an unlimited time for repurchase of the properties if the land was abandoned and ceased to be used for the public purposes for which it was acquired. After the Authority (P) ceased operation of its sewage treatment plant, it continued to maintain and possess the land, bringing this action to quiet title in the land. The trial court found that the restrictions did not violate the rule since the deed conveyed a fee simple interest subject to a condition subsequent. On appeal, the superior court held that the restrictions were options to purchase, which were subject to the rule. However, the court found that the restrictions were not invalid on public policy grounds. The Authority (P) appealed.

ISSUE: Is a restrictive covenant in a deed allowing unlimited time for repurchase of property conveyed a purchase option subject to the rule against perpetuities?

HOLDING AND DECISION: (Flaherty, J.) Yes. A restrictive covenant in a deed allowing unlimited time for repurchase of property conveyed is a purchase option subject to the rule against perpetuities. The superior court correctly found that the restrictions constituted a repurchase option subject to the rule against perpetuities. The court erred, however, in finding the restrictions valid on public policy grounds. The rule against perpetuities is a peremptory command of law, and thus is not subject to negation by a countervailing statement of public policy. Economic development and prosperity depend in part upon the free alienability of land. It is for this reason that the rule against perpetuities is to be remorselessly applied. The repurchase option is, therefore, void.

EDITOR'S ANALYSIS: The court found that the considerations delineated in Barton v. Thaw, 92 A.312 (Pa. 1914), are still valid today. The Barton court declared that unlimited options to repurchase isolated the property, and removed it from the market. In addition, it halted improvements, and prevented the land from answering to the needs of growing communities. It was for the express purpose of destroying such serious hindrances to material and social prosperity that the rule against perpetuities was developed.

[For more information on restrictive covenants, see Casenote Law Outline on Property, Chapter 8, § III, Real Covenants and Equitable Servitudes.]

NOTES:

TEXACO REFINING AND MARKETING, INC. v. SAMOWITZ
Conn. Sup. Ct., 570 A.2d 170 (1990).

NATURE OF CASE: Appeal from a judgment in an action for specific performance of an option in a commercial lease to purchase real property.

FACT SUMMARY: When Texaco Refining and Marketing, Inc. (P) exercised the option to purchase commercial property it was leasing, Samowitz (D) and the other successors in interest to the lessor refused to transfer the property, prompting this action by Texaco (P) for a judicial order of specific performance.

CONCISE RULE OF LAW: An option to purchase contained in a commercial lease, at least if the option must be exercised within the leasehold term, is valid without regard to the rule against perpetuities.

FACTS: Texaco (P) held a leasehold on commercial property for a term of fifteen years, renewable by Texaco (P) for three additional five-year periods. The lease also contained an exclusive right to purchase the land at any time during the term of the lease or an extension or renewal thereof. During the second renewal period, Texaco (P) informed Samowitz (D) and the other successors in interest to the lessor that Texaco (P) was exercising its option to purchase. When Samowitz (D) and the others refused to transfer the property, Texaco (P) brought this action for specific performance. Samowitz (D) and the others contended that the option violated the rule against perpetuities. The trial court held that the option did not violate the rule because the interest would vest within the time period specified by the rule. This appeal followed.

ISSUE: Is an option to purchase contained in a commercial lease, at least if the option must be exercised within the leasehold term, valid without regard to the rule against perpetuities?

HOLDING AND DECISION: (Peters, J.) Yes. An option to purchase contained in a commercial lease, at least if the option must be exercised within the leasehold term, is valid without regard to the rule against perpetuities. An option to purchase coupled with a long-term commercial lease is consistent with the policy objectives of the rule because it stimulates improvement of the property and thus renders it more rather than less marketable. Any extension of the rule against perpetuities would, furthermore, be inconsistent with the legislative adoption of the "second look" doctrine, pursuant to which an interest subject to the rule may be validated, contrary to the common law, by the occurrence of events subsequent to the creation of the interest. The option in this case was therefore enforceable.

EDITOR'S ANALYSIS: The fundamental purpose of the rule is founded on the public policy in favor of free alienability of property and against restricting its marketability over long periods of time. The trial court construed the lease agreement as a series of discrete undertakings, none of which exceeded ternty-one years in length. The state supreme court, however, found no reason of policy why it should extend the ambit of the rule to cover an option to purchase contained in a commercial lease of real property.

[For more information on options to purchase, see Casenote Law Outline on Property, Chapter 5, § IV, The Rule Against Perpetuities.]

NOTES:

CAMBRIDGE CO. v. EAST SLOPE INVESTMENT CORP.
Colo. Sup. Ct., 700 P.2d 537 (1985).

NATURE OF CASE: Appeal from a judgment in an action to set aside the conveyance of a condominium unit subject to a right of preemption.

FACT SUMMARY: When East Slope (D) sold its unit in a condominium complex to a third-party buyer, despite the exercise by Cambridge (P), one of the other unit owners, of its preemptive right to purchase the unit, Cambridge (P) brought suit to set aside the conveyance as violative of the rule against perpetuities.

CONCISE RULE OF LAW: The rule against perpetuities will be applied to preemptive rights only where the purposes of the rule are served.

FACTS: All owners of condominiums in a condominium complex were subject to the same covenants and conditions, one of which created a right of preemption in the unit owners, defined as a first right to purchase any other unit offered for sale upon the same terms and conditions offered by a third party buyer. When East Slope Investment Corp. (D) offered a unit it owned for sale, the condominium association notified all other unit owners. The Cambridge Co. (P), owner of a unit, exercised its right of preemption within the specified time period. East Slope (D) nonetheless conveyed its unit to the Burgetts (D), who were third-party buyers. The Cambridge Co. (P) instituted this action to set aside the conveyance, and for damages. At trial, East Slope (D) contended that the preemptive right clause violated the rule against perpetuities. This appeal followed the lower court's ruling.

ISSUE: Will the rule against perpetuities be applied to preemptive rights only where the purposes of the rule are served?

HOLDING AND DECISION: (Dubofsky, J.) Yes. The rule against perpetuities will be applied to preemptive rights only where the purposes of the rule are served. While the rule applies to preemptive rights, it must not be applied mechanically. Here, the owner is assured of receiving market value for his property and will not be deterred from improving it or offering it for sale. Moreover, the preemption here cannot be exercised unless the owner desires to sell. At that time, the only effect of the preemption is to change the identity of the buyer. In short, both the current and future owners of units subject to the preemptive right hold a title that is freely alienable at the full market price. Thus, because the preemptive right here poses no threat to the free alienability of the condominium units, no reason exists for invalidating the right under the rule against perpetuities.

EDITOR'S ANALYSIS: The rule against perpetuities holds that no interest in real property is valid unless it must vest, if at all, not later than twenty-one years after some life in being at the creation of the interest. The rule prevents the remote vesting of contingent interests in real property. The right at issue in the instant case has traditionally been viewed as a contingent equitable interest in real property subject to the rule. However, courts differ in their application of the rule.

_____

[For more information on the Rule Against Perpetuities, see Casenote Law Outline on Property, Chapter 5, § IV, The Rule Against Perpetuities.]

NOTES:

MOORE v. PHILLIPS
Kan. Ct. of App., 6 Kan. App. 2d 94, 627 P.2d 831 (1981).

NATURE OF CASE: Appeal from award of damages for waste.

FACT SUMMARY: Dorothy Moore (P) and her son sued as remaindermen to recover damages for the deterioration of a farmhouse resulting from neglect by the life tenant, Moore's (P) mother.

CONCISE RULE OF LAW: Laches is an equitable defense and will not bar recovery for permissive waste from mere lapse of time nor where there is a reasonable excuse for non-action of a party in making inquiry as to his rights and asserting them.

FACTS: Leslie Brannon died in 1962, and by will left his wife, Ada Brannon, a life estate in farmland containing a farmhouse, with remainder interests to Dorothy Moore (P) and Kent Reinhard. Ada Brannon resided in the farmhouse until 1964, then rented it out until 1965, whereupon the house subsequently became unoccupied. From 1969 through 1971, the house was leased to the remaindermen, but they did not live there, but from time to time they would inspect the premises. In 1976, Ada Brannon died leaving her property to others because she and her daughter, Moore (P), had been estranged since 1964. After Ada Brannon's death in 1976, Moore (P) sued her mother's executor, Phillips (D), on the theory of waste to recover damages for the deterioration of the farmhouse. Phillips (D) raised laches and estoppel as affirmative defenses, which the trial court sustained, but on appeal was reversed. Phillips (D) appealed.

ISSUE: Will laches be a bar to recovery in an action for permissive waste, when there was a reasonable excuse for not bringing the action earlier?

HOLDING AND DECISION: (Prager, J.) No. Permissive waste is the failure of the tenant to exercise the ordinary care of a prudent man for the preservation and protection of the estate. Where the right of action of the remaindermen is based upon permissive waste, as in this case, it is generally held that the statute of limitations does not commence to run in favor of the tenant until the expiration of the tenancy. Laches, is not merely delay, but delay that works a disadvantage to another, may be used in actions at law as well as in equitable proceedings. A mere lapse of time will not bar recovery where there is a reasonable excuse for non-action of a party in making inquiry as to his rights or in asserting them. Here, the evidence is clear that the life tenant, as a quasi-trustee, did not keep the property in reasonable repair, as was her responsibility. Furthermore, it was Moore's (P) position that she did not file an action against her elderly mother that would have aggravated her. Even though Moore (P) was estranged from her mother, the law should not require her to sue her mother during her lifetime under these circumstances. Affirmed.

EDITOR'S ANALYSIS: Waste may take on a variety of forms, voluntary, permissive, or ameliorating. While permissive waste was discussed above, voluntary waste occurs during the commission of some deliberate or voluntary destructive act while ameliorating waste occurs when there has been any material change in the nature of the property even though the change enhances the value of the property.

[For more information on voluntary waste, see Casenote Law Outline on Property, Chapter 5, § II, Present Possessory Estates.]

NOTES:

SHELLEY v. KRAEMER
334 U.S. 1 (1948).

NATURE OF CASE: On writ of certiorari in action to enjoin a sale of property.

FACT SUMMARY: The Kraemers (P) sought to oust the Shelleys (D), Negroes, from their recently purchased property on the grounds that it was subject to a racially restrictive covenant.

CONCISE RULE OF LAW: The Equal Protection Clause of the Fourteenth Amendment prohibits judicial enforcement by state courts of restrictive covenants based on race or color.

FACTS: In 1945, the Shelleys (D), Negroes, purchased property which, unknown to them, was subject to a racially restrictive covenant signed in 1911 for a 50-year period by the majority of property owners on the block. The Kraemers (P), also owners of property subject to the covenant, sued in the state court to restrain the Shelleys (D) from taking possession and to revest the title in others. The state court denied relief on the grounds that the covenant had never been finalized. However, the Missouri Supreme Court reversed. The U.S. Supreme Court granted the Shelley's (D) certiorari. They argued that the Equal Protection Clause of the Fourteenth Amendment prevented the judicial enforcement by state courts of racially restrictive covenants.

ISSUE: Does the Equal Protection Clause of the Fourteenth Amendment prohibit judicial enforcement by state courts of racially restrictive covenants?

HOLDING AND DECISION: (Vinson, J.) Yes. The Equal Protection Clause of the Fourteenth Amendment prohibits judicial enforcement by state courts of racially restrictive covenants. Equality in the enjoyment of property rights was clearly among the civil rights intended to be protected from discriminatory state action by the framers of the Fourteenth Amendment. And although past cases have struck down such discrimination when enacted by state legislatures or city councils, it may not be said that such discrimination, as in the instant case, may escape on the grounds that it was only an agreement between private individuals. Indeed, were it no more than that, no violation would exist, However, in this case state action is clearly present by reason of the active intervention of the state court to enforce the covenant. As early as 1880, in Ex Parte Virginia, this Court found state action in violation of the Fourteenth Amendment when a state judge restricted jury service to whites. Nor is the amendment ineffective simply because this action was taken according to the state's common law policy. We hold that in granting judicial enforcement of these restrictive covenants, the state has denied the Shelleys (D) equal protection of the laws. Reversed.

EDITOR'S ANALYSIS: In the 1961 case of Burton v. Wilmington Parking Authority, a state agency had built and owned a parking garage, and rented space in the garage to a private restaurant. The Supreme Court held that the restaurant's exclusion of blacks from service amounted to state action under the Fourteenth Amendment. The test announced was that of significant state involvement in private discrimination.

_____

[For more information on restrictions on use of land, see Casenote Law Outline on Property, Chapter 5, § II, Present Possessory Estates.]

NOTES:

EVANS v. ABNEY
396 U.S. 435 (1970).

NATURE OF CASE: Review of judgment terminating trust.

FACT SUMMARY: When Senator Bacon's intention to provide a park to be used exclusively by white people became unenforceable after being held unconstitutional, the Georgia Supreme Court ruled that the trust had failed. The trust property therefore reverted to Bacon's heirs.

CONCISE RULE OF LAW: The cy pres doctrine is not applicable when the testator would presumably have preferred to have the whole trust fail if the particular purpose of the trust became impossible to accomplish.

FACTS: In 1911, U.S. Senator Bacon of Georgia conveyed property in trust to his home town of Macon (D) for the creation of a public park for the exclusive use of the white people of Macon (D). The City (D) initially kept the park segregated, but then let the whites-only policy lapse. The Board of Managers (P), who supervised the operation of the park, sued the City (D), which actually managed the park, to remove the City (D) as trustee. Evans (D) and other black citizens of Macon (D) intervened, and the suit eventually reached the Supreme Court, which held that the park must be treated as a public institution subject to the Fourteenth Amendment. Since racial separation was found to an inseparable part of Bacon's intent, on remand the Georgia courts subsequently held that the cy pres doctrine could not be used to alter Bacon's will to permit racial integration in the park. The trust was therefore held to have failed, and the park reverted to Bacon's heirs. Evans et al. (D) petitioned for certiorari, arguing that termination of the trust violated their rights to equal protection and due process under the Fourteenth Amendment. The Supreme Court granted certiorari.

ISSUE: Is the cy pres doctrine applicable when the testator would presumably have preferred to have the whole trust fail if the particular purpose of the trust became impossible to accomplish?

HOLDING AND DECISION: (Black, J.) Yes. The cy pres doctrine is not applicable when the testator would presumably have preferred to have the whole trust fail if the particular purpose of the trust became impossible to accomplish. Cy pres operates to allow a court to carry out the "general" charitable intent of the testator where this intent might otherwise be thwarted by the impossibility of the plan or scheme provided by the testator. In this case, however, the language of Bacon's will indicates that his charitable intent was not "general" but extended only to the establishment of a segregated park for the benefit of white people only. Apparently, he would rather have had the whole trust fail than have the park integrated. Therefore, the Georgia court had no alternative but to end the trust and return the property to Bacon's heirs. State judicial action is unconstitutional when it affirmatively enforces a private scheme of racial discrimination. But here, all discrimination has been eliminated by eliminating the park itself; it is a loss shared equally by all citizens, regardless of race, and thus is not unconstitutional.

DISSENT: (Douglas, J.) This decision can only be regarded as a gesture toward a state-sanctioned segregated way of life that is passé.

DISSENT: (Brennan, Jr., J.) Under the Equal Protection Clause, a state may not close down a public facility solely to avoid its duty to desegregate that facility. In this case, it conveys an unambiguous message of community involvement in racial discrimination. Contrary to the majority's conclusion, the closing of the park is a discriminatory state action; it is not a case of private discrimination, and enforcement of the reverter is therefore unconstitutional.

EDITOR'S ANALYSIS: Historically, racially discriminatory covenants on use and occupancy were looked upon as private agreements. They did not fall within the scope of the Fourteenth Amendment, which applies only to state action, and were thus considered valid. However, the case of Shelley v. Kraemer, 334 U.S. 1 (1948), held that the state, via its courts, could not enforce a privately devised racial restriction if parties of different races were willing to deal with one another. Hence Justice Brennan's dissenting opinion that the majority's decision was prohibited by the Fourteenth Amendment.

[For more information on restrictions on use of land, see Casenote Law Outline on Property, Chapter 5, § II, Present Possessory Estates.]

NOTES:

LEWIS v. SEARLES
452 S.W.2d 153 (1970).

NATURE OF CASE: Action for declaratory judgment to quiet title and construe a will.

FACT SUMMARY: A testatrix bequeathed her property to Lewis (P) for as long as she remained unmarried, and if she married, the property was to go to named heirs; Lewis (P) claimed that the will gave her a fee simple determinable rather than a life estate.

CONCISE RULE OF LAW: The law will hold all devises as being in fee simple if no intent is expressed to create a life estate only, and also no further devise is made to take effect after the death of the devisee.

FACTS: Letita Lewis died in 1926 and left a will which devised all of her real and personal property to Hattie Lewis (P) for so long as Hattie Lewis (P) remained unmarried. In the event that Lewis (P) were to marry, then Lewis (P) would receive one-third of the property, and a third would go to each of two other heirs, La Forge and James Lewis. Both of these heirs died leaving children, one of which is Searles (D). Lewis (P) remained unmarried, and when she was 95, she instituted this action to have the court declare that the will left her a fee simple determinable which could only end if she married. Searles (D) and the other heirs argued that the will gave Lewis (P) and each of the other two heirs title in fee simple to an undivided third of the estate subject to Lewis' (P) life estate.

ISSUE: In a will, if there is no expressed intent to create a life estate only, and if no further devise is made to take effect after the death of the devisee, will the law presume that the testatrix manifested an intent to create a fee simple?

HOLDING AND DECISION: (Eager, J.) Yes. There exist several factors, all of which indicate that the devisee was to take a fee simple determinable rather than a life estate. First, no intention appears to indicate the conveyance of only a life estate. Second, no further devise is made to take effect after the death of Lewis (P). Third, if Lewis (P) were to marry, she would be immediately given an undivided third of the property in fee. Fourth, it is not stated whether the heirs had to survive Lewis (P) in order to receive a third if Lewis (P) were to marry. Fifth, if it were only a life estate, there could be a partial intestacy if she married because there was no gift or limitation over upon Lewis' (P) death. The law presumes a fee unless there are words in a subsequent and limiting clause which clearly and decisively indicate an intent to devise less than a fee. The words of the will when considered as a whole evinced an intent to pass the maximum estate possible consistent with the limitation on marriage. There are no express words to the contrary present in the will. The fact that the gift to the heirs would come about only by a marriage indicates that this was not meant to be a gift on Lewis'(P) death and, therefore, Lewis (P) had a fee simple determinable, not a life estate.

EDITOR'S ANALYSIS: A fee simple determinable is an estate which automatically terminates on the happening of a stated event and reverts back to the grantor or to whomever the grantor appoints. At common law, this possibility of reverter could not be devised or alienated, but modern law allows it. The basic rule is that a provision in restraint of marriage is void as being against public policy. But there are exceptions, such as where the grantor wishes to provide support to a devisee while single, or in many other situations where the restraint is imposed for legitimate purposes and not out of caprice. The court construed the will such that the testatrix merely wished to support Lewis (P) while she was single, and did not wish to restrain marriage.

[For more information on creation of a life estate, see Casenote Law Outline on Property, Chapter 5, § II, Present Possessory Estates.]

NOTES:

NOTES

CHAPTER 5
GOVERNMENTAL LAND USE PLANNING

QUICK REFERENCE RULES OF LAW

1. **Exclusionary Zoning.** Municipal land use regulations must provide a realistic opportunity for low and moderate income housing. (Southern Burlington County, NAACP v. Township of Mount Laurel)

   [For more information on exclusionary zoning, see Casenote Law Outline on Property, Chapter 10, § II, Validity of Zoning Laws.]

2. **Prior Nonconfroming Uses.** An existing nonconforming use may continue only where it is a continuance of substantially the same kind of use as that to which the premises were devoted when the zoning ordinance was passed. (Town of Belleville v. Parrillo's, Inc.)

   [For more information on nonconforming use of property, see Casenote Law Outline on Property, Chapter 10, § III, Changes in Zoning Laws.]

3. **Variances.** A variance may be granted where strict application of a zoning ordinance would result in exceptional and undue hardship upon the developer of the property. (Commons v. Westwood Zoning Board of Adjustment)

   [For more information on variances, see Casenote Law Outline on Property, Chapter 10, § III, Changes in Zoning Laws.]

4. **Vested Rights.** The validity of a police power enactment, such as zoning, depends on its reasonableness. (Stone v. City of Wilton)

   [For more information on the power to zone, see Casenote Law Outline on Property, Chapter 10, § I, The Power to Zone.]

5. **Environmental Regulations: Liability of Property.** Once the state has incurred assessment costs related to a contaminated site, it may place a lien securing both the costs already incurred and those which will be incurred in monitoring and supervision. (Acme Laundry Co., Inc. v. Secretary of Environmental Affairs)

5

SOUTHERN BURLINGTON COUNTY NAACP v. TOWNSHIP OF MOUNT LAUREL

N.J. Sup. Ct., 67 N.J. 151, 336 A.2d 713 (1975).

NATURE OF CASE: Appeal from invalidation of zoning ordinance.

FACT SUMMARY: The trial court held that a bona fide attempt by a municipality to provide zoned land for low-cost housing fulfilled its constitutional obligations.

CONCISE RULE OF LAW: Municipal land use regulations must provide a realistic opportunity for low and moderate income housing.

FACTS: The NAACP (P) sued Mount Laurel (D), contending the municipality's zoning scheme violated the New Jersey constitution by failing to provide for low-income housing outside of depressed areas. The New Jersey Supreme Court invalidated the ordinances and remanded for further proceedings. The trial court held that it was sufficient that Mount Laurel (D) had made a bona fide attempt to comply with the Supreme Court decision and upheld the new ordinance enacted in response. The NAACP (P) appealed, contending a mere attempt to provide such zoning did not discharge Mount Laurel's (D) constitutional obligations.

ISSUE: Must municipal land use regulations provide a realistic opportunity for low- and moderate-income housing?

HOLDING AND DECISION: (Hall, J.) Yes. Municipal land use regulations must provide a realistic opportunity for low- and moderate-income housing. Such obligation extends beyond attempting to provide for such housing. The housing must be in direct proportion to the percentage of lower income residents in the city. To reach this goal, affirmative governmental action may be required. The elimination of some obstacles and the creation of a new zoning scheme may be frustrated by other restrictions which effectively deprive the poor of adequate housing. Therefore, the zoning scheme which merely manifested an intent to abide by the original supreme court holding was insufficient to discharge Mount Laurel's (D) constitutional obligations. Reversed and remanded.

EDITOR'S ANALYSIS: The rationale behind the Mount Laurel case is that the use of all land is controlled by the State. The State has constitutional obligations to all its residents whether rich or poor. Municipalities, as state subjects, must set aside a fair share of its land for lower income housing. They cannot allocate only dilapidated land for the poor and retain valuable land for the rich exclusively. While this rationale appears clear in theory, in execution it has proven very difficult. The main difficulty is in developing an equitable formula for determining "fair share." Until a definitive formula is developed, this will prevent widespread application of this rule.

[For more information on exclusionary zoning, see Casenote Law Outline on Property, Chapter 10, § II, Validity of Zoning Laws.]

NOTES:

TOWN OF BELLEVILLE v. PARRILLO'S, INC.
N.J. Sup. Ct., 416 A.2d 388 (1980).

NATURE OF CASE: Appeal from the reversal of a conviction for continued operation of a nonconforming business whose usage underwent a change.

FACT SUMMARY: When Parrillo's (D) changed its existing nonconforming use from a restaurant to a discotheque, the Town of Belleville (P) filed charges which led to a conviction of Parrillo's (D) owners, however, the appellate division reversed the conviction, prompting this appeal.

CONCISE RULE OF LAW: An existing nonconforming use may continue only where it is a continuance of substantially the same kind of use as that to which the premises were devoted when the zoning ordinance was passed.

FACTS: Parrillo's (D) already operated as a restaurant when the Town of Belleville (P) enacted a zoning ordinance designating the area in which Parrillo's (D) was located as a residence zone. Parrillo's (D) owners later made certain renovations to the premises, which then opened as a discotheque. Shortly after opening under the new format, Parrillo's (D) owners applied for a discotheque license as required by the Town's (P) ordinance regulating dancehalls. Although the application was denied, Parrillo's (D) continued business as usual. The Town (P) filed charges that culminated in a conviction and a court-imposed fine. On a trial de novo after appeal, Parrillo's (D) was again found guilty. The court concluded that there had been a prohibited change in the use of the premises. The appellate division reversed. The Town (P) appealed.

ISSUE: May an existing nonconforming use continue only where it is a continuance of substantially the same kind of use as that to which the premises were devoted when the zoning ordinance was passed?

HOLDING AND DECISION: (Clifford, J.) Yes. An existing nonconforming use may continue only where it is a continuance of substantially the same kind of use as that to which the premises were devoted when the zoning ordinance was passed. Parrillo's (D) conversion of the premises from a restaurant to a discotheque resulted in a substantial, and therefore impermissible, change. The entire character of the business has been altered. What was once a restaurant is now a dancehall. Measured by the zoning ordinance, the general welfare of the neighborhood has been demonstrably affected adversely by the conversion of Parrillo's (D) business. Reversed and remanded for entry of a judgment of conviction.

EDITOR'S ANALYSIS: Because nonconforming uses are inconsistent with the objectives of uniform zoning, the courts have required that consistent with the property rights of those affected and with substantial justice, they should be reduced to conformity as quickly as is compatible with justice. In that regard, the courts have permitted municipalities to impose limitations upon nonconforming uses. The method generally used to limit nonconforming uses is to prevent any increase or change in the nonconformity.

[For more information on nonconforming use of property, see Casenote Law Outline on Property, Chapter 10, § III, Changes in Zoning Laws.]

NOTES:

COMMONS v. WESTWOOD ZONING BOARD OF ADJUSTMENT
N.J. Sup. Ct., 410 A.2d 1138 (1980).

NATURE OF CASE: Appeal from a judgment as to the validity of a denial for a zoning variance.

FACT SUMMARY: When the Commons' (P) application for a zoning variance to allow them to build a house on a nonconforming lot was denied by the Westwood Zoning Board of Adjustment (D), the Commons (P) appealed that denial.

CONCISE RULE OF LAW: A variance may be granted where strict application of a zoning ordinance would result in exceptional and undue hardship upon the developer of the property.

FACTS: The Commons (P) wanted to build a house on a vacant lot they and their predecessors in title had owned since 1927. The lot had a frontage of thirty feet and a total area of 5190 square feet. The Borough of Westwood (D) adopted a zoning ordinance in 1933, amended in 1947 to require a frontage of at least seventy-five feet and an area of no less than 7,500 square feet. Many of the existing homes were nonconforming. An unsuccessful attempt had been made to sell the vacant lot to an adjacent homeowner. Later, the developer who contracted to purchase the land unsuccessfully sought to purchase a 10-foot strip from another adjacent homeowner. Many neighbors opposed the application for a variance. The Board (D) denied the variance, finding no evidence to establish hardship. The trial court affirmed on the ground that the variance would be detrimental to the entire area where the property was situated. The appellate division affirmed. This appeal followed.

ISSUE: May a variance be granted where strict application of a zoning ordinance would result in exceptional and undue hardship upon the developer of the property?

HOLDING AND DECISION: (Schreiber, J.) Yes. A variance may be granted where strict application of a zoning ordinance would result in exceptional and undue hardship upon the developer of the property. When an undue hardship is found to exist, the Board (D) must also be satisfied that granting the variance will not impinge on the public good and will not substantially impair the intent and purpose of the zone plan and zoning ordinance. Here, one could reasonably conclude that the land would be zoned into inutility if a variance were not granted. Thus, it cannot be said that there was no evidence to establish hardship. However, the Board (D) did not consider the negative criteria, nor did the developer submit a detailed plan of the proposed house. These circumstances call for a remand to the Board (D) so that the record may be supplemented and adequate findings made.

EDITOR'S ANALYSIS: "Undue hardship" involves the underlying notion that no effective use can be made of the property in the event the variance is denied. Use of the property may of course be subject to reasonable restraint. Where denial of a variance would zone the property into inutility, the possibility exists that an exercise of eminent domain will be called for, and compensation must be paid.

[For more information on variances, see Casenote Law Outline on Property, Chapter 10, § III, Changes in Zoning Laws.]

NOTES:

STONE v. CITY OF WILTON

Iowa Sup. Ct., 331 N.W.2d 398 (1983).

NATURE OF CASE: Appeal from the dismissal of a petition for declaratory judgment, injunctive relief and damages in an action involving rezoning.

FACT SUMMARY: When the City of Wilton (D) considered a rezoning recommendation that would affect Stone's (P) property and his plan to construct a multi-family housing project, he filed a petition with the court, contending he had a vested right in developing his land.

CONCISE RULE OF LAW: The validity of a police power enactment, such as zoning, depends on its reasonableness.

FACTS: Stone (P) purchased land to develop a low-income, federally subsidized housing project consisting of several multi-family units. About one-fourth of the land was zoned single-family residential, while the remainder was zoned multi-family residential. After purchasing the land, Stone (P) incurred expenses for an architect and an engineer. Stone (P) also secured an FHA loan commitment for construction of the project. Later, the planning and zoning commission recommended rezoning part of the city to single-family residential due to alleged inadequacies of sewer, water, and electrical services. The rezoning recommendation affected all of Stone's (P) property. When the City of Wilton (D) denied Stone's (P) application for a building permit due to the pending rezoning recommendation, he filed a petition with the court. Stone (P) also contended that he had a vested right in developing his property. This appeal followed the trial court's ruling.

ISSUE: Does the validity of a police power enactment, such as zoning, depend on its reasonableness?

HOLDING AND DECISION: (McGiverin, J.) Yes. The validity of a police power enactment, such as zoning, depends on its reasonableness. A city's comprehensive plan is always subject to reasonable revisions designed to meet the ever-changing needs and conditions of a community. Here, the Council (D) rationally decided to rezone this section of the city to further the public welfare in accordance with a comprehensive plan. In addition, Stone's (P) efforts and expenditures prior to rezoning were not so substantial as to create vested rights in the completion of the housing project. Finally, the rezoning only deprived Stone (P) of the land's most beneficial use, which does not render it an unconstitutional taking. This court cannot substitute its view of reasonableness for that of the Council (D). Thus, the ordinance is valid and applicable to Stone's (P) land and project.

EDITOR'S ANALYSIS: The Wilton (D) city council was faced with a number of competing concerns in regard to the proper zoning of the area where Stone's (P) land was situated. Because legislative bodies are faced with balancing such competing concerns, courts refrain from reviewing the merits of their decisions if at least a debatable question exists as to the reasonableness of their action. However, where a discriminatory purpose is a motivating factor in the decision, such judicial deference is no longer justified.

―――――――――

[For more information on the power to zone, see Casenote Law Outline on Property, Chapter 10, § I, The Power to Zone.]

NOTES:

ACME LAUNDRY CO., INC. v.
SECRETARY OF ENVIRONMENTAL AFFAIRS
Mass. Sup. Ct., 575 N.E.2d 1086 (1991).

NATURE OF CASE: Appeal from judgment granting defendants' motion for summary judgment in an action seeking to have a lien declared invalid.

FACT SUMMARY: Acme Laundry (P) filed this action, protesting the placing of a lien on contaminated property owned by Acme (P) pursuant to the Massachusetts Oil and Hazardous Material Release Prevention Act.

CONCISE RULE OF LAW: Once the state has incurred assessment costs related to a contaminated site, it may place a lien securing both the costs already incurred and those which will be incurred in monitoring and supervision.

FACTS: Acme Laundry (P) operated a laundry business on the same parcel of land for almost seventy years. When Acme (P) proposed to sell the laundry site, the prospective purchasers engaged an environmental engineering firm to examine the site. Two fuel oil storage tanks were removed from underground. One tank had a hole in it, and the surrounding soil was discovered to be saturated with fuel oil. After examining the property, the Department of Environmental Quality Engineering (DEQE) (D) placed a lien on the property pursuant to the Mass. Oil and Hazardous Material Release Prevention Act, despite the fact that one of the owners stated that Acme (P) would clean up the contaminated site. Acme (P) filed this action requesting a declaration that the lien was invalid and that three other parcels of property unaffected by the release could not be subject to the lien. Acme (P) also requested an injunction to discharge the current lien and to prevent imposition of future liens. The trial court granted the Secretary's (D) motion for summary judgment. Acme (P) appealed.

ISSUE: Once the state has incurred assessment costs related to a contaminated site, may it place a lien securing both the costs already incurred and those that will be incurred in monitoring and supervision?

HOLDING AND DECISION: (Abrams, J.) Yes. Once the state has incurred assessment costs related to a contaminated site, it may place a lien securing both the costs already incurred and those that will be incurred in monitoring and supervision. Before summary judgment was entered, the DEQE (D) offered to release the lien if Acme (P) would provide alternative security in the form of a trust fund, letter of credit, escrow deposit, or surety bond. Acme (P) refused. The lien has thus secured the Commonwealth's recovery of its costs without interfering with Acme's (P) ability to finance cleanup operations. Placing of such a lien provides a powerful incentive to a responsible party to conclude the cleanup process as quickly and efficiently as possible. Affirmed.

DISSENT: (O'Connor, J.) The court's holding will defeat the legislative objective in enacting the statute, which is to encourage responsible parties to clean up their own mess. Moreover, the court's holding is unfaithful to the statutory language. Therefore, the summary judgment for the Secretary (D) should be reversed, and the liens declared invalid.

EDITOR'S ANALYSIS: Unlike the original § 9604 of the Comprehensive Environmental Response, Compensation and Liability Act (CERCLA), the state statute contained no language limiting the authority of the agency to act. Congress has since amended § 9604 of CERCLA so that it now more closely resembles the state statute at issue here. Liability for releases of hazardous material is imposed without fault on various parties, including persons who currently own a contaminated site, or did own such a site at the time hazardous material was stored or disposed of at the site, and any person who otherwise caused or is legally responsible for a release of oil or hazardous material.

NOTES:

CHAPTER 6
COMMON OWNERSHIP OF RESIDENTIAL PROPERTY

QUICK REFERENCE RULES OF LAW

1. **Conflicts over Rent and Ouster in the Context of Divorce.** In a divorce proceeding where a spouse departs a residence held as community property due to marital friction, a constructive ouster is effected, but if the spouse abandons the home for another intimate partner, a constructive ouster is not effected. (Olivas v. Olivas)

   [For more information on ouster of cotenant, see Casenote Law Outline on Property, Chapter 6, § V, Rights of Cotenants As between Themselves.]

2. **Family Conflicts over Use of Common Property.** Where a cotenant lawfully leases his own interest in the common property to another without the consent of the other tenant and without his joining in the lease, the nonjoining tenant may not demand exclusive possession as against the lessee, but may only demand to be let into co-possession. (Carr v. Deking)

   [For more information on cotenant right to lease, see Casenote Law Outline on Property, Chapter 6, § V, Rights of Cotenants As between Themselves.]

3. **Death.** A lease does not sever a joint tenancy and expires upon the death of the lessor joint tenant. (Tenhet v. Boswell)

   [For more information on severance of joint tenancy, see Casenote Law Outline on Property, Chapter 6, § III, The Joint Tenancy with Right of Survivorship.]

4. **Divorce.** Pursuant to a divorce proceeding where one party is awarded the entire ownership of certain lands, those lands are taken subject to leasehold interests in the ex-spouse's former ownership interest. (Kresha v. Kresha)

   [For more information on the right to lease, see Casenote Law Outline on Property, Chapter 6, § V, Rights of Cotenants As between Themselves.]

5. **Tenancy by the Entirety.** The interest of one spouse in an estate by the entireties is not subject to the claims of his or her individual creditors; thus, the spouses can jointly convey the property free of such claims. (Sawada v. Endo)

   [For more information on tenants by the entirety, see Casenote Law Outline on Property, Chapter 6, § IV, Tenants by the Entirety.]

6. **Rule against Unreasonable Restraints on Alienation.** No person shall be denied the right to purchase or lease a unit because of race, religion, sex, sexual preference, marital status or national origin. (Wolinsky v. Kadison)

   [For more information on power to restrict transfer of unit, see Casenote Law Outline on Property, Chapter 13, § I, Condominiums.]

7. **Requiring Prior Consent of the Condominium Association.** A clause in a condominium's declaration permitting the association to arbitrarily withhold its consent to transfer a unit constitutes an unreasonable restraint on alienation. (Aquarian Foundation, Inc. v. Sholom House, Inc.)

[For more information on restraint on alienation of unit, see Casenote Law Outline on Property, Chapter 13, § I, Condominiums.]

8. **Restrictions on Leasing.** A restriction adopted after the purchase of a condominium unit would not be enforceable against the purchaser except through the purchaser's acquiescence. (Breene v. Plaza Towers Association)

   [For more information on powers of the association, see Casenote Law Outline on Property, Chapter 13, § I, Condominiums.]

9. **Reasonableness Limits on Condominium Rules.** Condominium declarations and bylaws granting a board the authority to enact rules banning television antennae will withstand judicial scrutiny if they are deemed reasonable. (O'Buck v. Cottonwood Village Condominium Association)

   [For more information on the operation of condominium association, see Casenote Law Outline on Property, Chapter 13, § I, Condominiums.]

10. **Restraints on Alienation of Low-Income Housing.** Restrictions on alienation of property that are in keeping with the public policy of the state and that are clearly and directly related to the legitimate purposes for which a condominium project was established are reasonable and valid. (City of Oceanside v. McKenna)

    [For more information on restrictions on alienation of condominium property, see Casenote Law Outline on Property, Chapter 13, § I, Condominiums.]

OLIVAS v. OLIVAS

N.M. Sup. Ct., 780 P.2d 640 (1989).

NATURE OF CASE: Appeal of the property division in a divorce action.

FACT SUMMARY: Because of a lengthy delay between the Olivas's divorce decree and the property division, Mr. Olivas (D) waited several years before seeking rent from Mrs. Olivas (P), who had remained in their home.

CONCISE RULE OF LAW: In a divorce proceeding where a spouse departs a residence held as community property due to marital friction, a constructive ouster is effected, but if the spouse abandons the home for another intimate partner, a constructive ouster is not effected.

FACTS: Caroline (P) and Sam Olivas (D) were divorced by a partial decree entered December 18, 1984, but the district court did not enter its final order dividing property until August 31, 1987. The district court found that Sam Olivas (D) chose to move out of the family home and live in a separate home with another woman. The district court failed to find that he had been constructively ousted from the family home. Sam Olivas (D) requested findings and conclusions that the constructive ouster by Caroline (P) entitled him to half of the reasonable rental value of the home from the time of the initial separation.

ISSUE: In a divorce proceeding where a spouse departs a residence held as community property due to marital friction, a constructive ouster is effected, but if the spouse abandons the home for another intimate partner, is a constructive ouster also effected?

HOLDING AND DECISION: (Hartz, J.) No. If one of the parties in a divorce case remains in possession of the community residence between the date of the divorce and the date of the final judgment dividing the community assets, then there may be a form of constructive ouster which may render the divorced spouse in possession of the residence liable to the one not in possession for the use and occupation of the residence. However, where there is substantial evidence, as in this case, to support the inference that the husband's purpose in leaving the community residence was to live with a girlfriend and his departure was the reason his wife filed for divorce, then he was not pushed out but pulled. Affirmed.

EDITOR'S ANALYSIS: Common law precedents support the proposition that the remaining spouse should pay rent to the cotenant when both cannot be expected to live together on the property. For example, when it is impractical for all cotenants to occupy the premises jointly, it is unnecessary that those claiming rent from the cotenant in possession first demand the right to move in and occupy the premises.

[For more information on ouster of cotenant, see Casenote Law Outline on Property, Chapter 6, § V, Rights of Cotenants As between Themselves.]

NOTES:

CARR v. DEKING

Wash. Sup. Ct., 765 P.2d 40 (1988).

NATURE OF CASE: Action to declare that no valid lease existed and that tenant should vacate the property.

FACT SUMMARY: George Carr, owner of a parcel of land with his son, Joel Carr (P), as tenants in common, executed a written lease agreement with Deking (D) without Joel's (P) authorization.

CONCISE RULE OF LAW: Where a cotenant lawfully leases his own interest in the common property to another without the consent of the other tenant and without his joining in the lease, the nonjoining tenant may not demand exclusive possession as against the lessee, but may only demand to be let into co-possession.

FACTS: George Carr and his son, Joel Carr (P), owned a parcel of land as tenants in common. From 1974 to 1986 they leased the land to Deking (D) pursuant to a year-to year oral agreement, receiving one-third of the annual crop as rent. In 1986, Joel Carr (P) informed Deking (D) he wanted cash rent in place of crop rent. Shortly thereafter, George Carr (P) executed a written lease agreement with Deking (D) without his son's authorization. Joel Carr (P) commenced this action to declare that no valid lease existed and that Deking (D) had no right to farm the land.

ISSUE: Where a cotenant lawfully leases his own interest in the common property to another without the consent of the other tenant and without his joining in the lease, can the nonjoining tenant demand exclusive possession as against the lessee?

HOLDING AND DECISION: (Green, J.) No. Where a cotenant lawfully leases his own interest in the common property to another without the consent of the other tenant and without his joining in the lease, the nonjoining tenant may not demand exclusive possession as against the lessee, but may only demand to be let into copossession. Joel Carr (P) is not entitled to eject Deking (D) from his property. The proper remedy is partition, and until that occurs, Mr. Deking (D) is entitled to farm the land under the lease.

EDITOR'S ANALYSIS: It is well settled that each tenant in common of real property may use, benefit, and possess the entire property subject only to the equal rights of cotenants. Thus, a cotenant may lawfully lease his own interest in the common property to another without the consent of the other tenant and without his joining in the lease.

[For more information on cotenant right to lease, see Casenote Law Outline on Property, Chapter 6, § V, Rights of Cotenants As between Themselves.]

TENHET v. BOSWELL

Cal. Sup. Ct., 554 P.2d 330 (1976).

NATURE OF CASE: Joint tenant's action to have a lease declared invalid.

FACT SUMMARY: Johnson, a joint tenant with Tenhet (P), leased his interest in the joint tenancy property to Boswell (D) for a term of years and died during that term.

CONCISE RULE OF LAW: A lease does not sever a joint tenancy and expires upon the death of the lessor joint tenant.

FACTS: Johnson and Tenhet (P) owned a parcel of property as joint tenants. Without Tenhet's (P) knowledge or consent, Johnson leased the property to Boswell (D) for a period of ten years. Johnson died three months after execution of the lease, and Tenhet (P) sought to establish her sole right to possession of the property as the surviving joint tenant. After an unsuccessful demand upon Johnson (D) to vacate the premises, Tenhet (P) brought an action to have the lease declared invalid.

ISSUE: Although a lease does not sever a joint tenancy, does it expire upon the death of the lessor joint tenant?

HOLDING AND DECISION: (Mosk, J.) Yes. A lease expires upon the death of the lessor joint tenant. Even if they could not agree to act in concert, either Tenhet (P) or Johnson might have severed the joint tenancy, with or without the consent of the other, by an act that was clearly indicative of an intent to terminate, such as conveyance of her entire interest. Because a joint tenancy may be created only by express intent and because there are alternative and unambiguous means of altering the nature of that estate, the lease here in issue did not operate to sever the joint tenancy. However, when Johnson died the lease died with him, and therefore it is no longer enforceable against Tenhet (P).

EDITOR'S ANALYSIS: California Civil Code § 683 provides in part, "A joint interest is one owned by two or more persons in equal shares, by a title created by a single will or transfer, when expressly declared in the will or transfer to be a joint tenancy." This statute, requiring an express declaration for the creation of joint interests, does not abrogate the common law rule that four unities are essential to an estate in joint tenancy: unity of interest, unity of time, unity of title, and unity of possession.

[For more information on severance of joint tenancy, see Casenote Law Outline on Property, Chapter 6, § III, The Joint Tenancy with Right of Survivorship.]

NOTES:

KRESHA v. KRESHA

Neb. Sup. Ct., 371 N.W.2d 280 (1985).

NATURE OF CASE: Forcible entry and detainer action to obtain possession of lands.

FACT SUMMARY: A dissolution decree awarded land held in co-tenancy to Rose Kresha (P), who then attempted to terminate her son Joseph's (D) pre-dissolution lease on the property.

CONCISE RULE OF LAW: Pursuant to a divorce proceeding where one party is awarded the entire ownership of certain lands, those lands are taken subject to leasehold interests in the ex-spouse's former ownership interest.

FACTS: Adolph Kresha and Rose Kresha (P) were husband and wife and the co-owners of two tracts of land. Adolph, by written instrument and without the consent, knowledge or authority of Rose Kresha (P), leased the land to their son Joseph (D) for a six-year period. Within those six years the couple divorced, and a dissolution decree awarded the lands in question to Rose Kersha (P). She advised Joseph (D) that she was terminating his lease. Joseph (D) refused to vacate the premises, and Rose Kresha (P) brought a forcible entry and detainer action in the county court to obtain possession of the lands. The trial court ruled for Joseph (D), and Rose Kresha (P) appealed.

ISSUE: Pursuant to a divorce proceeding where one party is awarded the entire ownership of certain lands, are those lands taken subject to leasehold interests in the ex-spouse's former ownership interest?

HOLDING AND DECISION: (Caporale, J.) Yes. Pursuant to a divorce proceeding where one party is awarded the entire ownership of certain lands, those lands are taken subject to leasehold interests in the ex-spouse's former ownership interest. The situation here is similar to that presented in the acquisition of property from a fee owner which the purchaser knows to be encumbered by an existing lease. In such a situation, the purchaser acquires the property subject to the lease. Joseph's (D) lease survives the divorce. Affirmed.

EDITOR'S ANALYSIS: In George & Teas v. George, 591 S.W.2d 655 (1978), the court set aside a lease by the husband of real property owned jointly with his wife. The lease to the husband's mother was for a 99-year term and called for only a nominal rental. The mother knew her son was having marital difficulties, and the lease was entered into after the husband filed the last of two or three divorce actions. The wife did not learn of the lease until the final phases of the proceedings. The George court found that under these circumstances, the lease constituted a fraudulent conveyance.

[For more information on the right to lease, see Casenote Law Outline on Property, Chapter 6, § V, Rights of Cotenants As between Themselves.]

NOTES:

SAWADA v. ENDO

57 Haw. 608, 561 P.2d 1291 (1977).

NATURE OF CASE: Appeal from refusal to set aside a conveyance of land.

FACT SUMMARY: The Sawadas (P), who were injured when struck by a car driven by Endo (D) and unable to obtain satisfaction of their judgments from Endo's (D) personal property, sought to set aside a conveyance by Endo (D) and his wife of some land which had been held by them as tenants by the entirety.

CONCISE RULE OF LAW: The interest of one spouse in an estate by the entireties is not subject to the claims of his or her individual creditors; thus, the spouses can jointly convey the property free of such claims.

FACTS: In 1968, Endo (D) struck Masako and Helen Sawada (P) while driving his car. After Helen Sawada (P) filed suit, Endo (D) and his wife conveyed to their sons some real property which they held as tenants by the entirety. Masako Sawada (P) filed suit, and both she and Helen Sawada (P) obtained judgments against Endo (D). Unable to satisfy the judgments from Endo's (D) personal property, the Sawadas (P) sought to set aside the conveyance of land. The court refused to do so, and the Sawadas (P) appealed.

ISSUE: Is the interest of one spouse in real property, held in tenancy by the entirety, subject to levy and execution by his or her individual creditors absent consent of both spouses?

HOLDING AND DECISION: (Menor, J.) No. The tenancy by the entirety is an estate held by a husband and wife in single ownership; both and each hold the whole estate. Since the passage of the Married Women's Property Acts, this estate is indivisible except by joint action of the spouses. Thus, the spouses can jointly convey the property free of any judgment liens against the husband or wife as individuals. This is in accord with the purpose of the estate: to protect a spouse from the other spouse's improvident debts. Since the land in question here was held by Endo (D) and his wife in tenancy by the entirety, it was immune from claims by Endo's (D) separate creditors, the Sawadas (P). Affirmed.

DISSENT: (Kidwell, J.) The effect of the Married Women's Act, if properly interpreted, was not to take from the husband his common law right to transfer his interest but to give the wife the same right to alienate her interest in the estate. Thus, judgment creditors of either spouse should be able to levy and execute on the separate interests, at least to the extent of the husband's or wife's right of survivorship.

EDITOR'S ANALYSIS: About half the states continue to recognize tenancy by the entirety as a valid institution. The majority of these states are aligned with Sawada v. Endo on the interpretation of the Married Women's Act: one spouse alone cannot assign his or her interest in a tenancy by the entirety. This is of great significance for general creditors, as they can only reach property which the debtors can voluntarily assign. This consequence of tenancy by the entirety is one of its primary attractions.

[For more information on tenants by the entirety, see Casenote Law Outline on Property, Chapter 6, § IV, Tenants by the Entirety.]

NOTES:

WOLINSKY v. KADISON
Ill. App. Ct., 449 N.E.2d 151 (1983).

NATURE OF CASE: Appeal from dismissal of action for damages based on discrimination in purchase of property.

FACT SUMMARY: The Board of Directors (D) for a condominium complex exercised its right of first refusal regarding Wolinsky's (P) offer to purchase a condominium.

CONCISE RULE OF LAW: No person shall be denied the right to purchase or lease a unit because of race, religion, sex, sexual preference, marital status or national origin.

FACTS: In late August, 1978, Wolinsky (P) contracted to purchase a unit in the same condominium complex in which she was already living. In late September, the Board of Directors (D) notified her that it was exercising its right of first refusal, and the seller then terminated its contract with Wolinsky (P). She alleged that the Board (D) exercised its first refusal on the basis of the condominium management's report to the board that she was an unmarried woman who would occupy the unit with her children. Wolinsky (P) filed suit, and the case went before the appellate court.

ISSUE: May a person be denied the right to purchase or lease a unit because of race, religion, sex, sexual preference, marital status or national origin?

HOLDING AND DECISION: (Rizzi, J.) No. The Chicago condominium ordinance provides that no person shall be denied the right to purchase or lease a unit because of race, religion, sex, sexual preference, marital status or national origin. Wolinsky (P) alleged that the board exercised its right of first refusal because she was an unmarried female who would occupy the unit in question with her children. Her allegations bring her well within the scope of the ordinance, which the Board (D) has violated.

EDITOR'S ANALYSIS: A board of directors must exercise a right of first refusal reasonably upon consideration of the prospective purchaser's qualifications in light of the economic and social reasons that justify the restraint itself. The criteria for testing the reasonableness of an exercise of this power by a condominium association are (1) whether the reason for exercising the right of first refusal is rationally related to the protection, preservation or proper operation of the property and the purposes of the association as set forth in its governing instruments, and (2) whether the power was exercised in a fair and nondiscriminatory manner.

[For more information on power to restrict transfer of unit, see Casenote Law Outline on Property, Chapter 13, § I, Condominiums.]

NOTES:

AQUARIAN FOUNDATION, INC. v. SHOLOM HOUSE, INC.

Fla. Dist. Ct. App., 448 So.2d 1166 (1984).

NATURE OF CASE: Appeal from judgment nullifying a conveyance in action for ejectment and damages.

FACT SUMMARY: When a condominium owner sold her unit to Aquarian Foundation (P) without the consent of Sholom House's (D) board of directors, Sholom House (D) sued to set aside the conveyance.

CONCISE RULE OF LAW: A clause in a condominium's declaration permitting the association to arbitrarily withhold its consent to transfer a unit constitutes an unreasonable restraint on alienation.

FACTS: A provision of the declaration of condominium at Sholom House (P) required the written consent of the condo association's board of directors to any sale, lease, or transfer of a unit owner's interest. In the event of a violation, the fee simple title to the condominium reverted to the association upon payment of the unit's fair value to the owner. The clause stated that the association could "arbitrarily, capriciously, or unreasonably" withhold its consent. Bertha Albares sold her unit to Aquarian Foundation (D) without the board's consent. Sholom House (P) sued to set aside the sale. The trial court, having concluded that Albares had violated the declaration of condominium, nullified the sale to Aquarian (D). Aquarian (D) appealed.

ISSUE: Does a clause in a condominium's declaration permitting the association to arbitrarily withhold its consent to transfer constitute an unreasonable restraint on alienation?

HOLDING AND DECISION: (Pearson, J.) Yes. A clause in a condominium's declaration permitting the association to arbitrarily, capriciously, or unreasonably withhold its consent to transfer a unit constitutes an unreasonable restraint on alienation. By necessity, unit owners give up a certain degree of freedom of choice to ensure the happiness and peace of mind of all the residents who live close together and share the condominium's facilities. Accordingly, restrictions on the right to transfer property within the condominium are generally upheld by the court. They will, however, be invalidated when found to violate some external public policy or constitutional right of the individual. An association may reject perpetually any unit owner's prospective buyer for any or no reason, so long as the association provides another purchaser or purchases the property itself. Here, the reverter clause does not obligate the association to compensate the owner within a reasonable time. In fact, the clause is not even triggered until there is a sale, which would not ordinarily be expected to occur without the association's consent. Thus, the association's accountability to the unit owner is illusory. Therefore, the restraint on alienation is unlawful. Reversed.

EDITOR'S ANALYSIS: Courts may generally uphold provisions in condominium by-laws prohibiting alienation of units as per se

reasonable but will still review the reasonableness of refusals to grant such consent. One court has held that an association's refusal to consent to a time-share arrangement was unreasonable and impermissible. See Laguna Royale Owners Ass'n. v. Darger, 119 Cal. App. 3d 670 (1981).

_____

[For more information on restraint on alienation of unit, see Casenote Law Outline on Property, Chapter 13, § I, Condominiums.]

NOTES:

BREENE v. PLAZA TOWERS ASSOCIATION
N.D. Sup.Ct., 310 N.W.2d 730 (1981).

NATURE OF CASE: Appeal from a summary judgment invalidating amended housing bylaws/restrictions.

FACT SUMMARY: Breene (P) owned a condominium in the Plaza Tower complex and was prohibited from renting her unit by the Plaza Towers Association (D).

CONCISE RULE OF LAW: A restriction adopted after the purchase of a condominium unit would not be enforceable against the purchaser except through the purchaser's acquiescence.

FACTS: Breene (P) purchased a condominium in the Plaza Tower condominium complex in 1974. When Breene (P) purchased her interest in the condominium, there was no restriction relating to the sale or lease of the unit other than a provision giving the Association (D) the right of first refusal to purchase or lease the unit. In 1979, however, the Plaza Tower Association (D) passed and adopted an amendment to its bylaws providing that all units of the condominium were to be occupied by the unit owner and that the leasing of a unit to a nonowner was prohibited except in certain situations. Breene (P) requested permission to rent her unit to another party, and the Association (D) refused. Breene (P) brought suit and won on a summary judgment motion. The Association (D) appealed.

ISSUE: Would a restriction adopted after the purchase of a condominium unit be enforceable against the purchaser if the purchaser did not agree to it?

HOLDING AND DECISION: (Sand, J.) No. A restriction adopted after the purchase of a condominium unit would not be enforceable against the purchaser except through the purchaser's acquiescence. A prerequisite to the enforceability of a restriction is that the restriction be recorded prior to the conveyance of any condominium unit. A necessary corollary of this is that a restriction adopted after the purchase of a condominium unit would not be enforceable against the purchaser except through the purchaser's acquiescence. Here, amendments to the bylaws could be adopted that would be enforceable against those currently owning a condominium unit. However, these bylaws would have to relate to maintenance of common elements, limited elements, assessment of expenses, payment of losses, and similar matters. The action in the instant case is not within the scope of the subject matter of a bylaw and is, instead, governed by the provisions relating to restrictions. Affirmed.

EDITOR'S ANALYSIS: The statutory provisions relating to condominiums require that the declaration of condominium, the restrictions, and the bylaws must be recorded in the office of the register of deeds. These statutory provisions put prospective purchasers and owners on notice as to the restrictions and bylaws affecting their interest in a property. A prospective purchaser's decision to buy a particular unit in a condominium may be based upon the recorded restrictions that encumber the unit.

[For more information on powers of the association, see Casenote Law Outline on Property, Chapter 13, § I, Condominiums.]

NOTES:

O'BUCK v. COTTONWOOD VILLAGE CONDOMINIUM ASSOCIATION, INC.

Alaska Sup. Ct., 750 P.2d 813 (1988).

NATURE OF CASE: Appeal concerning action seeking damages and an injunction against adoption of condominium rules.

FACT SUMMARY: The Cottonwood Village Association (D) found that roof leakage was caused in part by badly mounted T.V. antennae and foot traffic on the roof related to the antennae and adopted a rule prohibiting the mounting of television antennae anywhere on the building. Consequently, the O'Bucks (P) lost reception in three of their four televisions.

CONCISE RULE OF LAW: Condominium declarations and bylaws granting a board the authority to enact rules banning television antennae will withstand judicial scrutiny if they are deemed reasonable.

FACTS: The Cottonwood Village Association (D) found that roof leakage was caused in part by badly mounted T.V. antennae and foot traffic on the roof related to the antennae and adopted a rule prohibiting the mounting of television antennae anywhere on the building. The purpose of this rule was to protect the roof and to enhance the marketablility of the condominium units. The Board (D) also decided to make a cable system available as an alternative to antennae. Without the antennae, the O'Bucks (P) lost reception in three of their four televisions. It would cost ten dollars per month per set to hook up to the newly offered cable. The O'Bucks (P) filed a complaint against the Association (D) seeking damages and an injunction against enforcement of the rule.

ISSUE: Will condominium declarations and bylaws granting a board the authority to enact rules banning television antennae withstand judicial scrutiny if they are deemed reasonable?

HOLDING AND DECISION: (Rabinowitz, J.) Yes. Condominium declarations and bylaws granting a board the authority to enact rules banning television antennae will withstand judicial scrutiny if they are deemed reasonable. In evaluating the reasonableness of a condominium association rule, it is necessary to balance the importance of the rule's objective against the importance of the interest infringed upon. In a case where a rule seriously curtails an important civil liberty, the court will look with suspicion on the rule and require a compelling justification. However, the antennae ban in the instant case curtails no significant interests. The only loss suffered is that the O'Bucks (P) and the other owners must now pay a small fee to receive television. Injunction denied.

EDITOR'S ANALYSIS: The absence of any provision explicitly authorizing a board to ban or prohibit certain uses or activities is not fatal to the board's right to do so. In Beachwood Villas Condominium v. Poor, 448 So.2d 1143, (Fla. Dist. Ct. App. 1984), the court held that "it would be impossible to list all restrictive uses in a declaration of condominium." As mentioned above, determinations in these situations are based on a reasonableness standard where the competing interests are balanced and analyzed.

[For more information on the operation of condominium association, see Casenote Law Outline on Property, Chapter 13, § I, Condominiums.]

NOTES:

CITY OF OCEANSIDE v. McKENNA
Cal. Ct. App., 264 Cal. Rptr. 275 (1990).

NATURE OF CASE: Appeal from summary judgment granting an injunction prohibiting alienation of property.

FACT SUMMARY: McKenna (D) attempted to rent a condominium unit he had recently purchased, but the City of Oceanside (P) filed an action intended to enjoin McKenna (D) from renting or leasing his unit.

CONCISE RULE OF LAW: Restrictions on alienation of property that are in keeping with the public policy of the state and that are clearly and directly related to the legitimate purposes for which a condominium project was established are reasonable and valid.

FACTS: Oceanside Beach Partners bought Sea Village Condominiums from the City of Oceanside (P) for significantly below-market value. In return for the reduced price, Oceanside Partners agreed to CC&Rs that, among other things, prohibited any Sea Village owner from failing to occupy the dwelling as the owner's principal place of residence and from renting or leasing the property at any time for any reason. The CC&Rs were designed to assure the continued affordability of the condominiums and to foster an owner-occupied environment in the redevelopment area. McKenna (D) attempted to rent a condominium unit he had recently purchased, and the City of Oceanside (P) filed an action to enjoin McKenna (D) from renting or leasing his unit. The trial court granted a motion for summary judgment in favor of the City of Oceanside (P), and McKenna (D) appealed.

ISSUE: Are restrictions on alienation of property that are in keeping with the public policy of the state and that are clearly and directly related to the legitimate purposes for which a condominium project was established reasonable and valid?

HOLDING AND DECISION: (Todd, J.) Yes. Restrictions on alienation of property that are in keeping with the public policy of the state and that are clearly and directly related to the legitimate purposes for which a condominium project was established are reasonable and valid. Certainly the provision of housing for low and moderate-income persons is in keeping with the public policy of this state. Thus the restrictions support rather than offend the policies of this state. Given this factor and the fact that they clearly and directly are related to the legitimate purposes for which the Sea Village condominium project was established, they are reasonable. Affirmed.

EDITOR'S ANALYSIS: Under California Civil Code § 1354, CC&Rs in the document creating a condominium project shall be enforceable equitable servitudes unless unreasonable. California Civil Code § 711 has been interpreted to indicate that "the day has long since passed when the rule was that all restraints on alienation were unlawful under the statute. It is now the settled law in this jurisdiction that only unreasonable restraints on alienation are invalid." Martin v. Villa Roma, Inc., 182 Cal. Rptr. 382, 383 (Ct. App. 1982)

[For more information on restrictions on alienation of condominium property, see Casenote Law Outline on Property, Chapter 13, § I, Condominiums.]

NOTES:

CHAPTER 7
LANDLORD-TENANT RELATIONS

QUICK REFERENCE RULES OF LAW

1. **Identifying Landlord-Tenant Relationships: Self-Help versus Judicial Process.** When a migrant farmworker's employment is terminated, he may be removed from employer-provided housing only through a judicial proceeding. (Vasquez v. Glassboro Service Association, Inc.)

   [For more information on eviction of tenant, see Casenote Law Outline on Property, Chapter 7, §
   IX, Other Rights and Duties of Landlord and Tenant.]

2. **Landlord's Duty to Mitigate Damages.** A landlord has an obligation to make a reasonable effort to mitigate damages when a lessee "surrenders," meaning that he must make a reasonable effort to relet the premises. (Sommer v. Kridel)

   [For more information on the mitigation rule, see Casenote Law Outline on Property, Chapter 7, §
   X, Wrongful Abandonment.]

3. **Statutory Interpretation: Who Is Protected?** The term "family" as utilized in relation to rent-control noneviction provisions encompasses two adult lifetime partners whose relationship is long term and characterized by an emotional and financial commitment and interdependence. (Braschi v. Stahl Associates Company)

   [For more information on housing discrimination, see Casenote Law Outline on Property, Chapter
   12, § III, State Law.]

4. **When the Lease Requires the Landlord's Consent.** Where a lease provides for assignment only with the prior consent of the lessor, such consent may be withheld only where the lessor has a commercially reasonable objection to the assignment. (Kendall v. Ernest Pestana, Inc.)

   [For more information on assignment of lease, see Casenote Law Outline on Property, Chapter 7, §
   VIII, Transfers of Leasehold Interests.]

5. **When the Lease Requires the Landlord's Consent.** A lease provision requiring the landlord's consent to an assignment or sublease permits the landlord to refuse arbitrarily or unreasonably. (Slavin v. Rent Control Board of Brookline)

   [For more information on assignment and sublease, see Casenote Law Outline on Property, Chap-
   ter 7, § VIII, Transfers of Leasehold Interests.]

6. **Tenant's Good Faith Duty to Operate.** A covenant of continued operations will be implied into commercial leases containing a guaranteed minimum plus a percentage if the covenant is contemplated by the parties and the guaranteed minimum is not substantial or adequate. (College Block v. Atlantic Richfield Co.)

   [For more information on the duty to pay rent, see Casenote Law Outline on Property, Chapter 7, §
   IX, Other Rights and Duties of Landlord and Tenant.]

7. **The Covenant of Quiet Enjoyment and Construction Eviction.** A tenant may assert the defense of constructive eviction for the nonpayment of rent, even if he or she has abandoned only a portion of the demised premises due to the landlord's acts. (Minjak Co. v. Randolph)

[For more information on constructive eviction, see Casenote Law Outline on Property, Chapter 7, § VI, Interference with the Tenant's Use and Enjoyment of the Premises.]

8. **The Covenant of Quiet Enjoyment and Construction Eviction.** Where a landlord permits conduct of third persons which substantially impairs the right of quiet enjoyment of other tenants, it is a constructive eviction. (Blackett v. Olanoff)

   [For more information on constructive eviction, see Casenote Law Outline on Property, Chapter 7, § VI, Interference with the Tenant's Use and Enjoyment of the Premises.]

9. **Doctrinal Development.** Leases of real property contain an implied warranty of habitability for the breach of which the payment of rent may be suspended. (Javins v. First National Realty Corp.)

   [For more information on the implied warranty of habitability, see Casenote Law Outline on Property, Chapter 7, § VI, Interference with the Tenant's Use and Enjoyment of the Premises.]

10. **Retaliatory Eviction.** Tenants may organize and join a tenant's association and may participate in activities designed to legitimately coerce a landlord into taking action to improve living conditions without fear of retaliation, but engaging in physical threats or violence is not a legitimate method of coercion. (Hillview Associates v. Bloomquist)

    [For more information on retaliatory eviction, see Casenote Law Outline on Property, Chapter 7, § VI, Interference with the Tenant's Use and Enjoyment of the Premises.]

11. **Retaliatory Eviction.** First Amendment rights of speech unrelated to the tenant's property interest do not arise from tenancy relatiionship and therefore are not protected under a retaliatory eviction defense. (Imperial Colliery Co. v. Fout)

    [For more information on retaliatory eviction, see Casenote Law Outline on Property, Chapter 7, § VI, Interference with the Tenant's Use and Enjoyment of the Premises.]

12. **Consumer Protection Legislation.** In a situation involving the rental of a dwelling unit in an owner-occupied two-family house where the landlord owns no other real property, the relationship between the landlord and tenant is of a private nature and in no way concerns a trade or business. (Billings v. Wilson)

    [For more information on motive for retaliatory eviction, see Casenote Law Outline on Property, Chapter 7, § VI, Interference with the Tenant's Use and Enjoyment of the Premises.]

13. **Consumer Protection Legislation.** (1) A landlord's attempt to evict a tenant based solely on her efforts to convince him to repair her apartment is considered a retaliatory eviction. (2) Where a landlord is in violation of Massachusetts General Laws ch. 93 A, treble damages shall be awarded for intentional infliction of emotional distress and violation of the warranty of habitability. (Haddad v. Gonzalez)

    [For more information on retaliatory eviction, see Casenote Law Outline on Property, Chapter 7, § VI, Interference with the Tenant's Use and Enjoyment of the Premises.]

14. **Landlord's Tort Liability to Tenants: Lead Paint Poisoning.** Claims under Massachusetts' lead poisoning prevention law, which imposes tort liability on landlords who violate its provisions, are within the scope of the state contribution statute. (Ankiewicz v. Kinder)

    [For more information on negligently made repairs, see Casenote Law Outline on Property, Chapter 7, § VII, Landlord's Liability in Tort for Tenant's Physical Injuries.]

VASQUEZ v. GLASSBORO SERVICE ASSOCIATION, INC.

N.J. Sup. Ct., 415 A.2d 1156 (1980).

NATURE OF CASE: Appeal from a judgment in an action seeking to enjoin farm owners from depriving farmworkers of the use of their quarters except through judicial process.

FACT SUMMARY: After Vasquez's (P) employment as a migrant farmworker was terminated, he was not allowed to remain overnight in the employer-provided barracks until he could find alternative housing.

CONCISE RULE OF LAW: When a migrant farmworker's employment is terminated, he may be removed from employer-provided housing only through a judicial proceeding.

FACTS: Glassboro (D) contracted to bring migrant farmworkers to New Jersey from Puerto Rico, supplying living quarters for those workers at its labor camp. No extra charge was imposed for such housing. Vasquez (P), who was recruited in Puerto Rico, worked for Glassboro (D). Later, Glassboro's (D) foreman told Vasquez (P) that his work was unsatisfactory and that he was to be discharged. After a hearing and discharge, Vasquez (P) was not allowed to remain in the camp overnight. Unable to speak English and without funds to return to Puerto Rico, Vasquez (P) sought the assistance of the Farmworkers Corporation. He also consulted with the Farmworkers Rights Project, which filed a complaint, seeking an order permitting Vasquez (P) to reenter his living quarters and enjoining Glassboro (D) from depriving him of the use of the quarters except through judicial process.

ISSUE: When a migrant farmworker's employment is terminated, may he be removed from employer-provided housing without a judicial proceeding?

HOLDING AND DECISION: (Pollock, J.) No. When a migrant farmworker's employment is terminated, he may not be removed from employer-provided housing without a judicial proceeding. The contract under which Vasquez (P) was brought from Puerto Rico is a contract of adhesion. The unconscionability of the contract inheres not only in its failure to provide a worker with a reasonable opportunity to find alternative housing, but in its disregard for his welfare after termination of his employment. In the absence of any concern demonstrated for the worker in the contract, public policy requires the implication of a provision for a reasonable time to find alternative housing. By abolishing self-help in such situations, the court provides a forum for an equitable resolution of a controversy between a farm labor service and a migrant farmworker on termination of employment.

EDITOR'S ANALYSIS: A migrant farmworker has even less bargaining power than a residential tenant. Although Vasquez (P) had found housing at the time of this court decision, other workers had been evicted, some at odd hours of the night. The lack of alternative housing emphasized the inequality between Glassboro (D) and the migrant farmworkers. Once his employment ended, a farmworker lost not only his job but his shelter. Moreover, a migrant farmworker is not a tenant under the applicable New Jersey statute.

―――――――――――――――

[For more information on eviction of tenant, see Casenote Law Outline on Property, Chapter 7, § IX, Other Rights and Duties of Landlord and Tenant.]

NOTES:

SOMMER v. KRIDEL

N.J. Sup. Ct., 74 N.J. 446, 378 A.2d 767 (1977).

NATURE OF CASE: Consolidated actions seeking damages from a defaulting tenant.

FACT SUMMARY: Sommer (P) did not attempt to relet the premises he had leased to Kridel (D), even though the opportunity to do so existed and Kridel (D) had specifically informed Sommer (P) that he was unable to go through with the leasing for personal reasons and asked for acceptance of his surrender.

CONCISE RULE OF LAW: A landlord has an obligation to make a reasonable effort to mitigate damages when a lessee "surrenders," meaning that he must make a reasonable effort to relet the premises.

FACTS: Sommer (P) and Riverview Realty Co. (P) were both landlords who leased to tenants, Kridel (D) and Perosio (D), respectively, who were forced by personal circumstances to attempt "surrenders." Sommer (P) received a letter explaining the situations and stating Kridel's (D) desire to surrender. Neither landlord made an attempt to relet their vacated units, even though a party expressed interest in renting the unit from Sommer (P). Instead, both landlords brought suits to recover damages from their respective "defaulting" tenants. Noting that Sommer (P) never responded to Kridel's (D) written offer of surrender and finding that such was tantamount to an acceptance of that offer, the court found that Kridel's (D) tenancy had been terminated along with his obligation to pay rent. From an appellate reversal of the judgment dismissing Sommer's (P) complaint and the counterclaim for return of the security deposit, Sommer (P) appealed. His appeal was consolidated with that of Perosio (D), there having been an appellate affirmance of the trial court decision granting Riverview (P) summary judgment.

ISSUE: Must a landlord make a reasonable effort to mitigate damages by attempting to relet the premises when a lessee "surrenders" same?

HOLDING AND DECISION: (Pashman, J.) Yes. If a lessee has effected a "surrender" of the leased premises, the landlord is under an obligation to make a reasonable effort to mitigate damages by attempting to relet the premises. Such mitigation of damages is his duty when he seeks to recover rents due from a defaulting tenant. While the historical rule, and that still followed in a majority of states, is that no such duty exists, the modern trend is in favor of finding such a duty. This trend is based on the recognition that a lease is no longer simply a conveyance giving the tenant control over an estate and making his abandonment of as little concern to the landlord as would be the tenant's abandonment of property he owned outright and not simply for a term. Leases now also are of contractual nature; the changes in society have created diverse problems that have come to be dealt with by utilizing specific clauses in residential leases to fit each particular set of circumstances. Thus, a contractual ingredient has been reintroduced into the law of estates for years. Contractual obligations bespeak a duty to mitigate damages, and in the case of a residential lease, this is accomplished, upon "surrender" by the lessee, by an attempt to relet the premises. As the landlord is in a better position to prove that he has used reasonable diligence in attempting to relet the premises, the burden of proof on that issue lies with him. The facts show that Sommer (P) was not diligent in that regard; thus, that judgment must be reversed. As to Riverdale (P), the lack of a factual determination as to any attempt to relet requires that the case be remanded for a determination of whether a reasonable attempt to mitigate damages was made.

EDITOR'S ANALYSIS: Some courts have found that such mitigation is not required when a landlord simply sues to recover unpaid rent. For example, in Winshall v. Ampco Auto Parks, Inc., 417 F. Supp. 334 (E.D. Mich. 1976), the court specifically held that mitigation was a concept applicable only to suits for damages and then went on to state that an action to recover unpaid rent was not a suit for damages.

[For more information on the mitigation rule, see Casenote Law Outline on Property, Chapter 7, § X, Wrongful Abandonment.]

NOTES:

BRASCHI v. STAHL ASSOCIATES COMPANY

544 N.Y.S.2d 784, 74 N.Y.2d 201, 543 N.E.2d 49 (1989).

NATURE OF CASE: Appeal from denial of motion for preliminary injunctive relief relative to contemplated eviction proceeding.

FACT SUMMARY: Braschi (P) appealed from an appellate decision denying his motion for preliminary injunctive relief to enjoin Stahl Associates Company (Stahl) (D) from evicting him from the rent-controlled apartment of Blanchard, contending he qualified as a family member of Blanchard for purposes of the rent-control noneviction provisions.

CONCISE RULE OF LAW: The term "family" as utilized in relation to rent-control noneviction provisions encompasses two adult lifetime partners whose relationship is long term and characterized by an emotional and financial commitment and interdependence.

FACTS: Braschi (P) and Blanchard were two men who lived together as permanent life partners for more than 10 years. The apartment where they lived was a rent-controlled apartment owned by Stahl (D), and Blanchard was the only tenant of record. Braschi (P) and Blanchard held themselves out as a couple, were known to the building's employees, and were considered by their respective families as spouses. Braschi (P) clearly considered the apartment his home, receiving his mail there, and listing the address on his driver's license and passport. Braschi (P) and Blanchard shared all financial obligation, maintaining a joint household budget. Blanchard died in 1986, and shortly thereafter, Stahl (D) served a notice to cure on Braschi (P) to recover the apartment. Braschi (P) instituted an action seeking a permanent injunction and a declaration of entitlement to stay in the apartment. He then sought a preliminary injunction to enjoin Stahl (P) from evicting him until a court determined whether he was a member of Blanchard's family within the meaning of the rent-control noneviction provisions. The lower court determined that the preliminary injunction should issue, but this decision was reversed by the appellate court. From that decision, Braschi (P) appealed.

ISSUE: Does the term "family" as utilized in relation to rent-control noneviction provisions encompass two adult lifetime partners whose relationship is long term and characterized by an emotional and financial commitment and interdependence?

HOLDING AND DECISION: (Titone, J.) Yes. The term "family" as utilized in relation to rent-control noneviction provisions encompasses two adult lifetime partners whose relationship is long term and characterized by an emotional and financial commitment and interdependence. Since the term "family" is undefined in the rent-control noneviction provisions, one must look to the legislative intent behind rent-control provisions in general, and in particular the noneviction provisions. The manifest intent behind the noneviction provisions is to restrict a landlord's ability to evict a narrow class of persons other than the actual tenant of record. Arguments that "family" should be interpreted in a manner consistent with intestacy

laws are misplaced, since the purposes behind the intestacy laws differ from the overall remedial purposes of rent-control provisions. To further that purpose, the term "family" should find its foundation in the reality of family life. The factors to be considered should demonstrate a level of emotional and financial commitment and interdependence characteristic of the typical family. Everything about the relationship between Braschi (P) and Blanchard demonstrated that commitment and interdependence. As such, Braschi (P) has shown the likelihood of success on the merits necessary for the preliminary injunction to issue. Reversed; case remitted.

CONCURRENCE: (Bellacosa, J.) The anti-eviction public policy enactment of the rent-control scheme is furthered by affording Braschi (P) its remedial protection upon the facts presented.

DISSENT: (Simons, J.) Rent regulation is accomplished by the systems of rent control and rent stabilization. The intent behind the provision in question was to create succession rights to a possessory interest in rent-controlled property. To balance that provision with the purpose underlying rent stabilization, the term "family" must be defined by objectively verifiable criteria, such as those of blood, marriage, or adoption.

EDITOR'S ANALYSIS: Rent control is primarily of two types, the first which allows for some type of vacancy decontrol, such as the one in the present case, and those which merely impose ceilings and limits on rents and rent increases. To prevent abuses, most schemes require rental property to be registered. Note that it is less likely that the dispute in the present case would arise less often in jurisdictions employing the second type of rent control, since the impetus for eviction is usually the decontrol of the unit in question. Since many local rent-control schemes combine elements of both, the best protection for tenants who are unmarried but involved in a lifelong, family-like, committed relationship is to make certain that both partners names appear on the lease or rent agreement.

[For more information on housing discrimination, see Casenote Law Outline on Property, Chapter 12, § III, State Law.]

NOTES:

KENDALL v. ERNEST PESTANA, INC.
Cal. Sup. Ct., 709 P.2d 837 (1985).

NATURE OF CASE: Appeal from judgment in an action for declaratory and injunctive relief for a landlord's refusal to consent to a lease assignment.

FACT SUMMARY: When Pestana (D) refused to allow Bixler to assign his interest in a commercial leasehold to Kendall (P) and two others, they filed suit, seeking a declaration that Pestana's (D) refusal was unreasonable.

CONCISE RULE OF LAW: Where a lease provides for assignment only with the prior consent of the lessor, such consent may be withheld only where the lessor has a commercially reasonable objection to the assignment.

FACTS: Ernest Pestana (D) held an assigned lease interest in hangar space at the San Jose Municipal Airport. The original holders of the lease had also entered into a 25-year sublease with Bixler, who was to use the premises for an airplane maintenance business. Bixler later decided to sell the business to Kendall (P) and two others. The proposed sale included the existing lease. Kendall (P) had a stronger financial statement and greater net worth than Bixler and was willing to be bound by the terms of the lease. However, Pestana (D) refused to consent to the assignment, maintaining that he had an absolute right arbitrarily to refuse any such request. Kendall (P) and the others brought suit, seeking a declaration that Pestana's (D) refusal was unreasonable and an unlawful restraint on the freedom of alienation. This appeal followed the lower court's decision.

ISSUE: Where a lease provides for assignment only with the prior consent of the lessor, may such consent be withheld only where the lessor has a commercially reasonable objection to the assignment?

HOLDING AND DECISION: (Broussard, J.) Yes. Where a lease provides for assignment only with the prior consent of the lessor, such consent may be withheld only where the lessor has a commercially reasonable objection to the assignment. Some of the factors that the trier of fact may properly consider in applying the standards of good faith and commercial reasonableness are (1) financial responsibility of the proposed assignee, (2) suitability of the use for the particular property, (3) legality of the proposed use, (4) need for alteration of the premises, and (5) the nature of the occupancy. Pestana (D) is trying to get more than he bargained for in the lease. A lessor is free to build periodic rent increases into a lease, as was done here. Any increased value of the property beyond this belongs to the lessor only in the sense that the lessor's reversionary estate will benefit from it upon the expiration of the lease. The minority rule applied here is the preferable one.

DISSENT: (Lucas, J.) The weight of authority should be followed which allows the commercial lessor to withhold his consent to an assignment or sublease arbitrarily or without reasonable cause.

EDITOR'S ANALYSIS: The impetus for change in the majority rule has come from two directions, reflecting the dual nature of a lease as a conveyance of a leasehold interest and a contract. The Restatement Second of Property adopts the minority rule on the validity of approval clauses in leases, requiring that withholding of consent be reasonable. In addition, where a contract confers on one party a discretionary power affecting the rights of the other, a duty is imposed to exercise that discretion in good faith and in accordance with fair dealing.

[For more information on assignment of lease, see Casenote Law Outline on Property, Chapter 7, § VIII, Transfers of Leasehold Interests.]

NOTES:

SLAVIN v. RENT CONTROL BOARD OF BROOKLINE
Mass. Sup. Ct., 548 N.E.2d 1226 (1990).

NATURE OF CASE: Appeal from a ruling refusing to issue an eviction certificate requested by a landlord.

FACT SUMMARY: When Slavin (P) sought a certificate of eviction in an attempt to evict a tenant for violation of a lease provision requiring the landlord's consent for another person to occupy the premises, the Board (D) refused to issue the certificate on the ground that Slavin (P) had acted unreasonably.

CONCISE RULE OF LAW: A lease provision requiring the landlord's consent to an assignment or sublease permits the landlord to refuse arbitrarily or <u>unreasonably</u>.

FACTS: Slavin (P) applied to the Rent Control Board of Brookline (D) for a certificate of eviction, seeking to evict a tenant, Myers (D), on the ground that Myers (D) violated an obligation of his tenancy by allowing an unauthorized person to occupy his apartment without first obtaining Slavin's (P) written consent as stipulated in the lease. The Board (D) refused to issue the certificate on the ground that Slavin (P) had acted unreasonably because she had categorically refused to allow Myers (D) to bring in someone new after the original cotenant had moved out. Thus, Myers (D) could not be said to have violated the lease. Slavin (P) appealed.

ISSUE: Does a lease provision requiring the landlord's consent to an assignment or sublease permit the landlord to refuse arbitrarily or unreasonably?

HOLDING AND DECISION: (O'Connor, J.) Yes. A lease provision requiring the landlord's consent to an assignment or sublease permits the landlord to refuse arbitrarily or unreasonably. All but two of the cases cited by the Board (D) involved a commercial, not a residential lease. In several of the cases, the court specifically states that its holding is limited to the commercial lease context. In 68 Beacon St., Inc. v. Sohier, 194 N.E. 303 (Mass. 1935), this court ruled that a commercial lease provision requiring a landlord's consent prior to an assignment, with no limitation on the landlord's ability to refuse, is not an unreasonable restraint on alienation. In light of that decision and in the absence of a demonstrable trend involving residential leases in other jurisdictions, there appears no need to impose on residential landlords a reasonableness requirement. The question is one of public policy which the legislature is free to address.

EDITOR'S ANALYSIS: The court noted that in Kruger v. Page Management Co., 432 N.Y.S.2d 295 (Sup. Ct. 1980) — the only purely residential lease case cited by the Board (D) — the reasonableness requirement in New York has been statutorily imposed. Valid arguments can be made in support of a reasonableness rule in the residential context. But there are also valid counter-arguments, not the least of which is that such a rule would be likely to engender a plethora of litigation about whether the landlord's withholding of consent was reasonable.

_____

[For more information on assignment and sublease, see Casenote Law Outline on Property, Chapter 7, § VIII, Transfers of Leasehold Interests.]

NOTES:

COLLEGE BLOCK v. ATLANTIC RICHFIELD COMPANY

Cal. Ct. of App., 206 Cal. App. 3d 1376 (1988).

NATURE OF CASE: Appeal from award of damages.

FACT SUMMARY: College (P) entered into a 20-year lease with ARCO (D), which obligated ARCO (D) to build and operate a service station.

CONCISE RULE OF LAW: A covenant of continued operations will be implied into commercial leases containing a guaranteed minimum plus a percentage if the covenant is contemplated by the parties and the guaranteed minimum is not substantial or adequate.

FACTS: College (P) owned a parcel of undeveloped property. College (P) signed a 20-year lease with ARCO (D), which provided that ARCO (D) would build and operate a service station on the property. One provision provided that the rent would be determined by a percentage of the gasoline delivered to the station but that College (P) would receive a minimum of $1,000 regardless of the amount delivered. Another provision prohibited College (P) from operating a gasoline station on other properties it owned or operated and limited ARCO's (D) use of the property to that of a service station. Pursuant to the lease, ARCO (D) built and operated a station on the property for seventeen years. ARCO (D) closed the station 39 months prior to the end of the lease term. ARCO (D) paid College (P) $1,000 per month for the months remaining on the lease, on the basis that it was responsible only for the minimum monthly rental because the lease did not contain an express provision requiring continued operation of the station. College (P) sued ARCO (D) for additional sums College (P) would have received had the station remained open until the end of the lease term. College (P) contended that, as a matter of law, a covenant of continued operations was implied into the lease. The court ruled that, as a matter of law, there was an implied covenant in the lease which required ARCO (D) to operate the station as a gas station for the entire 20-year lease period and awarded College (P) damages. ARCO (D) appealed.

ISSUE: Should a covenant of continued operations be implied into commercial leases containing a guaranteed minimum plus a percentage, where the covenant was contemplated by the parties and the guaranteed minimum is not substantial or adequate?

HOLDING AND DECISION: (Ashby, J.) Yes. The lease between College (P) and ARCO (D) required ARCO (D) to build and operate a service station on College's (P) underdeveloped property. The rent was tied to the operation of the station. Without the station's continued operations, no basis would exist to calculate the rent. The lease limited College's (P) abilities to obtain and lease other properties it owned or controlled as gas stations (thus foreclosing College [P] from securing another station if ARCO [D] ceased operations) and limited ARCO's (D) ability to operate another type of business on the property. Such provisions are incongruent to a conclusion that ARCO (D) could cease service station operations whenever it desired. A "substantial minimum" cannot be precisely defined, and factual information on this issue must be examined. Before we find that an implied covenant existed, we must find that $1,000, the guaranteed minimum, was not substantial and did not provide College (P) with a fair return on its money. Remanded so additional evidence may be heard on this issue.

EDITOR'S ANALYSIS: In an analogous case, a tenant conducting sales operations under the lease paid rent to the lessor based on a percentage of its sales revenues. The lessee abandoned its sales operations and started using the property as a warehouse. The lease contained provisions stipulating that if the tenant assigned or sublet the premises the lessor would receive as rent "the average monthly rental paid . . . during the twelve months . . . preceding" the subletting or assignment. The lease also provided that if the lessee abandoned the premises prematurely, the tenant would pay as damages the differences between the best rent obtainable by a reletting and the "rent herein reserved." The court treated these provisions as providing for liquidated damages for loss of the lessor's percentage of rent if the lessee ceased occupying the premises and reasoned that the parties intended the same measure of damages to apply when the loss resulted from the lessee's abandoning its retail sales operations.

[For more information on the duty to pay rent, see Casenote Law Outline on Property, Chapter 7, § IX, Other Rights and Duties of Landlord and Tenant.]

NOTES:

MINJAK CO. v. RANDOLPH
N.Y. App. Div., 528 N.Y.S.2d 554 (1988).

NATURE OF CASE: Appeal from reversal of an award in tenant's favor of rent abatement and punitive damages in a landlord's action for nonpayment of rent.

FACT SUMMARY: After Randolph (D) and Kikuchi (D) withheld their rent due to the condition of the loft space they were leasing, Minjak Co. (P), the landlord, brought this action for non-payment, and Randolph (D) and Kikuchi (D) counterclaimed for breach of warranty of habitability.

CONCISE RULE OF LAW: A tenant may assert the defense of constructive eviction for the nonpayment of rent, even if he or she has abandoned only a portion of the demised premises due to the landlord's acts.

FACTS: Randolph (D) and Kikuchi (D) leased a loft in a building owned by Minjak Co. (P). Two-thirds of the loft space was used as a music studio by Kikuchi (D), and the remainder of the space was used as their residence. At one point, water poured into the bedroom and closets from the tenant's loft above them. After Minjak (P) started construction on the building, huge clouds of dust came pouring into the loft, settling everywhere. Kikuchi's (D) musical equipment had to be covered at all times to protect it from the dust. When Randolph (D) and Kikuchi (D) withheld their rent payments, Minjak (P) commenced a summary nonpayment proceeding against them. Randolph (D) and Kikuchi (D) counterclaimed for breach of warranty of habitability. After trial, the jury awarded Randolph (D) and Kikuchi (D) a rent abatement as compensatory damages on the theory of constructive eviction, along with punitive damages. The appellate term reversed. This appeal followed.

ISSUE: May a tenant assert the defense of constructive eviction for the nonpayment of rent, even if he or she has abandoned only a portion of the demised premises due to the landlord's acts?

HOLDING AND DECISION: (Memorandum Decision) Yes. A tenant may assert the defense of constructive eviction for the nonpayment of rent, even if he or she has abandoned only a portion of the demised premises due to the landlord's acts. The evidence fully supported a finding that Randolph (D) and Kikuchi (D) had to abandon the music studio portion of the loft due to the Minjak's (P) wrongful acts. Moreover, the record supports the jury's finding of morally culpable conduct allowing punitive damages in light of the dangerous and offensive manner in which the landlord permitted the construction work to be performed. Accordingly, the award of punitive damages is sustained.

EDITOR'S ANALYSIS: The appellate term held that the doctrine of constructive eviction could not provide a defense to the non-payment proceeding because Randolph (D) and Kikuchi (D) had not abandoned possession of the demised premises. However, the appellate division found that compelling considerations of social policy and fairness dictated the rule it applied here. Punitive damages may be awarded in breach of warranty of habitability cases where the landlord's actions were intentional and malicious.

[For more information on constructive eviction, see Casenote Law Outline on Property, Chapter 7, § VI, Interference with the Tenant's Use and Enjoyment of the Premises.]

NOTES:

BLACKETT v. OLANOFF

Mass. Sup. Jud. Ct., 371 Mass. 714, 358 N.E.2d 817 (1977).

NATURE OF CASE: Action for rent due and owing.

FACT SUMMARY: Tenants (D) alleged that Blackett (P), the landlord, had breached his covenant of quiet enjoyment as a defense to an action for rent.

CONCISE RULE OF LAW: Where a landlord permits conduct of third persons which substantially impairs the right of quiet enjoyment of other tenants, it is a constructive eviction.

FACTS: Olanoff (D) and other tenants vacated an apartment building owned by Blackett (P) and others. Blackett (P) sued for rent due and owing. The tenants (D) alleged that their right to quiet enjoyment had been substantially impaired by the landlords (P). Blackett (P) had rented nearby property as a bar. The noise from the bar was often very loud and significantly disturbed the apartment tenants. Blackett (P) periodically warned the bar tenants to keep the noise down as they were obligated to do under the lease. The noise would be abated for a while, but it always became loud again. The tenants (D) finally vacated the apartments and Blackett (P) sued for rent. The court found that the tenants' right to quiet enjoyment had been substantially interfered with and that this constituted a constructive eviction which was a defense to an action for rent. Blackett (P) appealed, alleging that there could be no constructive eviction where the landlord had not, by his actions, caused the breach of the covenant.

ISSUE: Can a constructive eviction be found where the landlord permits a third party to substantially impair the rights of other tenants?

HOLDING AND DECISION: (Wilkins, J.) Yes. Normally, there must be some action by the landlord himself which causes the constructive eviction. Intent to deprive the tenants of their rights is not required. Where the landlord permits an activity to continue, which he can control, which causes significant impairment of the rights of other tenants, this constitutes a breach of the landlord's covenants. Here, Blackett (P) permitted a bar next to a residential apartment. Blackett (P) had the power to control the noise in the bar under the terms of its lease. Blackett (P) knew that the noise from the bar was disturbing tenants and failed to correct the matter. Under these circumstances, a constructive eviction may be found. Affirmed.

EDITOR'S ANALYSIS: Other examples of nonconduct by the landlord which have been held to constitute constructive eviction are: failure to supply adequate light, heat, etc. Burt, Inc. v. Seven Grand Corp., 340 Mass. 124 (1959); authorization by the landlord for a tenant to obstruct the view, light and air of another tenant to a substantial extent. Case v. Minot, 158 Mass. 577 (1893); and a defective boiler causing excessive soot and smoke for a long period of time. Westland Housing Corp. v. Scott, 312 Mass. 375 (1942).

[For more information on constructive eviction, see Casenote Law Outline on Property, Chapter 7, § VI, Interference with the Tenant's Use and Enjoyment of the Premises.]

NOTES:

JAVINS v. FIRST NATIONAL REALTY CORP.
428 F.2d 1071 (D.C. Cir. 1970);
cert. denied, 400 U.S. 925 (1970).

NATURE OF CASE: Actions to recover past-due rents.

FACT SUMMARY: Javins (D) refused to pay rent due to numerous housing code violations.

CONCISE RULE OF LAW: Leases of real property contain an implied warranty of habitability for the breach of which the payment of rent may be suspended.

FACTS: Javins (D) and other tenants refused to pay rent due to approximately 1,500 housing code violations in the building. The landlord, First National Realty (P), brought suit to recover possession and past-due rent. The trial court refused Javins' (D) offer of proof as to the violations, finding that their presence was not a defense. Judgment was rendered for First National (P).

ISSUE: Are defects in leased property which make it unfit for habitation grounds for withholding rent?

HOLDING AND DECISION: (Wright, J.) Yes. Urban tenants require more than a roof to live under. They pay rent for a place to live rather than for a conveyance in an interest in real property. What is leased is a place to live in, and the lease contains an implied warranty that the apartment is habitable. The presence of numerous housing code violations was a breach of this warranty and justified the withholding of rent by the tenant pending the completion of repairs by the landlord. The outmoded concept that the duty is owed by the landlord to effectuate such repairs absent a contractual provision to the contrary is rejected. Possession will only be returned to First National (P) if the court finds that amounts still remain due and unpaid and Javins (D) and the other tenants refuse to pay for them. Remanded for a proof of the defects and an inquiry into whether they existed during the time that the rent was withheld.

EDITOR'S ANALYSIS: The implied warranty of habitability is found to be coextensive with the requirements of the housing code in some jurisdictions. In others it is mere evidence of breach of warranty. The breach of one covenant by the landlord excuses the tenant's counterperformance (breaches of mutually dependent covenants). The lease is treated as a contract rather than as a conveyance of real property under these theories. Some states require that the rent withheld be placed in an escrow account pending repairs.

[For more information on the implied warranty of habitability, see Casenote Law Outline on Property, Chapter 7, § VI, Interference with the Tenant's Use and Enjoyment of the Premises.]

HILLVIEW ASSOCIATES v. BLOOMQUIST
440 N.W.2d 867 (1989).

NATURE OF CASE: Summary action for eviction and detainer where the tenants raised the defenses of retaliatory eviction and waiver.

FACT SUMMARY: Following a physical altercation between a tenant and a manager at a tenant's meeting, a number of tenants (D) received eviction notices from Hillview Associates (P).

CONCISE RULE OF LAW: Tenants may organize and join a tenant's association and may participate in activities designed to legitimately coerce a landlord into taking action to improve living conditions without fear of retaliation, but engaging in physical threats or violence is not a legitimate method of coercion.

FACTS: Tenants at Gracious Estates formed a tenant's association and contacted the Iowa Attorney General's office and their state representative regarding concerns over the physical condition of their trailer park and recent rent increases. At an April 15, 1987, meeting, a heated argument between tenants and management escalated into a physical altercation between tenant Davenport (D) and a manager. Hillview Associates (P) attempted to evict some of the tenants who attended the meeting in question, including Davenport (D). The tenants raised the defenses of retaliatory eviction and waiver.

ISSUE: May tenants organize and join a tenant's association and participate in activities designed to legitimately coerce a landlord into taking action to improve living conditions without fear of retaliation?

HOLDING AND DECISION: (Andreasen, J.) Yes. Tenants may organize and join a tenant's association and may participate in activities designed to legitimately coerce a landlord into taking action to improve living conditions without fear of retaliation. However, engaging in physical threats or violence is not a legitimate method of coercion, and termination due to this sort of activity will not be deemed retaliatory. The resolution of landlord-tenant grievances will normally involve some conflicts and friction between the parties. Arguments — even heated ones with raised voices — cannot fairly be described as being in violation of proper conduct. There is, however, a limit to the type of conduct that will be tolerated. Davenport (D) crossed this line, and his lease was appropriately terminated. Bloomquist (D) and the other tenants have established their affirmative defense of retaliatory eviction.

EDITOR'S ANALYSIS: In 1968, the United States Court of Appeals for the District of Columbia held that a landlord was not free to evict a tenant in retaliation for the tenant's report of housing code violations. As a matter of statutory construction and for reasons of public policy, such an eviction would not be permitted. See Edwards v. Habib, 397 F.2d 687 699 (D.C. Cir. 1968).

[For more information on retaliatory eviction, see Casenote Law Outline on Property, Chapter 7, § VI, Interference with the Tenant's Use and Enjoyment of the Premises.]

IMPERIAL COLLIERY CO. v. FOUT
W.Va. Sup. Ct. 373 S.E.2d 489 (1988).

NATURE OF CASE: Appeal of a summary judgment dismissing claim of retaliatory eviction based on provisions of state summary eviction statute.

FACT SUMMARY: Imperial Colliery Co. (P) instituted an eviction proceeding against Fout (D), who claimed the eviction was in retaliation for his participation in a labor strike.

CONCISE RULE OF LAW: First Amendment rights of speech unrelated to the tenant's property interest do not arise from tenancy relatiionship and therefore are not protected under a retaliatory eviction defense.

FACTS: Fout (D) worked for Milburn Colliery Company as a coal miner. For six years, he had a month-to-month lease on a dwelling owned by Imperial Colliery Co. (P), an interrelated company. After several exten-sions, Imperial Colliery Co. (P) instituted an eviction proceeding that Fout (D) claimed was in retaliation for his participation in a labor strike and a violation of his First Amendment rights of speech and assembly. Fout (D) also counterclaimed, seeking an injunction against Imperial Colliery Co. (P) and damages for annoyance and inconvenience.

ISSUE: Are First Amendment rights of speech and association unrelated to a tenant's property interest protected under a retaliatory eviction defense?

HOLDING AND DECISION: (Miller, J.) No. First Amendment rights of speech and association unrelated to a tenant's property interest are not protected under a retaliatory eviction defense in that they do not arise from the tenancy relationship. The retaliatory eviction defense must relate to activities of the tenant incidental to the tenancy. Such rights may, of course, be vindicated on other independent grounds. Affirmed.

EDITOR'S ANALYSIS: A few courts recognize that even where a tenant's activity is only indirectly related to the tenancy relationship, it may be protected against retaliatory conduct if such conduct would undermine the tenancy relationship. Typical of these cases is Windward Partners v. Delos Santos, 577 P.2d 326 (Haw. 1978). In that case, a group of month-to-month tenants gave testimony before a state land use commission in opposition to a proposal to redesignate their farm property from "agricultural" to "urban" uses. The court determined that the legislative policy encouraging such input would be jeopardized if landlords were permitted to retaliate against tenants for opposing land use changes in a public form.

[For more information on retaliatory eviction, see Casenote Law Outline on Property, Chapter 7, § VI, Interference with the Tenant's Use and Enjoyment of the Premises.]

BILLINGS v. WILSON
Mass. Sup. Ct., 493 N.E.2d 187 (1986).

NATURE OF CASE: Counterclaim to breach of warranty and retaliation summary process action seeking possession and rent.

FACT SUMMARY: Billings (P) commenced an eviction proceeding against Wilson (D), who rented the first floor of Billings' (P) home.

CONCISE RULE OF LAW: In a situation involving the rental of a dwelling unit in an owner-occupied two-family house where the landlord owns no other real property, the relationship between the landlord and tenant is of a private nature and in no way concerns a trade or business.

FACTS: Wilson (D) rented an apartment from Billings (P) that consisted of the first floor of a two-family house. Billings (P) owned the house and occupied the second floor. This one apartment was the only rental property with which Billings (P) was concerned. Billings (P) commenced a summary process action seeking possession and rent. Wilson (D) filed an answer and counterclaim alleging, among other things, a violation of Massachusetts General Laws ch. 93A, which pertains to entities engaging in "trade or commerce."

ISSUE: In a situation involving the rental of a dwelling unit in an owner-occupied two-family house where the landlord owns no other real property, is the relationship between the landlord and tenant of a private nature that in no way concerns a trade or business?

HOLDING AND DECISION: (Hennessey, J.) Yes. In a situation involving the rental of a dwelling unit in an owner-occupied two-family house where the landlord owns no other real property, the relationship between the landlord and tenant is of a private nature and in no way concerns a trade or business. In this case, the commercial activity of Billings (D) is at a low level, and his motivation is of a personal rather than a business nature.

EDITOR'S ANALYSIS: In Commonwealth v. DeCotis, 316 N.E.2d 748 (Mass. 1974), the court stated that Massachusetts General Laws ch. 93(A) is one of several legislative attempts in recent years to regulate business activities with the view to providing proper disclosure of information and a more equitable balance in the relationship of consumers to persons conducting business activities.

[For more information on motive for retaliatory eviction, see Casenote Law Outline on Property, Chapter 7, § VI, Interference with the Tenant's Use and Enjoyment of the Premises.]

HADDAD v. GONZALEZ

Mass. Sup. Ct., 576 N.E.2d 658 (1991).

NATURE OF CASE: Appeal from award of damages to tenant on counterclaims filed in response to a summary process action.

FACT SUMMARY: Haddad (P) commenced a summary process action against tenant Gonzalez (D), and Gonzalez (D) counterclaimed alleging that Haddad's (P) actions were retaliatory in nature and violated Massachusetts General Laws Ch. 93A, which pertains to entities engaging in "trade or commerce."

CONCISE RULES OF LAW: (1) A landlord's attempt to evict a tenant based solely on her efforts to convince him to repair her apartment is considered a retaliatory eviction. (2) Where a landlord is in violation of Massachusetts General Laws ch. 93 A, treble damages shall be awarded for intentional infliction of emotional distress and violation of the warranty of habitability.

FACTS: In 1983, Gonzalez (D) and her four children leased an apartment from Haddad (P). At the time of the lease, the apartment was in deplorable condition, but Haddad (P) promised he would remedy the problems. Haddad (P) fixed nothing after repeated complaints about lack of adequate heating and sanitation. At some point in their interaction, Haddad engaged in sexual innuendos that scared Gonzalez (D). Eventually, Gonzalez (D) refused to pay the rent in full until Haddad (P) made the promised repairs. The landlord commenced a summary process action against Gonzalez (D), and Gonzalez (D) counterclaimed, alleging amongst other things that Haddad's (P) actions were retaliatory in nature and violated Massachusetts General Laws Ch. 93A, which pertains to entities engaging in "trade or commerce."

ISSUES: (1) Is a landlord's attempt to evict a tenant based solely on her efforts to convince him to repair her apartment considered a retaliatory eviction? (2) Where a landlord is in violation of Massachusetts General Laws ch. 93 (A), can treble damages be awarded for intentional infliction of emotional distress and violation of the warranty of habitability?

HOLDING AND DECISION: (Greaney, J.) (1) Yes. A landlord's attempt to evict a tenant based solely on her efforts to convince him to repair her apartment is considered a retaliatory eviction. (2) Where a landlord is in violation of Massachusetts General Laws ch 93A, treble damages shall be awarded for intentional infliction of emotional disstress and violation of the warranty of habitability. Haddad's (P) attempt to evict Gonzalez (D) based solely on her efforts to convince him to repair her apartment is considered a retaliatory eviction and is in violation of Massachusetts General Laws ch. 186 § 18. Here, Gonzalez (D) proved her counterclaims for intentional infliction of emotional distress and violation of the warranty of habitability, and the court correctly added both these base awards and then trebled the total. Affirmed.

DISSENT: (Lynch, J.) The purpose of the multiple damages provision of ch. 93A is to remove economic disincentives to consumer actions, which typically involve small dollar amounts. The multiplication of damages for the intentional infliction of emotional distress does not serve the purpose of transforming petty lawsuits into cost-justified ones.

EDITOR'S ANALYSIS: Before 1979, Massachusetts General Laws ch. 93A, § 9(I), provided, "Any person who purchases or leases goods, services or property, real or personal, primarily for personal, family of household purposes and thereby suffers any loss of money or property...as a result of...an unfair or deceptive act or practice...may...bring an action...for damages." In other words, in order to make a claim based on allegations of severe emotional distress, a plaintiff must show a loss of money or property. The legislature later deleted this requirement; thus, any intentionally wrongful act in violation of ch. 93A, § 2 will result in multiple damages.

_____

[For more information on retaliatory eviction, see Casenote Law Outline on Property, Chapter 7, § VI, Interference with the Tenant's Use and Enjoyment of the Premises.]

NOTES:

ANKIEWICZ v. KINDER
Mass. Sup. Ct., 563 N.E.2d 684 (1990).

NATURE OF CASE: Appeal from trial court's dismissal of claim for contribution on a statutory cause of action.

FACT SUMMARY: The Ankiewiczs (P) filed a tort claim against their landlord, Kinder (D), following the lead poisoning of their child.

CONCISE RULE OF LAW: Claims under Massachusetts' lead poisoning prevention law, which imposes tort liability on landlords who violate its provisions, are within the scope of the state contribution statute.

FACTS: This case arises out of the alleged lead poisoning of Stanley Ankiewicz, Jr. (P), a minor under the age of six. The complaint asserted that Kinder (D), the landlord of the apartment occupied by Stanley (P) and his parents (P) was negligent, in breach of the implied warranty of habitability, and violated the state's lead poisoning prevention law. Kinder (D) filed a third-party complaint against Mrs. Ankiewicz (P) for contribution, alleging she negligently allowed her child to ingest lead-based paint in the apartment. The trial court dismissed Kinder's (D) contribution claim, and he appealed.

ISSUE: Are claims under Massachusetts' lead poisoning prevention law, which imposes tort liability on landlords who violate its provisions, within the scope of the state contribution statute?

HOLDING AND DECISION: (Lynch, J.) Yes. Claims under Massachusetts' lead poisoning prevention law, which imposes tort liability on landlords who violate its provisions, are within the scope of the state contribution statute. All torts share the elements of duty, breach of that duty, and damages arising from that breach. The cause of action created by the statute in question contains all those elements, and it is clearly tort-like in nature. Reversed.

DISSENT: (Liacos, J.) The Legislature did not intend that the owners of residential properties, who breach their statutory duty of maintaining their apartments free of lead contamination, should be allowed to seek contribution from the parents of children poisoned by the lead-based paint.

EDITOR'S ANALYSIS: Only Louisiana and California have imposed a general standard of strict liability on landlords for injuries caused by defective premises, thus making the landlord liable if a defect in the premises caused the plaintiff's injuries, regardless of whether the landlord could have prevented or foreseen the harm by reasonable maintenance. In Becker v. IRM, 698 P.2d 116 (Cal.1985), a tenant was injured when he slipped and fell through a shower door made of untempered glass. The court held that the landlord was strictly liable for damages arising out of a latent defect in the premises.

[For more information on negligently made repairs, see Casenote Law Outline on Property, Chapter 7, § VII, Landlord's Liability in Tort for Tenant's Physical Injuries.]

NOTES:

8

CHAPTER 8
REAL ESTATE TRANSACTIONS

QUICK REFERENCE RULES OF LAW

1. **What Constitutes an Agreement: The Statute of Frauds versus Part Performance and Estoppel.** To establish the doctrine of part performance, the performance must unequivocally refer to the agreement, and must not be reasonably susceptible of other possible meanings. (Burns v. McCormick)

    [For more information on the statute of frauds, see Casenote Law Outline on Property, Chapter 14, § I, Negotiating the Contract for Sale.]

2. **What Constitutes an Agreement: The Statute of Frauds versus Part Performance and Estoppel.** An oral contract for the transfer of interest in land may be specifically enforced despite the Statute of Frauds if the party seeking performance changed his position in reasonable reliance on the contract and injustice can be avoided only through specific performance. (Hickey v. Green)

    [For more information on the statute of frauds, see Casenote Law Outline on Property, Chapter 14, § I, Negotiating the Contract for Sale.]

3. **What Constitutes an Agreement: The Statute of Frauds versus Part Performance and Estoppel.** A party who partially performs under a real estate agreement may avoid the Statute of Frauds and introduce evidence of the oral contract. (Gardner v. Gardner)

    [For more information on partial performance, see Casenote Law Outline on Property, Chapter 14, § I, Negotiating the Contract for Sale.]

4. **Misrepresentation and Fraudulent Nondisclosure.** Where the seller of a home knows of facts materially affecting the value of the property that are not readily observable and are not known to the buyer, the seller is under a duty to disclose them to the buyer. (Johnson v. Davis)

5. **Chain of Title Problems.** A deed outside the chain of title is not constructive notice and a subsequently recorded deed will take priority. (Sabo v. Horvath)

    [For more information on the recording system, see Casenote Law Outline on Property, Chapter 14, § III, The Real Estate Closing.]

6. **Fraud and Forgery.** Absent a duty to act, a delay in filing suit is not unreasonable and is not grounds for laches. (Martin v. Carter)

    [For more information on marketable title, see Casenote Law Outline on Property, Chapter 14, § II, Preparing for Closing.]

7. **Fraud and Forgery.** Fraud in the inducement renders a legally effective deed merely voidable and not void. (McCoy v. Love)

8. **Regulating the Foreclosure Process.** Mere inadequacy of price is not sufficient to set aside a foreclosure sale unless the price is so inadequate as to shock the conscience of the court. (Central Financial Services, Inc. v. Spears)

9. **Forfeiture.** Liquidated damages provisions in land sale contracts are enforceable if the amount is a fair estimate of the seller's actual damages. (Stonebraker v. Zinn)

[For more information on sellers' remedies for breach, see Casenote Law Outline on Property, Chapter 14, § II, Preparing for Closing.]

10. **Making Mortgage Protection Nondisclaimable.** The seller's interest in an installment land sale contract should be treated as a lien in order to protect the buyer from unfair forfeiture. (Sebastian v. Floyd)

[For more information on liquidated damage provision, see Casenote Law Outline on Property, Chapter 14, § II, Preparing for Closing.]

11. **Equitable Mortgages.** A conveyance of property by deed may be treated as mortgage if it appears that the parties did not intend to make an absolute transfer. (Koenig v. Van Reken)

[For more information on equitable conversion, see Casenote Law Outline on Property, Chapter 14, § II, Preparing for Closing.]

BURNS v. McCORMICK
233 N.Y. 230 (1922).

NATURE OF CASE: Appeal from decision denying specific performance.

FACT SUMMARY: Burns (P) agreed to take care of Halsey (now deceased) for life in exchange for Halsey's house and furnishings after his death.

CONCISE RULE OF LAW: To establish the doctrine of part performance, the performance must unequivocally refer to the agreement, and must not be reasonably susceptible of other possible meanings.

FACTS: Halsey told the Burnses (P) that if they would board and care for him during his life, he would give them his house and furniture at his death. Halsey died without will, deed, or memorandum of the alleged transfer. The Burnses (P) sued for specific performance of the oral contract, and other parties in interest raised the statute of frauds. McCormick (D) was successful and the trial court denied specific performance. The Burnses (P) appealed.

ISSUE: Is performance which is susceptible to several different interpretations sufficient to remove an oral contract from the statute of frauds?

HOLDING AND DECISION: (Cardozo, J.) No. Not every act of part performance will move a court of equity to grant specific performance, even though legal remedies are deemed inadequate. The performance must be unequivocally referable to the agreement. An act which admits of explanation without reference to the alleged oral contract will not generally be deemed to have satisfied the statute of frauds. The performance must be such that the actions alone and without the alleged words of promise would be unintelligible, or at least extraordinary if no incidents of ownership were involved. Here, the Burnses' (P) board and care of Halsey could have been in exchange for the partial use of his house, i.e., rent. Since the Burnses' (P) actions could be otherwise explained, their performance will not satisfy the statute. Since no fraud is alleged or involved, the decision of the trial court must be upheld.

EDITOR'S ANALYSIS: Hardship, estoppel, and numerous casual remarks by a decedent may be recognized in various jurisdictions as proving the existence of the alleged oral contract to pass property after death. Some jurisdictions, notably California, have held that hardship alone may remove an oral contract from the statute through estoppel. However, a majority of courts still strictly construe the statute of frauds and the doctrine of part performance.

[For more information on the statute of frauds, see Casenote Law Outline on Property, Chapter 14, § I, Negotiating the Contract for Sale.]

NOTES:

95

HICKEY v. GREEN
Mass. App. Ct., 14 Mass. App. Ct. 671, 442 N.E.2d 37 (1982).

NATURE OF CASE: Appeal from grant of specific performance of a real estate contract.

FACT SUMMARY: Green (D) contended that the real estate sales contract she orally entered into with Hickey (P) was unenforceable based on the statute of frauds.

CONCISE RULE OF LAW: An oral contract for the transfer of interest in land may be specifically enforced despite the statute of frauds if the party seeking performance changed his position in reasonable reliance on the contract and injustice can be avoided only through specific performance.

FACTS: Green (D) orally agreed to sell a parcel to Hickey (P), and accepted a check as a deposit. In reliance on the contract Hickey (P) accepted a deposit on his home from a purchaser, intending to build a new home on the land he purchased from Green (D). Subsequently, Green (D), knowing Hickey (P) sold his house in reliance on the contract, refused to sell the land to Hickey (P). Hickey (P) sued for specific performance, and Green (D) defended, contending the contract was unenforceable under the statute of frauds. The trial court granted specific performance, and Green (D) appealed.

ISSUE: Can an oral contract for the sale of real estate be specifically enforced if the party seeking enforcement changed his position in reasonable reliance upon the contract?

HOLDING AND DECISION: (Cutter, J.) Yes. An oral contract for the transfer of an interest in land may be specifically enforced, despite the statute of frauds requirement of a writing, if the party seeking enforcement changed his position in reasonable reliance on the contract and injustice can be avoided only through specific performance. In this case, Hickey (P) clearly changed his position in reliance on the contract by selling his house in anticipation of occupying another on Green's (D) land. The reliance was reasonable, and Green (D) was fully aware of this change in position when she refused to honor the contract. As a result, it would be manifestly unjust to refuse specific performance in this case. Therefore, it must be ordered. Affirmed.

EDITOR'S ANALYSIS: This case could have been decided on different grounds. Some commentators, spurred by dicta in the opinion, contend that the check which Hickey (P) gave Green (D) as a deposit on the land constituted an adequate memorandum to satisfy the requirements of the statute of frauds.

[For more information on the statute of frauds, see Casenote Law Outline on Property, Chapter 14, § I, Negotiating the Contract for Sale.]

GARDNER v. GARDNER
Iowa Sup. Ct., 454 N.W.2d 361 (1990).

NATURE OF CASE: Appeal from denial of action to compel reconveyance.

FACT SUMMARY: Mark and James Gardner (P) agreed to convey land to their brother Harry Gardner (D) to be used for security for a loan, and Harry (D) agreed to reconvey the land back to them if the loan was not granted.

CONCISE RULE OF LAW: A party who partially performs under a real estate agreement may avoid the Statute of Frauds and introduce evidence of the oral contract.

FACTS: In 1985, Harry Gardner (D) was heavily indebted to the Citizens' State Bank of Oakland Iowa. The bank refused to lend him more money and called his loan due. Harry Gardner (D) told his brothers, Mark and James Gardner (P), of the problem and they agreed to convey land to Harry Gardner (D) to be used as security in an attempt to refinance with the Federal Land Bank. Harry Gardner (D) agreed to reconvey the land if the loan was not approved. When the federal government denied Harry Gardner's (D) loan application, he refused to reconvey the land. Mark and James Gardner (P) filed an action to compel the reconveyance. At trial, the court refused to allow evidence regarding the oral agreement pursuant to the Statute of Frauds. Mark and James (P) appealed.

ISSUE: May a party who partially performs under a real estate agreement avoid the Statute of Frauds and introduce evidence of the oral contract?

HOLDING AND DECISION: (Larson, J.) Yes. A party who partially performs under a real estate agreement may avoid the Statute of Frauds and introduce evidence of the oral contract. Under the Iowa Statute of Frauds, it is well established that a party who partially performs under a real estate agreement may avoid the Statute of Frauds and introduce evidence of the oral contract. Mark and James (P) in this case performed their part of the alleged oral agreement by conveying their remainder interests in the land. This was sufficient performance to take the alleged oral agreement from the operation of the Statute of Frauds. Reversed in favor of Mark and James Gardner (P).

EDITOR'S ANALYSIS: In this case the court also explained that parol evidence establishing an agreement for the creation of an interest in real estate may be admitted where the agreement is established by oral evidence of the adverse party. The court wrote that although Harry (D) disputed the fact at trial, there was some evidence that he admitted an agreement to reconvene and as such, the trial court erred in refusing to admit the evidence of the alleged oral agreement.

[For more information on partial performance, see Casenote Law Outline on Property, Chapter 14, § I, Negotiating the Contract for Sale.]

JOHNSON v. DAVIS

Fla. Sup. Ct., 480 So.2d 625 (1985).

NATURE OF CASE: Appeal from trial court decision finding fraudulent misrepresentation and granting respondents the return of their deposit.

SUMMARY OF FACTS: The Davises (P) agreed to purchase the Johnsons' (D) home after the Johnsons (D) assured them that buckling around a family room window and stains on the ceiling resulted from a minor problem that had long since been fixed.

CONCISE RULE OF LAW: Where the seller of a home knows of facts materially affecting the value of the property that are not readily observable and are not known to the buyer, the seller is under a duty to disclose them to the buyer.

FACTS: In May of 1982, the Davises (P) entered into a contract to buy the Johnsons' (D) home. The contract required a $5,000 deposit payment and an additional $26,000 deposit payment within five days. Before making the additional $26,000 payment, the Davises (P) noticed ceiling stains and buckling around a family room window. The Johnsons (D) assured them that these problems resulted from a minor problem that had long since been fixed. Several days later during a heavy rain, water came gushing into the house through various parts of the family room. Two roofers hired by the Johnsons (D) concluded that the problem could be solved for under $1,000. Three roofers hired by the Davises (P) determined that the roof was inherently defective and any repairs would be temporary because the roof was slipping. The Davises (P) filed a complaint alleging breach of contract, fraud, and misrepresentation and sought recession of the contract and return of their deposit. The trial court ruled for the Davises (P), and the Johnsons (D) appealed.

ISSUE: Where the seller of a home knows of facts materially affecting the value of the property which are not readily observable and are not known to the buyer, is he under a duty to disclose them to the buyer?

HOLDING AND DECISION: (Adkins, J.) Yes. Where the seller of a home knows of facts materially affecting the value of the property which are not readily observable and are not known to the buyer, he is under a duty to disclose them to the buyer. This duty is equally applicable to all forms of real property, new and used. In the case at bar, the evidence shows that the Johnsons (D) knew of and failed to disclose that there had been problems with the roof of the house. The Davises (P) detrimentally relied on this concealment. Affirmed.

DISSENT: (Boyd, J.) Homeowners who attempt to sell their houses are typically in no better position to measure the quality, value, or desirability of their houses than are the prospective purchasers with whom they come into contact. This ruling will give rise to a flood of litigation and will facilitate unjust outcomes in many cases.

EDITOR'S ANALYSIS: In the state of Florida, relief for a fraudulent misrepresentation may be granted only when the following elements are present: (1) a false statement concerning a material fact; (2) the representor's knowledge that the representation is false; (3) an intention that the representation induce another to act on it; and (4) consequent injury by the party acting in reliance on the representation. Those opposed to this sort of regulation argue that it is unnecessary since prudent purchasers inspect property, with expert advice if necessary, before the agree to buy, and prudent lenders require inspections before agreeing to provide purchase money.

NOTES:

SABO v. HORVATH

Alaska Sup. Ct., 559 P.2d 1038 (1976).

NATURE OF CASE: Action to determine title to real property.

FACT SUMMARY: Horvath (P) recorded his deed prior to a patent being granted the seller so that the recorded deed was outside the chain of title.

CONCISE RULE OF LAW: A deed outside the chain of title is not constructive notice and a subsequently recorded deed will take priority.

FACTS: Lowery filed for a federal land patent on real property he was homesteading in Alaska. Prior to the issuance of the patent, Lowery conveyed his interest in the land to Horvath (P) by quitclaim deed. Horvath (P) recorded the deed, which was then outside the chain of record title since Lowery had not yet obtained patent title to the land. After patent title was obtained, Horvath (P) did not re-record the deed. Lowery subsequently "sold" the land a second time to Sabo (D) by quitclaim deed. Sabo (D) recorded his deed. Sabo (D) had no notice of the earlier conveyance. Horvath (P) brought a quiet title action. Sabo (D) alleged that a deed recorded out of chain of title was not constructive notice and that under the state's notice recording law he had no notice of the earlier sale and should be given preference.

ISSUE: Is a deed recorded outside the chain of title given preference to a subsequent bona fide purchaser without actual notice?

HOLDING AND DECISION: (Boochever, J.) No. The purpose of our recording statute is to protect innocent purchasers without notice of an earlier unrecorded sale. Normally, a recordation gives the subsequent purchaser constructive notice of the earlier conveyance. However, we hold that a deed recorded outside the chain of title is not constructive notice to an innocent purchaser for value without actual notice. It is less burdensome for one recording outside the chain of title to re-record than to force purchasers to check all conveyances outside the chain of the title. Quitclaim deedholders are entitled to protection under the recording statutes (the majority rule). While Horvath (P) originally received Lowrey's equitable interest in the land, his failure to re-record after the patent was granted requires us to find for Sabo (D). Reversed.

EDITOR'S ANALYSIS: Sabo would be useful only where the jurisdiction does not use a tract index system. Under a tract index system, every document affecting land is recorded. Some jurisdictions hold that the grantee of a quitclaim deed is not a bona fide purchaser. In Crossly v. Campion Mining Co., 1 Alaska 391 (1901), a quitclaim grantee with knowledge of a superior unrecorded claim was held not to be in good faith.

[For more information on the recording system, see Casenote Law Outline on Property, Chapter 14, § III, The Real Estate Closing.]

NOTES:

MARTIN v. CARTER

D.C. Sup. Ct., 400 a.2d 326 (1979).

NATURE OF CASE: Appeal from denial of action seeking return of property based on a laches defense.

FACT SUMMARY: Martin (P) and Fletcher owned property as joint tenants. Fletcher forged Martin's (P) signature on the sales contract and the deed and sold the land without notifying Martin (P).

CONCISE RULE OF LAW: Absent a duty to act, a delay in filing suit is not unreasonable and is not grounds for laches.

FACTS: Martin (P) and Fletcher owned property as joint tenants. Fletcher forged Martin's (P) signature on the sales contract and the deed and sold the land to Spicer Real Estate Inc. without notifying Martin (P). When Martin (P) learned of the forgery, she immediately advised Spicer that she was a joint owner of the property and had never signed a conveyance. Spicer denied any knowledge of her name and denied her any interest in the property. Martin (P) consulted an attorney who advised her to take legal action to protect her interests, but for financial reasons she did not pursue the issue at that time. Four months later, Spicer conveyed the property to the Carters (D). The Carters (D) had no knowledge of Martin's (P) interest in the property. Nineteen months later, Martin (P) filed an action seeking to have the property returned to her. The trial court ruled for the Carters (D), and Martin (P) appealed.

ISSUE: Absent a duty to act, is a delay in filing suit unreasonable and a grounds for laches?

HOLDING AND DECISION: (Kelly, J.) No. Absent a duty to act, a delay in filing suit is not unreasonable and is not grounds for laches. Laches, which bars stale claims asserted by the plaintiff, comes into play when two prerequisites have been met: the defendant has been prejudiced by plaintiff's delay, and plaintiff's delay must have been unreasonable. Here, Martin (P) did give prompt notice to Spicer, the only claimant of whom she had specific knowledge. Absent a showing that she had specific knowledge of the Carters (D), her duty went no further and her delay in filing suit was not unreasonable. Reversed.

EDITOR'S ANALYSIS: As regards the prejudice aspect of the laches defense in this case, the court stated that there was some prejudice to the Carters (D), but to a significant extent it could be remedied. The court suggested it may find it appropriate to protect the Carters (D) by creating an equitable lien on the property, reflecting the improvements that the Carters had made, including their services as caretakers of the residence. The reliance interest of the Carters (D) may be protected by pursuit of their cross-claim against Spicer for failure to notify them of the claims against the title he offered to them.

[For more information on marketable title, see Casenote Law Outline on Property, Chapter 14, § II, Preparing for Closing.]

McCOY v. LOVE
Fla. Sup. Ct., 382 So.2d 647 (1980).

NATURE OF CASE: Appeal from finding that a deed was voidable.

FACT SUMMARY: Russell drew up a fraudulent sales contract wherein Elliott (P) unknowingly conveyed all of her interest in mineral rights to Russell.

CONCISE RULE OF LAW: Fraud in the inducement renders a legally effective deed merely voidable and not void.

FACTS: Elliott (P), who was unable to read or write, agreed to sell Russell a small portion of her mineral rights in a property. Russell drew up a sales contract wherein Elliott (P) unknowingly conveyed all of her interest to Russell. Russell notified Elliott (P) that a mistake had been made, but in the meantime sold part of Elliott's (P) mineral rights to other parties, including Love (D). Elliott (P) remained ignorant of these subsequent transactions until she wanted to sell more of her mineral rights and a title search revealed them. She sued for cancellation of the deed. The trial court concluded that the deed was void and granted summary judgment to Elliott (P). On appeal, the district court held the deed voidable rather than void. Elliott (P) appealed.

ISSUE: Does fraud in the inducement render a legally effective deed merely voidable and not void?

HOLDING AND DECISION: (Boyd, J.) Yes. Fraud in the inducement renders a legally effective deed merely voidable and not void. Where all essential legal requisites of a deed are present, it conveys legal title. In this case, Elliott (P) knew she was executing and delivering a deed of mineral rights. She was responsible for informing herself of its legal effect. The district court was correct in holding that the deed was merely voidable and that it conveyed a legal title to Russell. The case should be remanded for trial on the factual issue of whether Love (D) and the other buyers were bona fide purchasers.

EDITOR'S ANALYSIS: A deed is either void or voidable if obtained by forgery or fraud. The deed will be set aside at the previous owner's request if no further conveyances have occurred. Where the property has been conveyed to a bona fide purchaser (BFP), if the deed is void, no title is conveyed to the grantee; thus, the grantee cannot convey the title to another. If the deed is considered merely voidable by an owner who had a fraud perpetrated against him, a subsequent BFP will obtain good title.

CENTRAL FINANCIAL SERVICES, INC. v. SPEARS
Miss. Sup. Ct., 425 So.2d 403 (1983).

NATURE OF CASE: Appeal from order to pay damages based on the difference between fair market value and the price paid for a property at a foreclosure sale.

FACT SUMMARY: After Spears (P) borrowed $1,250 from Central Financial Services (D) to purchase certain real property, he fell in arrears on payment of the loan, and Central Financial Services (D) bought the property back through a foreclosure sale.

CONCISE RULE OF LAW: Mere inadequacy of price is not sufficient to set aside a foreclosure sale unless the price is so inadequate as to shock the conscience of the court.

FACTS: Spears (P) borrowed $1,250 from Central Financial Services (D) to purchase certain real property; however, he fell in arrears on payment of the loan. Central Financial Services (D) bought the property back through a foreclosure sale for a total of $1,458, the amount of the indebtedness due plus costs of foreclosure. Two days later, upon notice of the sale, Spears (P) offered to pay the amount of the delinquency, but was told he was too late. Two weeks later, CFS (D) sold the property to Stewart for $4,000. Stewart then sold the property to Henderson for $6,500. Spears (P) filed a bill of complaint praying that the foreclosure sale be set aside alleging inadequate sale price. After a demurrer, appeal, and remand, the trial court found that the fair market value of the property was $7,000 and the consideration paid to Spears (P) was so grossly inadequate as to shock the conscience. The trial court ordered CFS (D) to pay Spears (P) the difference between the fair market value and the price paid at the foreclosure sale. CFS (D) appealed.

ISSUE: Is mere inadequacy of price sufficient grounds to set aside a foreclosure sale?

HOLDING AND DECISION: (Sugg, J.) No. Mere inadequacy of price is not sufficient to set aside a foreclosure sale unless the price is so inadequate as to shock the conscience of the court. A sale of mortgaged property within twelve days of the foreclosure sale at a price two and one-half times the bid of the mortgage is so inadequate, it would be impossible to state it to a man of common sense without producing an exclamation at the inequality of it. However, the decree should be modified to reduce the amount of recovery against CFS (D) to the difference between the initial amount bid and the $4,000 received at the private sale.

EDITOR'S ANALYSIS: In the majority of jurisdictions, after the foreclosure proceedings have begun but prior to the sale of the property, the debtor may redeem the mortgage or trust deed by paying all sums due on the debt. If the debtor can pay all outstanding debts, the foreclosure proceedings will be stopped.

STONEBRAKER v. ZINN
W. Va. Sup. Ct., 286 S.E.2d 911 (1982).

NATURE OF CASE: Action regarding forfeiture of liquidated damages.

FACT SUMMARY: A land sale contract between the Zinns (D) and Stonebrakers (P) included a liquidated damages provision if the buyer breached.

CONCISE RULE OF LAW: Liquidated damages provisions in land sale contracts are enforceable if the amount is a fair estimate of the seller's actual damages.

FACTS: The Zinns (D) contracted to sell the Stonebrakers (P) real property for $25,000. The Stonebrakers (P) paid $1,500 as a down payment and agreed to pay $189 a month, representing the balance at 9% annual interest. The contract provided that if the Stonebrakers (P) abandoned the property, the Zinns's (D) liquidated damages would be the amount of money paid to that point. The Stonebrakers (P) abandoned the property after making payments for one year. They then sought to avoid the forfeiture by asserting that the liquidated damages provision was unconscionable.

ISSUE: Are liquidated damages provisions in land sale contracts enforceable if the amount is a fair estimate of the seller's actual damages?

HOLDING AND DECISION: (Miller, J.) Yes. Liquidated damages provisions in land sale contracts are enforceable if the amount is a fair estimate of the seller's actual damages. Liquidated damages clauses are appropriate where damages are uncertain and not easily ascertainable due to the nature of the subject or case. A liquidated damages provision is an unconscionable penalty only where the amount is grossly disproportionate to the actual damages suffered by the nonbreaching party. In the context of land sale contracts, courts must be careful to consider all of the costs suffered by a seller when the buyer defaults, and each case must be judged on its own facts. In this case, the Zinns (D) collected a total of $3,850 from the Stonebrakers (P) before the abandonment. Taking into account the fair rental value of the property for one year and the Zinns's (D) various expenses in selling the home a second time, this was not an excessive retention. Thus, the liquidated damages provision will be enforced.

EDITOR'S ANALYSIS: A buyer's default not only brings up the forfeiture question but often the issue of the buyer's right of redemption; i.e., the right to continue in possession of the property if he or she pays off the rest of the contract price. Some jurisdictions treat installment land contracts as if they were mortgages, permitting redemption, requiring notice prior to foreclosure, and upholding the right of the buyer to receive any excess profit from a foreclosure sale. Other jurisdictions limit such protections to those installment land contracts where the property has been maintained and improved, the default is unintentional, and the buyer has built up a substantial amount of equity. Still others, as in the case above, never permit redemption.

[For more information on sellers' remedies for breach, see Casenote Law Outline on Property, Chapter 14, § II, Preparing for Closing.]

NOTES:

SEBASTIAN v. FLOYD
Ky. Sup. Ct., 585 S.W.2d 381 (1979).

NATURE OF CASE: Appeal from judgment enforcing a forfeiture.

FACT SUMMARY: Sebastian (D) sought to have an installment land contract treated as a mortgage after he defaulted.

CONCISE RULE OF LAW: The seller's interest in an installment land sale contract should be treated as a lien in order to protect the buyer from unfair forfeiture.

FACTS: Sebastian (D) contracted to buy real property from Floyd (P) for $3,800 down and the balance of $10,900 in monthly installments at 8°% interest. The agreement contained a forfeiture clause providing that if Sebastian (D) defaulted on any payments, Floyd (P) could terminate the contract and retain all previous payments as liquidated damages. Sebastian (D) defaulted after paying out a total of $5,480 ($4,300 of principal). Floyd (P) sued to enforce the forfeiture. The trial court ruled for Floyd (P), and Sebastian (D) appealed.

ISSUE: Should the seller's interest in an installment land sale contract be treated as a lien in order to protect the buyer from unfair forfeiture?

HOLDING AND DECISION: (Aker, J.) Yes. The seller's interest in an installment land sale contract should be treated as a lien in order to protect the buyer from unfair forfeiture. In a typical installment land contract, legal title to the property remains with the seller until the buyer has paid the entire contract price, but equitable title is transferred at the outset of the agreement. There is no practical difference between this type of contract and a purchase money mortgage in which the buyer gets legal title immediately and the seller holds a lien on the property as security. However, under a mortgage, the buyer's interest in the property is not forfeited at default. Instead, the buyer is entitled to any remaining equity in the property after the seller has been paid the contract amount and any expenses. Since this arrangement protects both the buyer and seller, an installment land contract should treated as giving the seller a lien on the property. Therefore, in the present case, the forfeiture clause may not be enforced by Floyd (P), and Sebastian (D) is entitled to any equity interest in the property that remains after Floyd (P) exercises his lien. Reversed.

EDITOR'S ANALYSIS: Other states treat only some installment land contracts as mortgages based on a range of factors, including the buyer's equity in the property and the length of the default period. See Grombone v. Krekel, 754 P.2d 777 (Colo. Ct. App. 1988). In that case, the court of appeals held the decision to be within the lower court's discretion pending an analysis of those factors.

[For more information on liquidated damage provision, see Casenote Law Outline on Property, Chapter 14, § II, Preparing for Closing.]

NOTES:

KOENIG v. VAN REKEN

Mich. Ct. App., 279 N.W.2d 590 (1979).

NATURE OF CASE: Appeal from judgment in action for declaration of an equitable mortgage.

FACT SUMMARY: Koenig (P) claimed an equitable mortgage should be imposed because she did not intend to grant an absolute deed to Van Reken (D).

CONCISE RULE OF LAW: A conveyance of property by deed may be treated as mortgage if it appears that the parties did not intend to make an absolute transfer.

FACTS: Koenig (P) owned a home with a market value of $60,000. There were three mortgages on the property totalling $26,000. Koenig (P) was unable to pay the property taxes and the mortgage payments. Van Reken (D) then approached Koenig (P) and proposed a complex arrangement whereby Van Reken (D) would purchase the property, redeem it from tax sale and foreclosure, and give Koenig (P) a lease with an option to repurchase the property. The lease agreement provided that Koenig (P) would pay $300 per month for three years, after which she could repurchase the premises for $32,000. Van Reken (D) prepared all of the contracts and deeds and Koenig (P) was unrepresented by counsel. After almost two years under the agreement, Koenig (P) defaulted and was evicted. Koenig (P) brought suit to impose an equitable mortgage based on the agreement with Van Reken (D).

ISSUE: May conveyances of property by deed be treated as mortgages if it appears that the parties did not intend to make an absolute transfer?

HOLDING AND DECISION: (Brennan, J.) Yes. Conveyances of property by deed may be treated as mortgages if it appears that the parties did not intend to make an absolute transfer. The controlling factor as to whether an absolute deed should be construed as a mortgage is the intention of the parties. This intention may be determined by looking at the circumstances of the transaction and the relative positions of the parties. If the adverse financial position of the seller is combined with an inadequate purchase price, a deed should be considered a mortgage. In the present case, Koenig (P) was in financial distress and entered into an agreement whereby her $30,000 in equity was conveyed for less than $4,000. This indicates that the conveyance was not meant to be absolute and that an equitable mortgage should be imposed. Judgment for Koenig (P).

EDITOR'S ANALYSIS: Equitable mortgages are not affected by the statute of frauds. Other courts have identified other factors that should be considered when imposing an equitable mortgage, such as the relationship of the parties, the sophistication of the parties, and who retained possession.

[For more information on equitable conversion, see Casenote Law Outline on Property, Chapter 14, § II, Preparing for Closing.]

NOTES:

NOTES

CHAPTER 9
LAWS REGULATING DISCRIMINATORY PRACTICES

QUICK REFERENCE RULES OF LAW

1. **Discrimination by Housing Providers.** The Fair Housing Act is violated where the plaintiff proves a prima facie case of intent to discriminate based on race and the defendant is unable to demonstrate legitimate nondiscriminatory reasons. (Asbury v. Brougham)

   [For more information on the Fair Housing Act, see Casenote Law Outline on Property, Chapter 12, § II, Federal Law.]

2. **Discrimination by Housing Providers.** The FHA may prevent the use of rigid racial quotas of indefinite duration to maintain a fixed level of integration in public housing when such practices restrict minority access to public housing. (United States v. Starrett City Associates)

   [For more information on the race discrimination and quotas, see Casenote Law Outline on Property, Chapter 12, § II, Federal Law.]

3. **Civil Rights Act of 1866.** Section 1982 is not violated unless a municipal action impairs significant property interests. (City of Memphis v. Greene)

   [For more information on violation of section 1982, see Casenote Law Outline on Property, Chapter 12, § II, Federal Law.]

4. **Sex Discrimination: Sexual Harassment.** Section 3617 of the Fair Housing Act bars threats pursuant to sexual harassment by a landlord. (Grieger v. Sheets)

   [For more information on sexual harassment by landlord, see Casenote Law Outline on Property, Chapter 12, § II, Federal Law.]

5. **Familial Status: Families with Children.** The exception against familial status discrimination for senior housing does not apply unless there are significant facilities specially designed for older persons at the site. (Park Place Home Brokers v. P-K Mobile Home Park)

   [For more information on familial status discrimination, see Casenote Law Outline on Property, Chapter 12, § II, Federal Law.]

6. **Marital Status: Unmarried Couples.** Landlords may not discriminate against unmarried couples on the basis of claimed religious beliefs. (Smith v. Fair Employment and Housing Commission)

   [For more information on discrimination based on religious freedom, see Casenote Law Outline on Property, Chapter 12, § III, State Law.]

7. **Persons with AIDS.** Discrimination against homosexuals is illegal if it is based on the fear they will acquire AIDS. (Poff v. Caro)

   [For more information on disability and group homes, see Casenote Law Outline on Property, Chapter 12, § II, Federal Law.]

8. **Welfare Recipients.** Landlords are not automatically guilty of illegal discrimination because they refuse to rent to Section 8 certificate holders. (Attorney General v. Brown)

9. **Racially Discriminatory Zoning Practices.** Town zoning regulations may not restrict multifamily housing projects to largely minority areas. (Huntington Branch, NAACP v. Town of Huntington)

    [For more information on exclusionary zoning, see Casenote Law Outline on Property, Chapter 10, § II, Validity of Zoning Laws.]

10. **Sex Discrimination: Shelters for Battered Women.** The Fair Housing Act prohibits discrimination based on familial status, which may include single-parent families living communally. (Doe v. City of Butler)

    [For more information on group homes, see Casenote Law Outline on Property, Chapter 12, § II, Federal Law.]

11. **Federal Constitution.** Zoning legislation does not violate the equal protection clause if it is reasonable, not arbitrary, and bears a rational relationship to a permissible state objective. (Village of Belle Terre v. Boraas)

    [For more information on fundamental rights and equal protection, see Casenote Law Outline on Property, Chapter 12, § I, The United States Constitution.]

12. **State Constitutions.** The Michigan Constitution is violated by a law that allows only one unrelated person per home since it is not rationally related to a legitimate goal. (Charter Township of Delta v. Dinolfo)

    [For more information on housing discrimination and state laws, see Casenote Law Outline on Property, Chapter 12, § III, State Law.]

13. **AIDS Hospices.** Zoning regulations may not be invoked as a pretext for discrimination based upon fear of AIDS. (Association of Relatives and Friends of AIDS Patients v. Regulations and Permits Administration)

    [For more information on disability and groups homes, see Casenote Law Outline on Property, Chapter 12, § II, Federal Law.]

14. **Group Homes for Persons with Mental Illness.** Legislation which requires dispersal of group homes is a legitimate means whereby a state may achieve its goal of deinstitutionalization of the mentally ill, and does not violate the Fair Housing Amendments Act of 1988. (Familystyle of St. Paul, Inc. v. City of St. Paul)

    [For more information on disability and group homes, see Casenote Law Outline on Property, Chapter 12, § II, Federal Law.]

ASBURY v. BROUGHAM
866 F.2d 1276 (10th Cir. 1989).

NATURE OF CASE: Appeal from award of damages for illegal discrimination.

FACT SUMMARY: Asbury (P) claimed that she was denied an opportunity to rent a home at Brougham Estates (D) because she was black.

CONCISE RULE OF LAW: The Fair Housing Act is violated where the plaintiff proves a prima facie case of intent to discriminate based on race and the defendant is unable to demonstrate legitimate nondiscriminatory reasons.

FACTS: Asbury (P), a black woman, went to Brougham Estates (D), a housing complex, looking to rent a home. Asbury (P) was told that there were no vacancies and was refused an application. The following day, a white woman inquired about the same housing and was told that there were immediate openings. Other evidence presented at trial also indicated that white persons were given different information than Asbury (P). Brougham Estates (D) responded that there was no appropriate housing available for Asbury (P) at the time she inquired. The jury awarded damages, including punitives damages, against Brougham (D) to Asbury (P), and Brougham (D) appealed.

ISSUE: Is the Fair Housing Act violated where the plaintiff proves a prima facie case of intent to discriminate based on race and the defendant is unable to demonstrate legitimate nondiscriminatory reasons?

HOLDING AND DECISION: (Parker, J.) Yes. The Fair Housing Act is violated where the plaintiff proves a prima facie case of intent to discriminate based on race and the defendant is unable to demonstrate legitimate nondiscriminatory reasons. Under the Fair Housing Act and § 1982, persons may not use race as a factor to discriminate against minority applicants for rental housing. The plaintiff has the burden of bringing proof of a prima facie case. Then the defendant has the burden of showing that the refusal to rent or provide information was motivated by legitimate nonracial reasons. Finally, the burden shifts back to the plaintiff to demonstrate that the reasons claimed by the defendant were not the true considerations. Asbury (P) made her prima facie case by proving that she was denied access to housing although it remained available to white applicants. Brougham Estates's (D) defense that Asbury (P) was not qualified for housing was rebutted by evidence that exceptions were often made for persons in her position and she was not even provided with the conditions for obtaining an exception. Thus, the jury had a valid basis for deciding that Brougham Estates's (D) reasons were not legitimate. Accordingly, the award of damages to Asbury (P) is affirmed.

EDITOR'S ANALYSIS: The award of punitive damages against Brougham (D), the owner of the complex, was upheld despite his assertion that he could not be held responsible for the actions of his employees. The court found that there was ample evidence that Brougham (D) had adopted the discriminatory policy and ratified the employees' actions.

[For more information on the Fair Housing Act, see Casenote Law Outline on Property, Chapter 12, § II, Federal Law.]

NOTES:

UNITED STATES v. STARRETT CITY ASSOCIATES

840 F.2d 1096 (2d Cir. 1988), cert. denied 488 U.S. 946 (1988).

NATURE OF CASE: Appeal from grant of summary judgment and permanent injunction in housing discrimination case.

FACT SUMMARY: Starrett City Associates (Starrett) (D) appealed from a decision granting summary judgment and a permanent injunction in favor of the United States (Government) (P), preventing it from discriminating on the basis of race in the rental of apartments. Starrett (D) contended that its tenant selection procedures, designed to achieve racial integration, did not violate the Fair Housing Act (FHA).

CONCISE RULE OF LAW: The FHA may prevent the use of rigid racial quotas of indefinite duration to maintain a fixed level of integration in public housing when such practices restrict minority access to public housing.

FACTS: Starrett (D) owned and operated Starrett City, the largest public housing complex in the nation. To prevent "white flight" and to maintain a racial balance of 64% white, 22% black, and 8% Hispanic, Starrett (D) adopted a selection process whereby as vacancies arose, applicants of a similar race or national origin to those tenants departing were selected. It was undenied that this practice restricted minority access to the complex. The Government (P) brought suit against Starrett (D) alleging that the selection process discriminated on the basis of race, in violation of the FHA. The parties made cross-motions for summary judgment. The Government's (P) motion was granted and the court permanently enjoined the selection process which it determined had adversely impacted minority participation in the complex solely on the basis of race. From this decision, Starrett (D) appealed.

ISSUE: May the FHA prevent the use of rigid racial quotas of indefinite duration to maintain a fixed level of integration in public housing when such practices restrict minority access to public housing?

HOLDING AND DECISION: (Miner, J.) Yes. The FHA may prevent the use of rigid racial quotas of indefinite duration to maintain a fixed level of integration in public housing when such practices restrict minority access to public housing. Housing practices violative of the FHA include not only those motivated by racially discriminatory purposes, but also those that disproportionately affect minorities. Quotas bring the dual goals of the FHA — antidiscrimination and integration — into conflict. A racial classification is presumptively discriminating, but a race-conscious affirmative action plan does not necessarily violate federal constitutional or statutory law. Such plans must be temporary in nature and must terminate when a defined goal is reached. Access quotas which increase or ensure minority participation are generally upheld, while integration maintenance plans which restrict minority participation are of doubtful validity. Finally, quotas, when used, address the history of racial discrimination or imbalance. In the present case, Starrett's (D) selection process has as its only goal integration maintenance. There is no adequate

explanation as to why it was in force for over fifteen years. Furthermore, the selection process redresses no prior discrimination or racial imbalance. In fact, it acts as a ceiling on minority access to Starrett's complex. Fear of "white flight" cannot justify the use of inflexible racial quotas in the present case. While race is not always an inappropriate factor, Starrett's (D) use of racial quotas in the present case is. Affirmed.

DISSENT: (Newman, J.) The FHA, which was promulgated to bar the perpetuation of segregation, was never designed or intended to apply to actions like Starrett's (D), which do not promote segregated housing, but rather maintain integrated housing.

EDITOR'S ANALYSIS: Housing practices need not be motivated by a racially discriminatory purpose to be violative of the FHA; they may also be violative if they disproportionately affect minorities. Race-based factors, which are not motivated by a racially discriminating purpose, may not be violative of the FHA, even if they adversely affect minorities. A justifiable rental increase may decrease minority participation in a complex, but the increase, if not racially motivated, may not run afoul of the FHA.

[For more information on the race discrimination and quotas, see Casenote Law Outline on Property, Chapter 12, § II, Federal Law.]

NOTES:

CITY OF MEMPHIS v. GREENE
451 U.S. 100 (1981).

NATURE OF CASE: Section 1982 action.

FACT SUMMARY: Black residents (P) of Memphis (D) complained that a street closing was designed to keep them out of a white neighborhood.

CONCISE RULE OF LAW: Section 1982 is not violated unless a municipal action impairs significant property interests.

FACTS: Memphis (D) closed one end of West Drive, a street crossing a white neighborhood, preventing traffic from a predominantly black community from obtaining access to the street. Black residents (P) filed suit claiming that the closing violated § 1982 since Memphis (D) had acted with discriminatory intent.

ISSUE: Is § 1982 violated when municipal action impairs any property interests?

HOLDING AND DECISION: (Stevens, J.) No. Section 1982 is not violated unless a municipal action impairs significant property interests. The threshold inquiry under §1982 is whether any property interest of the minority community members are implicated by a municipal action. A town action would be illegal if the action depreciated the value of the minority citizen's property or if it hampered their use of property. Convenience is not the type of property interest the Court has identified as being within §1982. In the present case, the only injury claimed by the black residents (P) of Memphis (D) is inconvenience. Therefore, the street closing by Memphis (D) is not a violation of section 1982.

DISSENT: (Marshall, J.) The majority ignores the significant symbolic and psychological harm to which the street closure subjects the black residents (P). It defies the lessons of history and law to hold that courts cannot recognize symbolic harm.

EDITOR'S ANALYSIS: Justice Marshall pointed to the Court's decision in Brown v. Board of Education, 347 U.S. 483 (1954), where the Court stated that separation "solely because of their race generates a feeling of inferiority" as evidence that the court had previously stepped in to remedy such harm. Section 1982 refers to 42 U.S.C. § 1982, § 1 of the Civil Rights Act of 1866. The Act provides, in part, that "[a]ll citizens of the United States shall have the same right, in every state and territory, as is enjoyed by white citizens thereof to inherit, purchase, lease, sell, hold and convey real and personal property."

[For more information on violation of § 1982, see Casenote Law Outline on Property, Chapter 12, § II, Federal Law.]

GRIEGER v. SHEETS
689 F.Supp. 835 (N.D. Ill. 1988).

NATURE OF CASE: Motion to dismiss sexual harassment claim.

FACT SUMMARY: Sheets (D), a landlord, asserted that § 3617 of the Fair Housing Act did not apply to allegations that he directly harassed a tenant.

CONCISE RULE OF LAW: Section 3617 of the Fair Housing Act bars threats pursuant to sexual harassment by a landlord.

FACTS: Greiger (P) and Carter (P), a married couple with two kids, rented a house owned and managed by Sheets (D). Two weeks into their tenancy, Sheets (D) demanded sexual favors from Grieger (P) as a condition to performing promised repairs on the house. When she refused, Sheets (D) not only failed to make the repairs but also threatened both Carter (P) and Grieger (P) and forced them to get rid of their dog. Greiger (P) and Carter (P) sued Sheets (D) for sexual harassment under the Fair Housing Act, specifically §§ 3617 and 3612. Sheets (D) brought a motion to dismiss based on the fact that § 3617 does not apply to direct discrimination by a landlord against a tenant.

ISSUE: Does § 3617 of the Fair Housing Act bar threats pursuant to sexual harassment by a landlord?

HOLDING AND DECISION: (Aspen, J.) Yes. Section 3617 of the Fair Housing Act bars threats pursuant to sexual harassment by a landlord. Section 3617 prohibits coercion, intimidation, or interference with a person's exercise of rights granted under the Fair Housing Act. Clearly, both Grieger (P) and Carter (P) alleged that they were harassed and threatened by Sheets (D) in addition to the allegations of quid pro quo sexual harassment. Therefore, both plaintiffs have alleged valid § 3617 violations. Sheets's (D) motion to dismiss is denied.

EDITOR'S ANALYSIS: The court in People of the State of New York v. Merlino, 694 F. Supp. 1101 (S.D.N.Y. 1988), also found that the Fair Housing Act covers sexual harassment. The Merlino court analogized the Fair Housing Act to Title VII of the 1964 Civil Rights Act, which prohibits sex discrimination in employment, and concluded that proof of severe and pervasive sexual harrassment would trigger the Act's protection. Isolated or trivial instances not related to housing, however, would not.

[For more information on sexual harassment by landlord, see Casenote Law Outline on Property, Chapter 12, § II, Federal Law.]

PARK PLACE HOME BROKERS v. P-K MOBILE HOME PARK

773 F. Supp. 46 (N.D. Ohio 1991).

NATURE OF CASE: Action for injunction barring discrimination.

FACT SUMMARY: P-K Mobile Home Park (D) did not allow families with children and claimed to be housing for seniors only.

CONCISE RULE OF LAW: The exception against familial status discrimination for senior housing does not apply unless there are significant facilities specially designed for older persons at the site.

FACTS: Park Place (P), a housing broker, sought to arrange the sale of mobile homes in P-K Mobile Home Park (D) but was prevented by P-K's (D) policy of not admitting families with children. P-K (D) responded that it was exempt from the Fair Housing Act's prohibition against discrimination based on family status because the P-K Park (D) was housing for seniors. P-K (D) asserted that it provided significant facilities specially designed for the needs of older persons by the park's proximity to off-site facilities for seniors.

ISSUE: Can the exception against familial status discrimination for senior housing apply if there aren't significant facilities specially designed for older persons at the site?

HOLDING AND DECISION: (Potter, J.) No. The exception against familial status discrimination for senior housing does not apply unless there are significant facilities specially designed for older persons at the site. The 1988 amendments to the Fair Housing Act banned discrimination in housing on the basis of familial status. Thus, housing providers may not discriminate based on the fact that children will be present. However, Congress did provide for an exemption for "housing for older persons." 42 U.S.C. § 607(b)(1) provides that housing is exempt from the familial status discrimination prohibition if 80% of the units are occupied by at least one resident over 55 years old and significant facilities and services specially designed to meet the needs of seniors are provided. The latter is not satisfied by reliance on nearby off-site facilities. Otherwise, multiple housing providers could claim the same sites as the basis for the exemption. In the present case, the services cited by P-K (D) are only those that any landlord would provide to tenants of any age. Their reliance on off-site facilities and services for older persons is misplaced. Accordingly, P-K (D) does not qualify for the exemption and a permanent injunction is granted in favor of Park Place Brokers (P). The case will proceed to a trial for damages.

EDITOR'S ANALYSIS: The court also rejected P-K's (D) claim that providing special facilities and services was impractical. Simply because such services would be expensive is not sufficient to demonstrate impracticability.

[For more information on familial status discrimination, see Casenote Law Outline on Property, Chapter 12, § II, Federal Law.]

SMITH v. FAIR EMPLOYMENT AND HOUSING COMMISSION
913 P.2d 909 (1996).

NATURE OF CASE: Appeal from judgment in a complaint for unlawful housing discrimination.

FACT SUMMARY: Smith (D), a landlord, refused to rent to an unmarried couple because she claimed it violated her religious beliefs.

CONCISE RULE OF LAW: Landlords may not discriminate against unmarried couples on the basis of claimed religious beliefs.

FACTS: Gail Randall and Kenneth Phillips, an unmarried man and woman, responded to an advertisement for an apartment placed by Smith (D). Smith (D) owned four rental apartments in two duplexes in Chico, California. After learning that Smith (D) would not rent to an unmarried couple, Phillips falsely represented to Smith (D) that he and Randall were married and signed her name "Gail Phillips" on the lease agreement. Later the same day, Phillips phoned Smith (D) and told her that they were not married. Smith (D) told Randall that as a Christian she believed that extramarital sex was sinful and claimed it would violate these beliefs if she rented her apartments to unmarried men and women. Smith (D) promptly returned Randall's and Phillip's security deposit, and they filed a complaint against Smith (D) with the Fair Employment and Housing Commission (P) for unlawful discrimination based on marital status. The court of appeals ruled that Smith (D) was exempt from this discrimination law because it burdened her religious beliefs. The Commission (P) appealed.

ISSUE: May landlords discriminate against unmarried couples on the basis of claimed religious beliefs?

HOLDING AND DECISION: (Werdegar, J.) No. Landlords may not discriminate against unmarried couples on the basis of claimed religious beliefs. The Supreme Court has decided that the First Amendment right to free exercise of religion does not relieve an individual of the obligation to comply with valid and neutral laws of general applicability on the ground that the law causes a conflict with the person's religious beliefs. In response to this decision, Congress passed the Religious Freedom Restoration Act (RFRA). This law provides that the government may not substantially burden a person's exercise of religion, even if the burden results from a rule of general applicability, unless there is a compelling state interest and it is the least restrictive means of furthering that interest. In the present case, there is a conflict between the Fair Housing Law prohibiting discrimination against persons based on marital status and Smith's (D) religious beliefs. However, there is no substantial burden on Smith (D) because if she does not wish to comply with the antidiscrimination laws she can simply redirect her investment in the apartment buildings. Since there is no substantial burden on Smith's (D) religious exercise, the Commission's (P) complaint must be upheld. Reversed.

CONCURRENCE: (Mosk, J.) Any inquiry into whether government action substantially burdens an individual's free exercise of religion unavoidably entails a court to pass judgment on the nature of the religious conduct and particular beliefs. The Supreme Court has already ruled that such an inquiry is unconstitutional.

CONCURRENCE AND DISSENT: (Kennard, J.) The Fair Housing Laws do substantially burden Smith's (D) religious beliefs because they impose some economic pressure on her. The Commission (P) failed to show that the discrimination law was a compelling state interest.

DISSENT: (Baxter, J.) The state tolerates many other forms of discrimination against unmarried people. Smith's (D) federally guaranteed religious free exercise rights should similarly be sufficient reason for allowing such discrimination.

EDITOR'S ANALYSIS: Since the Smith holding, the Supreme Court has struck down the RFRA, holding that Congress cannot overrule Supreme Court interpretations of the First Amendment by statute. Thus, the disagreement among the California justices is moot as the discrimination laws apply to all landlords regardless of their religious beliefs. The majority could have reached the same conclusion by deciding that Christian religious beliefs actually say nothing about renting apartments.

[For more information on discrimination based on religious freedom, see Casenote Law Outline on Property, Chapter 12, § III, State Law.]

NOTES:

POFF v. CARO
N.J. Super. Ct. Law Div., 549 A.2d 900 (1987).

NATURE OF CASE: Action alleging illegal housing discrimination.

FACT SUMMARY: A landlord refused to rent to homosexual men out of fear of AIDS.

CONCISE RULE OF LAW: Discrimination against homosexuals is illegal if it is based on the fear they will acquire AIDS.

FACTS: [Named parties not identified] A landlord refused to rent his available apartments to three homosexual men because he believed that they would likely acquire AIDS.

ISSUE: Is discrimination against homosexuals illegal if it is based on the fear they will acquire AIDS?

HOLDING AND DECISION: (Humphreys, J.) Yes. Discrimination against homosexuals is illegal if it is based on the fear they will acquire AIDS. The New Jersey Law Against Discrimination protects the physically handicapped against discrimination based on their disability. AIDS attacks the body's immune system and is a debilitating disease that causes death. Clearly, a person with AIDS has a physical handicap within the meaning of the Law Against Discrimination. This law also prohibits discrimination based on the perception, accurate or not, of a handicap. Therefore, the landlord's decision not to rent to the homosexual men based on his belief that they will acquire AIDS is discrimination against them based on the perception they are disabled. Accordingly, the landlord's actions are illegal.

EDITOR'S ANALYSIS: The Federal Rehabilitation Act of 1973 prohibits discrimination based on disabilities in federally funded programs, including housing. Subsequent decisions have found that this includes receiving funds from the government. The Federal Fair Housing Act was amended to include physically and mentally handicapped individuals as a protected class in 1988.

[For more information on disability and group homes, see Casenote Law Outline on Property, Chapter 12, § II, Federal Law.]

NOTES:

ATTORNEY GENERAL v. BROWN
Mass. Sup. Ct., 511 N.E.2d 1103 (1987).

NATURE OF CASE: Appeal from summary judgment finding illegal discrimination and awarding declaratory and injunctive relief.

FACT SUMMARY: Brown (D), a landlord, refused to rent to Section 8 certificate holders because they could not make an advance payment of their last month's rent.

CONCISE RULE OF LAW: Landlords are not automatically guilty of illegal discrimination because they refuse to rent to Section 8 certificate holders.

FACTS: Brown (D), a landlord in Boston, refused to rent apartments to holders of Section 8 certificates. These certificates entitled those with low incomes to public housing assistance. Brown (D) asserted that he refused their applications because of his policy of renting only to those who make an advance payment of the last month's rent and those who sign his standard leases. Section 8 regulations do not allow for advance payment of rent and do not allow certain of the provisions in Brown's (D) leases. The Attorney General (P) of Massachusetts filed suit against Brown (D), claiming that he had violated Massachusetts law prohibiting housing discrimination against recipients of public assistance "solely because the individual is a recipient." The trial court granted summary judgment to the Attorney General (P), and Brown (D) appealed.

ISSUE: Are landlords automatically guilty of illegal discrimination when they refuse to rent to Section 8 certificate holders?

HOLDING AND DECISION: (Lynch, J.) No. Landlords are not automatically guilty of illegal discrimination because they refuse to rent to Section 8 certificate holders. A landlord is entitled to discriminate against recipients of public assistance if there are legitimate business reasons for doing so apart from their status as recipients. In the present case, Brown (D) claimed that he lost cash flow from collecting rent payments in advance. Although Section 8 regulations provide security to landlords if a tenant breaches the lease, the deprivation of cash flow may be a sufficient legitimate reason for Brown's (D) discrimination. Accordingly, summary judgment is inappropriate in these circumstances. Reversed.

EDITOR'S ANALYSIS: The court also dismissed the State's (P) assertion that Brown's (D) loss would be de minimis because Massachusetts requires that a tenant's security deposit be placed in a separate account and the tenant is paid 5% interest. The court ruled that Brown (D) might be able to earn more than 5% on the money.

HUNTINGTON BRANCH, NAACP v. TOWN OF HUNTINGTON
844 F.2d 926 (2d Cir. 1988).

NATURE OF CASE: Appeal from judgment denying an injunction.

FACT SUMMARY: Huntington (D) zoning regulations did not allow housing projects in white neighborhoods.

CONCISE RULE OF LAW: Town zoning regulations may not restrict multifamily housing projects to largely minority areas.

FACTS: Huntington (D), New York was a town of 200,000 people in 1980. Ninety-five percent of the residents were white. The 3.35% of black residents were concentrated in two neighborhoods. Because there was a shortage of low-income housing in Huntington (D), Housing Help Inc. (HHI) (P) decided to sponsor an integrated housing project. HHI (P) determined that it could only foster integration by locating the project in a white neighborhood. HHI (P) purchased a parcel of land and obtained HUD approval for the project. However, Huntington (D) zoning regulations allowed this type of housing only in a single area already occupied by black residents. HHI (P) and the NAACP (P) brought suit against Huntington (D), claiming that it was violating the Fair Housing Act because its zoning regulations had a disparate impact on racial minorities. Specifically, 24% of blacks living in Huntington (D) required subsidized housing as opposed to only 7% of the white residents. The trial court ruled for Huntington (D), and the HHI (P) and the NAACP (P) appealed.

ISSUE: May town zoning regulations restrict multifamily housing projects to largely minority areas?

HOLDING AND DECISION: (Kaufman, J.) No. Town zoning regulations may not restrict multifamily housing projects to largely minority areas. Disparate impact analysis under the Fair Housing Act examines a facially neutral policy or practice that has a different impact on particular groups of people. Intent to discriminate is not necessary to prove illegal discrimination. The prima facie case is established by showing that the practice has a discriminatory effect. Then a court must weigh the adverse impact against legitimate government interests and any possible alternatives with less discriminatory effects. In the present case, Huntington (D) zoning regulations promote racial segregation in housing by refusing to permit projects in white neighborhoods. At trial, Huntington (D) presented no evidence as to why preventing projects in white neighborhoods would impair any legitimate interests. Huntington's (D) objections to certain specific provisions of HHI's (P) plan could be resolved, and there was no support for evidence that the site chosen by HHI (P) was inappropriate for the housing project. Accordingly, the district court is ordered to direct judgment for HHI (P) and mandate that Huntington (D) re-zone the site to allow the project. Reversed and remanded.

EDITOR'S ANALYSIS: The circuit courts are split on whether the Fair Housing Act requires discriminatory intent. Most agree with this case — that a plaintiff may make a prima facie case based on disparate impact only. But see Metropolitan Housing Development Corp. v. Village of Arlington Heights, 558 F.2d 1283 (7th Cir. 1977), for an opposing view.

———————————————

[For more information on exclusionary zoning, see Casenote Law Outline on Property, Chapter 10, § II, Validity of Zoning Laws.]

NOTES:

DOE v. CITY OF BUTLER
892 F.2d 315 (3rd Cir. 1989).

NATURE OF CASE: Appeal from judgment denying injunction in Title VIII challenge.

FACT SUMMARY: Three battered women (P) claimed that a Butler (D) ordinance restricting shelters to six persons was sex and familial status discrimination.

CONCISE RULE OF LAW: The Fair Housing Act prohibits discrimination based on familial status, which may include single-parent families living communally.

FACTS: The City of Butler (D) had zoning ordinances that provided that transitional dwellings, defined as residential facilities providing temporary special care, were limited to six unrelated persons. The Volunteers Against Abuse Center (VAAC) (P) sought to use a building in Butler (D) as a temporary shelter for abused women and children. The Butler (D) City Council denied the application. Three battered women using the fictitious Doe (P) name brought suit, asserting that the Butler (D) ordinance violated the Fair Housing Act's prohibition against sex discrimination. The district court ruled that there was no sex discrimination. Doe (P) appealed. Meanwhile, Congress amended the Fair Housing Act to prohibit discrimination based on familial status, which Doe (P) added to their claims.

ISSUE: Does the Fair Housing Act's prohibition against discrimination based on familial status include single-parent families living communally?

HOLDING AND DECISION: (Sloviter, J.) Yes. The Fair Housing Act prohibits discrimination based on familial status, which may include single-parent families living communally. In order to show disparate impact discrimination under the Fair Housing Act, it must be demonstrated that the challenged law has a different effect on a protected group. In the present case, Doe (P) did not present any evidence that the Butler (D) ordinance had a different effect on women than men. Accordingly, there was no discrimination based on sex. The 1988 amendments to the Fair Housing Act adding "familial status" as an illegal basis for discrimination makes it possible that the Doe (P) women may have a valid argument that a six-person limit will adversely effect the ability of women with children to take advantage of transitional dwellings and shelters. Further evidence must be developed on the record at the trial level to adjudicate this issue. Remanded.

DISSENT: (Roth, J.) Nothing in the Fair Housing Act supports the proposition that it was intended to extend protection to families who wish to live in groups.

EDITOR'S ANALYSIS: The plaintiffs will have a difficult time demonstrating that the Butler (D) ordinance has a disparate impact on women with children. First, Butler (D) had never ruled that children counted against the six-person limit. Second, the Supreme Court has ruled that restrictions on the number of unrelated persons in a household are generally allowable. See Village of Belle Terre, 416 U.S. 1 (1974).

_____

[For more information on group homes, see Casenote Law Outline on Property, Chapter 12, § II, Federal Law.]

NOTES:

VILLAGE OF BELLE TERRE v. BORAAS
416 U.S. 1 (1974).

NATURE OF CASE: Appeal from an action seeking a declaratory judgment and an injunction.

FACT SUMMARY: Boraas (P) and other co-lessees of a house in the Village of Belle Terre (D) brought this action for an injunction and a judgment declaring an ordinance restricting land use to one-family dwellings unconstitutional.

CONCISE RULE OF LAW: Zoning legislation does not violate the equal protection clause if it is reasonable, not arbitrary, and bears a rational relationship to a permissible state objective.

FACTS: Belle Terre (D) had restricted land use to one-family dwellings. The word "family" as used in the ordinance meant one or more persons related by blood or a number of persons not exceeding two living together as a single housekeeping unit though not related by blood. The Dickmans (P), owners of a house in the Village of Belle Terre (D), leased it to two single males, a single female, and three others, Boraas (P) among them. The Village (D) served the Dickmans (P) with an "Order To Remedy Violations" of the ordinance. Thereupon, Boraas (P) and two of the other tenants, as well as the Dickmans (P), brought this action seeking an injunction and a judgment declaring the ordinance unconstitutional as violative of the equal protection clause. The district court held the ordinance constitutional and the court of appeals reversed. The Village (D) appealed to the Supreme Court.

ISSUE: Does zoning legislation violate the equal protection clause if it is reasonable and bears a rational relationship to a permissible state objective?

HOLDING AND DECISION: (Douglas, J.) No. The ordinance now before the court does not discriminate against unmarried couples in violation of the equal protection clause. The ordinance is not aimed at transients so as to interfere with a person's right to travel. It involves no procedural disparity inflicted on some but not on others. It involves no fundamental right guaranteed by the constitution. Economic and social legislation does not violate the equal protection clause if the law be reasonable, not arbitrary, and bears a rational relationship to a permissible state objective. Boraas (P) argues that if two unmarried people can constitute a family under the ordinance, there is no reason why three or four may not. But every line drawn by a legislature leaves some out that might well have been included. That exercise of discretion, however, is a legislative, not a judicial, function. A quiet place where yards are wide, people few, and motor vehicles restricted are legitimate guidelines in a land-use project addressed to family needs. This goal is a permissible one. The police power is not confined to elimination of filth, stench, and unhealthy places. It is ample to lay out zones where family values make the area a sanctuary for people. Therefore, the decision of the court of appeals is reversed.

DISSENT: (Brennan, J.) Since the tenants in the instant case have quit the house, this raises a serious question of whether there now exists a cognizable case and controversy.

DISSENT: (Marshall, J.) The disputed classification burdens the tenants' fundamental rights of association and privacy guaranteed by the first and fourteenth amendments. Therefore, strict equal protection scrutiny should be applied. The first amendment provides some limitation on zoning laws which, for example, seek to restrict occupancy to individuals adhering to particular religious, political, or scientific beliefs. Zoning officials properly concern themselves with the uses of land and can restrict the number of persons who reside in certain dwellings. But they cannot validly consider who those persons are or how they choose to live.

DISSENT: (Marshall, J.) The Belle Terre (D) ordinance unnecessarily burdens the First Amendment rights of freedom of association and privacy. The town has the option to reach its goals of peace and quiet through more even handed laws, such as a straight limit on the number of persons in a home.

EDITOR'S ANALYSIS: The freedom of association is often inextricably entwined with the constitutionally guaranteed right of privacy. In Meyer v. Nebraska, 262 U.S. 390 (1923), the Supreme Court held that the right to establish a home is an essential part of the liberty guaranteed by the fourteenth amendment. In Stanley v. Georgia, 394 U.S. 557, in the concurring opinion, Justice Goldberg stated that the constitution secures to an individual a freedom to satisfy his intellectual and emotional needs in the privacy of his own home. Both these cases were used in the dissent to support the argument of discrimination.

[For more information on fundamental rights and equal protection, see Casenote Law Outline on Property, Chapter 12, § I, The United States Constitution.]

NOTES:

CHARTER TOWNSHIP OF DELTA v. DINOLFO
Mich. Sup. Ct., 351 N.W.2d 831 (1984).

NATURE OF CASE: Action to enforce occupancy ordinance.

FACT SUMMARY: Delta (P) had a zoning ordinance limiting households to a family plus one unrelated person.

CONCISE RULE OF LAW: The Michigan Constitution is violated by a law that allows only one unrelated person per home since it is not rationally related to a legitimate goal.

FACTS: The Dinolfo (D) "family," a household consisting of parents, children and six unrelated single adults, moved into a home in Delta (P). This unconventional arrangement was adopted as part of their religious commitment to the Work of Christ Community. Their home was located in an area of Delta (P) zoned for single-family dwellings, defined as blood relatives and no more than one unrelated person. Delta (P) sent the Dinolfos (D) a violation notice and refused their application for a variance. The Dinolfos (D) responded that the zoning ordinance violated their rights of privacy, free association, and free exercise of religion under the U.S. and Michigan Constitutions. [No procedural history of the case is provided.]

ISSUE: Is it a violation of the Michigan Constitution to limit households to a family plus one unrelated person?

HOLDING AND DECISION: (Brickley, J.) Yes. The Michigan Constitution is violated by a law that allows only one unrelated person per home since it is not rationally related to a legitimate goal. In Village of Belle Terre v. Boraas, 416 U.S. 1 (1974), the Supreme Court upheld a nearly identical ordinance. However, this court must examine it under the Michigan Constitution as well. Laws must be rationally and reasonably related to legitimate government objectives. The preservation of family values, the maintenance of property values, and population control are legitimate state goals. However, the Delta (P) zoning ordinance assumes that unrelated persons act differently from biological families. Despite the parade of horrors brought out by the town, there is no evidence that there is any factual basis behind the assumption. Therefore, the ordinance is arbitrary and capricious and violates the due process clause of the Michigan Constitution. The rational way to reach the same goals is to limit the number of persons in a house.

EDITOR'S ANALYSIS: A minority of states, including California, New Jersey, and New York, have ruled that their state constitutions provide more protection than the Supreme Court found in Village of Belle Terre v. Boraas. Note that the holding in Belle Terre affects only unrelated individuals. The Supreme Court has explicitly stated that ordinances intrusively regulating blood relatives will not be tolerated. See Moore v. City of East Cleveland, 431 U.S. 494 (1977).

[For more information on housing discrimination and state laws, see Casenote Law Outline on Property, Chapter 12, § III, State Law.]

NOTES:

ASSOCIATION OF RELATIVES AND FRIENDS OF AIDS PATIENTS (AFAPS) v. REGULATIONS AND PERMITS ADMINISTRATION (ARPE)

740 F. Supp. 95 (D.P.R. 1990).

NATURE OF CASE: Action for injunction barring discrimination on the basis of handicap.

FACT SUMMARY: Government agency Regulations and Permits Administration (ARPE) (D) denied an application for an AIDS hospice claiming that zoning regulations prohibited it.

CONCISE RULE OF LAW: Zoning regulations may not be invoked as a pretext for discrimination based upon fear of AIDS.

FACTS: AFAPS (P) sought to establish an AIDS hospice in Sabana Ward, Puerto Rico. ARPE (D), the government agency in charge of permits, refused to grant AFAPS (P) permission after holding hearings on the issue. The hearings featured strong pressure by the Residents Committee, who opposed the hospice because they believed it was undesirable to have homosexuals and drug users in the area and were afraid that floods and mosquitoes would spread the disease. Although it was never discussed, ARPE (D) now claims that a zoning regulation limiting the area to agricultural use was the sole factor in denying AFAPS's (P) application. AFAPS (P) filed suit, asserting that the decision was based on illegal discrimination against people with AIDS.

ISSUE: May zoning regulations be invoked to prevent AIDS hospices from locating in certain areas?

HOLDING AND DECISION: (Fuste, J.) No. Zoning regulations may not invoked as a pretext for discrimination based upon fear of AIDS. Discrimination against people with AIDS is illegal because AIDS is considered a disability. In the present case, it is clear that the motives of the Residents Committee pressuring ARPE (D) were to keep AIDS patients from living near them. The absence of any discussion about zoning ordinances prior to ARPE's (D) denial, coupled with their discussion of the importance of public opinion, is persuasive evidence that the zoning regulation was used as a mere pretext. Finally, evidence shows that zoning laws were selectively enforced and exceptions routinely allowed. Thus, ARPE's (D) actions were obviously an intent to discriminate against people with AIDS. Judgment for AFAPS (P).

EDITOR'S ANALYSIS: The court also ruled that the denial of the permit had a disparate impact on persons with disabilities, using the four-prong test enunciated in Metropolitan Housing Development Corp. v. Village of Arlington Heights, 558 F.2d 1283 (7th Cir. 1977). The court found that the permit denial adversely affected persons with disabilities, there was evidence of discriminatory intent, and the state's interest was weak when balanced against the privately financed project being promoted by AFAPS (P).

[For more information on disability and groups homes, see Casenote Law Outline on Property, Chapter 12, § II, Federal Law.]

NOTES:

FAMILYSTYLE OF ST. PAUL, INC. v. CITY OF ST. PAUL
923 F.2d 91 (8th Cir. 1991).

NATURE OF CASE: Appeal from validation of deinstitutionalization ordinance.

FACT SUMMARY: When Familystyle (P) was denied a permit to expand its capacity to house mentally ill persons by adding three homes to its existing campus, it challenged St. Paul's (D) requirement that group homes be located at least a quarter mile apart.

CONCISE RULE OF LAW: Legislation which requires dispersal of group homes is a legitimate means whereby a state may achieve its goal of deinstitutionalization of the mentally ill, and does not violate the Fair Housing Amendments Act of 1988.

FACTS: The State of Minnesota (D) required that all residential services for people with mental illness and retardation be licensed. In an attempt to deinstitutionalize the mentally ill and integrate them back into mainstream society, Minnesota (D) enacted a licensing regulation requiring new group homes to be spaced at least a quarter of a mile apart St. Paul's (D) zoning code contains the same dispersal requirement. Familystyle (P) operated group homes and provided rehabilitative services for mentally ill persons on its campus located in St. Paul (D). Familystyle (P) applied for a license to add three new homes to its campus, but St. Paul (D) denied the application because it violated the dispersal requirement. Familystyle (P) filed suit alleging that Minnesota's (D) and St. Paul's (D) dispersal requirements result in a disparate impact on and discriminatory treatment of the mentally ill, in violation of the Fair Housing Amendments Act of 1988. The district court found that the government's interest in deinstitutionalization sufficiently rebutted any discriminatory effect of the laws. Familystyle (P) appealed.

ISSUE: Is legislation which requires dispersal of group homes a legitimate means for a state to achieve its goal of deinstitutionalization of the mentally ill, and not a violation of the Fair Housing Amendments Act of 1988?

HOLDING AND DECISION: (Wollman, J.) Yes. Legislation which requires dispersal of group homes is a legitimate means whereby a state may achieve its goal of deinstitutionalization of the mentally ill and does not violate the Fair Housing Amendments Act of 1988. First of all, in a Title VIII case, the plaintiff has the initial burden of establishing the discriminatory effect of the challenged law. Once such an effect is shown to disparately impact a nonsuspect class like the mentally ill, the burden shifts to the government to demonstrate that its legislation was rationally related to a legitimate government purpose. In this case, although local and state dispersal requirements for group homes on their face limit housing choices for the mentally ill, the government's method of dispersing group homes was rationally related to its goal of integrating the mentally ill into the mainstream of society. Affirmed.

EDITOR'S ANALYSIS: The Fair Housing Act prohibits discrimination on the basis of race, color, religion, sex, familial status, handicap, or national origin. Most FHA cases involve alleged discrimination on the basis of race, color or national origin. Very few cases are brought under the FHA based on gender. However, in Doe v. City of Butler, 892 F.2d 315 (3d Cir. 1989), a zoning ordinance that limited group homes to six persons was challenged as gender discrimination when applied to a home for abused women. The court validated the ordinance, finding no intention to discriminate against women, since the provision applied equally to group homes for men. On the other hand, the court condemned as discriminatory a landlord's refusal to rent to a goup of males because he believed that men tenants were dirtier than women tenants, in Baumgardner v. HUD, 960 F.2d 572 (6th Cir. 1992).

[For more information on disability and group homes, see Casenote Law Outline on Property, Chapter 12, § II, Federal Law.]

NOTES:

10

CHAPTER 10
FAMILY PROPERTY

QUICK REFERENCE RULES OF LAW

1. **Eviction.** Public housing interests are not forfeited when the lessee is unaware of drug activities at the apartment. (United States v. Leasehold Interest in 121 Nostrand Avenue)

2. **The Innocent Joint Owner: Spousal Rights and Domestic Violence.** The innocent owner defense to forfeiture is not available to a person who has knowledge of illegal activities and remains silent. (United States v. Sixty Acres in Etowah County)

3. **The Innocent Joint Owner: Spousal Rights and Domestic Violence.** States may take property under civil forfeiture laws without any showing that a co-owner of the property was culpable in the wrongdoing that led to the forfeiture. (Bennis v. Michigan)

4. **Child Support: Higher Education.** Alabama trial courts may order divorcing parents to provide for the college educations of their children. (Bayliss v. Bayliss)

5. **Domestic Violence and Protective Orders.** An order barring one spouse from the marital home does not constitute a taking of property requiring just compensation. (Cote v. Cote)

   [For more information on takings by government, see Casenote Law Outline on Property, Chapter 11, § I, Eminent Domain.]

6. **Equitable Distribution of "Property" Acquired during Marriage.** A professional license may constitute marital property. (O'Brien v. O'Brien)

7. **Community Property: The Problem of the Migratory Couple.** The validity and effect of a contract are governed by the law of the state having the most significant relationship with the contract. (Pacific Gamble Robinson Co. v. Lapp)

8. **Property Rights on Separation.** An unmarried cohabitant may assert a contract claim against the other cohabitant so long as the claim is independent of the sexual relationship and is supported by separate consideration. (Watts v. Watts)

9. **State Constitutions.** A group of college students living together may constitute the functional equivalent of a traditional family unit. (Borough of Glassboro v. Vallorosi)

   [For more information on "family" rights as fundamental, see Casenote Law Outline on Property, Chapter 12, § I, The United States Constitution.]

NOTES

UNITED STATES v. LEASEHOLD INTEREST IN 121 NOSTRAND AVENUE
760 F. Supp. 1015 (E.D.N.Y. 1991).

NATURE OF CASE: Trial for forfeiture of public housing rights.

FACT SUMMARY: Smith (D) was threatened with the loss of her public housing apartment after her relatives were convicted for selling drugs on the premises.

CONCISE RULE OF LAW: Public housing interests are not forfeited when the lessee is unaware of drug activities at the apartment.

FACTS: Clara Smith (D) leased an apartment in the Macy Housing Project for 32 years. Smith (D) lived with her children, grandchildren, and great-grandchildren. An undercover officer bought crack from one of Smith's (D) grandchildren. A subsequent search of the apartment uncovered other drugs stored there. Two members of the household were convicted of felony possession. The government (P) then sought to enforce the antidrug forfeiture statute by forcing Smith (D) to relinquish her apartment. Smith (D) responded that she was an innocent owner and not subject to the statute.

ISSUE: May public housing be forfeited if drug activities take place in the apartment but the lessee is unaware?

HOLDING AND DECISION: (Weinstein, J.) No. Public housing interests are not forfeited for drug activities of which the lessee is unaware. Congress designed the antidrug forfeiture statute as a powerful deterrent against drugs. The forfeiture clause provides that real property used to facilitate the commission of drug crimes may be seized by the government (P). In addition, there are statutes that specifically apply to public housing property interests. The government (P) is only required to show probable cause that property is subject to forfeiture. Then the burden shifts to the owner to establish by a preponderance of the evidence that the property may not be seized. The innocent owner defense created by Congress allows the owner to avoid forfeiture by establishing a lack of knowledge of the crimes or that the owner did not consent to the activities. In the present case, Smith (D) provided evidence that she had many responsibilities as head of a very large household and was not aware of everything that took place in the apartment. Therefore, since Smith (D) did not have knowledge, she has a defense to the forfeiture. Judgment for Smith (D).

EDITOR'S ANALYSIS: The court did rule that any rights that Smith's (D) grandchildren who were convicted of drug crimes had to occupy the apartment were forfeited. The great-grandchildren retained their rights through their relationship with Smith (D) only. Note that the government (P) is not even required to prove that a crime was even committed in the apartment in order to obtain forfeiture; it is sufficient to show that the premises "facilitated" the drug activity — i.e., made it easier.

UNITED STATES v. SIXTY ACRES IN ETOWAH COUNTY
930 F.2d 857 (11th Cir. 1991).

NATURE OF CASE: Appeal from judgment denying forfeiture.

FACT SUMMARY: Evelyn Ellis (D) was faced with forfeiture of her property because her husband sold drugs on the premises and she was too scared to stop him.

CONCISE RULE OF LAW: The innocent owner defense to forfeiture is not available to a person who has knowledge of illegal activities and remains silent.

FACTS: Hubert Ellis was convicted of selling drugs on real property owned by his wife Evelyn (D). The United States (P) sought forfeiture of that property under 21 U.S.C. §881 (a)(7), the anti-drug property forfeiture statute. Evelyn (D) responded that while she knew of her husband's activities she remained silent because she was afraid of her husband. Evelyn (D) presented evidence that Hubert had threatened her and physically harmed her. Others testified that Hubert was a scary and violent man. The district court concluded that Evelyn (D) was unable to stop the illegal acts and thus did not consent pursuant to the innocent owner exception to forfeiture. The United States (P) appealed.

ISSUE: Is the innocent owner defense to forfeiture available to a person who has knowledge of illegal activities and remains silent?

HOLDING AND DECISION: (Hill, J.) No. In order to qualify as an innocent owner to avoid property forfeiture, the owner may not remain silent about drug activities unless there are threats of immediate retaliation. The innocent owner defense to property forfeiture is available only where property owners have no knowledge or do not consent to the illegal acts. A person is considered to have consented to the activities if they remain silent, unless this silence is imposed by duress. Legal duress requires an immediate threat of death or serious injury and the lack of an opportunity to escape. A generalized fear such as the "battered woman syndrome" does not qualify. Evelyn Ellis (D) feared her husband but presented no evidence that he threatened immediate retaliation if she did not consent to his drug schemes. Therefore, Evelyn (D) was not under legal duress and cannot use the innocent owner defense to the forfeiture. Reversed.

EDITOR'S ANALYSIS: States have also found similar difficulties in balancing their interests in protecting innocent property owners and providing a strong incentive for families to police the activities of all members of the household. See Spence v. O'Brien, 446 N.E.2d 1070 (1983). The Spence court stated that O'Brien's unsuccessful attempts to stop her boyfriend from engaging in drug activity were not sufficient to prevent her eviction. "Consent" to illegal conduct has been defined as the failure to take all reasonable steps to prevent the illicit use of premises. See U.S. v. Certain Real Property, 922 F.2d 129 (2d Cir. 1990).

BENNIS v. MICHIGAN
116 S. Ct. 994 (1996).

NATURE OF CASE: Appeal from civil forfeiture action.

FACT SUMMARY: Michigan (D) confiscated and sold a car co-owned by Tina (P) and John Bennis as a public nuisance because John engaged in sexual activity with a prostitute in the vehicle.

CONCISE RULE OF LAW: States may take property under civil forfeiture laws without any showing that a co-owner of the property was culpable in the wrongdoing that led to the forfeiture.

FACTS: Tina (P) and John Bennis, a married couple, owned a car together. John was arrested when police observed him with a prostitute in the car. John was convicted of gross indecency, and the car was declared a public nuisance and confiscated by the state pursuant to civil forfeiture laws. Tina (P) complained that Michigan (D) could not take her half interest in the car because she did not know that John would use it to violate the law. The trial court rejected her argument, and the state received the proceeds of the sale. Tina (P) appealed.

ISSUE: May states take property under civil forfeiture laws without any showing that a co-owner of the property was culpable in the wrongdoing that led to the forfeiture?

HOLDING AND DECISION: (Rehnquist, C.J.) Yes. States may take property under civil forfeiture laws without any showing that a co-owner of the property was culpable in the wrongdoing that led to the forfeiture. Since 1827, this Court has recognized that an owner's interest in property may be forfeited by reason of the use to which the property is put, even though the owner had no knowledge of this use. Forfeiture serves a deterrent purpose distinct from any punitive purpose. It prevents illegal uses by preventing further illicit use of the property, and by imposing an economic penalty, rendering illegal behavior unprofitable. The Michigan (D) forfeiture laws at issue are consistent with these principles, especially since the trial court has wide discretion to recognize an "innocent" co-owner's interests, if they so choose. Therefore, the trial court's action in taking Tina's (P) interest in the car was not unconstitutional. Affirmed.

CONCURRENCE: (Thomas, J.) This case is a reminder that the Constitution does not bar all undesirable results. However, the history of forfeiture as a crime deterrent is well documented.

CONCURRENCE: (Ginsburg, J.) John had just as much of an ownership right as Tina (P) and had her consent to use the car. Furthermore, forfeiture proceedings are equitable in nature in that they permit the state courts to police exorbitant applications of the statute.

DISSENT: (Stevens, J.) Fundamental fairness prohibits the punishment of innocent people. Vicarious liability is limited in situations in which no deterrent function is likely to be served. The absence of any deterrent value in regards to Tina (P) shows that forfeitures can be punitive against those who have not done anything wrong.

EDITOR'S ANALYSIS: The dissent makes a very persuasive point. The circumstances of this case show that there was little Tina (P) could have done to prevent John's illegal conduct. Thus, it is difficult to see how there was any deterrent function in the forfeiture of the car. Recent laws mandating eviction from rental properties for drug offenses have caused similar problems for family members who reside at these apartments but were not involved with the drug activities.

NOTES:

BAYLISS v. BAYLISS

Ala. Sup. Ct., 550 So.2d 986 (1989).

NATURE OF CASE: Proceeding for modification of divorce judgment.

NOTES:

FACT SUMMARY: Cherry Bayliss (P) sought to have her ex-husband (D) contribute to their son's college costs.

CONCISE RULE OF LAW: Alabama trial courts may order divorcing parents to provide for the college educations of their children.

FACTS: Cherry Bayliss (P) and John Bayliss (D) were divorced when their son Patrick was 12 years old. Six years later, Cherry (P) filed a petition to modify the divorce judgment to require that John (D) help pay for Patrick's college costs. Cherry (P) asserted that John (D) had refused to pay although he had ample financial resources.

ISSUE: May Alabama trial courts order divorcing parents to provide for the college educations of their children?

HOLDING AND DECISION: (Houston, J.) Yes. Alabama trial courts may order divorcing parents to provide for the college educations of their children. Alabama law provides that the courts may give custody and education to either parent upon granting a divorce. Since 1926, state courts have increasingly determined that college education is a legally necessary expense. Since 1983, Alabama courts have acknowledged that certain necessary support may be required for children who have reached 18 years old, the age of majority. It is a reasonable interpretation of "children" to include offspring over the age of majority. In the present case, the trial court may order John Bayliss (D) to pay Patrick's college costs if it appears that he probably would assist if there had been no divorce. Therefore, the case is remanded to make this determination.

EDITOR'S ANALYSIS: States are split on this issue. At least 19 states agree with Alabama's position. On the other hand, some courts have ruled that when children reach the age of majority, all support duties are ended. See, e.g., Dowling v. Dowling, 679 P.2d 165 (Colo. 1987).

COTE v. COTE
Md. Ct. Spec. App., 599 A.2d 869 (1992).

NATURE OF CASE: Appeal from an injunction issued in dissolution action.

FACT SUMMARY: Charles Cote (P) claimed that an order barring him from the marital home during a pending divorce constituted a taking requiring compensation.

CONCISE RULE OF LAW: An order barring one spouse from the marital home does not constitute a taking of property requiring just compensation.

FACTS: Paula Cote (D) and Charles Cote (P) married in 1966. In 1990 the Cotes had a physical altercation. Charles (P) filed for divorce, and Paula (D) filed a petition for a restraining order. The trial court issued an order barring Charles (P) from entering the family home. Charles (P) argued that this order constitutes an illegal taking of property without just compensation. Charles (P) appealed the injunction barring his entry into the home.

ISSUE: Does an order barring one spouse from the marital home constitute a taking requiring government compensation?

HOLDING AND DECISION: (Bell, J.) No. An order barring one spouse from the marital home does not constitute a taking of property requiring just compensation. Three elements must be established in order to demonstrate a government taking. It must be 1) a state action; 2) that affects a property interest; and 3) deprives the owner of all beneficial use of the property. An order barring a person from a home affects a property interest even though the owner does not lose title to the property. Where an owner obtains some tangible benefits in the property, there is no taking. In the present case, Charles (P) does not have to provide Paula (D) with an alternative residence because he is letting her remain in the house. Thus, Charles (P) is receiving some tangible benefits from the house and has not lost all beneficial use of his property. Therefore, there is no taking and the injunction may remain.

EDITOR'S ANALYSIS: The court followed the analysis of the earlier decision of Pitsenberger v. Pitsenberger, 410 A.2d 1052 (1980), regarding the accepted method to use to determine a taking question. In that case, minor children were involved, but the Cote court found that fact did not create a meaningful distinction.

[For more information on takings by government, see Casenote Law Outline on Property, Chapter 11, § I, Eminent Domain.]

O'BRIEN v. O'BRIEN
N.Y. Ct. of App., 66 N.Y.2d 576 (1985).

NATURE OF CASE: Review of property division ordered pursuant to marital dissolution.

FACT SUMMARY: The divorcing wife (D) of Dr. O'Brien (P) claimed a marital property interest in his medical license.

CONCISE RULE OF LAW: A professional license may constitute marital property.

FACTS: While the O'Briens were married, the husband (P) attended medical school full-time. Ms. O'Brien (D) worked and contributed most of the funds to maintain the household and the husband's (P) studies. Not long after Dr. O'Brien (P) obtained his license to practice, he filed for divorce. The trial court held Dr. O'Brien's (P) license to be marital property and awarded Ms. O'Brien (D) 40% of the present value of Dr. O'Brien's (P) expected lifetime earnings. The appellate division reversed, holding that a professional license was not marital property. Ms. O'Brien (D) appealed.

ISSUE: May a professional license constitute marital property?

HOLDING AND DECISION: (Simons, J.) Yes. A professional license may constitute marital property. New York's Equitable Distribution Law is not bound by traditional concepts of property. It provides that spouses have an equitable claim to things of value arising out of the marital relationship, whether or not such things of value fit into the common law notion of property. In fact, one of the reasons for the adoption of the law was the realization that application of traditional property concepts had led to inequities upon dissolution of a marriage. Here, Dr. O'Brien's (P) professional license constitutes the most valuable marital asset, and an equitable division of its value was proper. Reversed.

CONCURRENCE: (Meyer, J.) A court needs to be able to retain jurisdiction to modify an award of this nature in the event that circumstances force the licensed former spouse into a less remunerative situation than originally anticipated.

EDITOR'S ANALYSIS: Whether a professional license is "property" has been a hotly debated topic during the 1980s. This is because it has some attributes of traditional property but not all. Like property, it has value that can be measured. Unlike property, it cannot be alienated and becomes nonexistent upon the licensee's death or loss of license.

NOTES:

PACIFIC GAMBLE ROBINSON CO. v. LAPP
Wash. Sup. Ct., 622 P.2d 850 (1980).

NATURE OF CASE: Appeal from dismissal of judgment in an action to collect a business debt incurred while spouses were domiciled in a foreign, noncommunity state.

FACT SUMMARY: After the Lapps (D) moved from a noncommunity property state to a community property state, Pacific Gamble (P) brought this action to recover the balance due and owing on a promissory note that Conrad Lapp (D) had executed in relation to a business that was his sole property.

CONCISE RULE OF LAW: The validity and effect of a contract are governed by the law of the state having the most significant relationship with the contract.

FACTS: Before the Lapps (D) were married, Conrad Lapp (D) acquired a Colorado corporation. The Lapps (D), Colorado residents, later married. In Colorado, a noncommunity property state, the company remained Mr. Lapp's (D) sole property. When the company experienced severe financial difficulty, Pacific Gamble (P) agreed to continue to supply produce if Lapp (D) signed a promissory note on which he would be personally liable, along with the company. Mr. Lapp's (D) earnings and property alone were subject to that debt. Mrs. Lapp (D) did not sign the note. After the company and Lapp (D) defaulted on the note, the Lapps (D) moved to Washington, a community property state. Pacific Gamble (P) brought this action against the company, Conrad Lapp (D) individually, and the Lapp (D) marital community to recover the balance due on the note. The lower court ruled that the Lapps' (D) community property was protected from the debt, and Pacific Gamble (P) appealed.

ISSUE: Are the validity and effect of a contract governed by the law of the state having the most significant relationship with the contract?

HOLDING AND DECISION: (Williams, J.) Yes. The validity and effect of a contract are governed by the law of the state having the most significant relationship with the contract. It is plain that Colorado has numerous governmental interests in this transaction. It occurred in Colorado, Pacific Gamble (P) was doing business in Colorado, and the Lapps (D) were domiciled in Colorado at the time of the execution of the note, which was signed in Colorado by Mr. Lapp (D) individually and on behalf of a Colorado corporation. Moreover, both parties apparently contemplated that all performance was to be in Colorado. In Colorado, all property of the Lapps (D) would be subject to Mr. Lapp's (D) debt to Pacific Gamble (P), except Mrs. Lapp's (D) separate property, including her earnings. The same property subject to payment of a debt in Colorado is likewise subject to payment of the debt in Washington, notwithstanding such property is characterized as "community" under Washington law. Mr. Lapp's (D) noncommunity debt may thus be satisfied from the marital community's property.

DISSENT: (Horowitz, J.) This state's public policy is to protect the community marital property against a debt not incurred for its benefit.

Washington's interest in this decision and its impact on our citizens' marital property rights is far greater than any continuing interest by Colorado in the remedy available for breach of a transitory contract sued upon in this state. Thus, Washington is the state with the most significant relationship to the single issue of the source of funds available for contract damages, and Mr. Lapp's (D) noncommunity debt cannot be satisfied from the marital community's property.

EDITOR'S ANALYSIS: Pacific Gamble's (P) principal place of business was in Washington. But the company was doing business in Colorado and had willingly subjected itself to Colorado law by entering into a contract with a Colorado resident and could justifiably assume that the Colorado law would likewise apply to the company's business debtor. According to the court, a creditor need not anticipate that a debtor may avoid a debt by moving to any of the 49 other states.

NOTES:

WATTS v. WATTS
Wis. Sup. Ct., 405 N.W.2d 303 (1987).

NATURE OF CASE: Appeal in a breach of contract action by an unmarried cohabitant to obtain an equal share in the wealth accumulated during the relationship.

FACT SUMMARY: When the nonmarital cohabitation of Sue Ann Evans Watts (P) and James Watts (D) ended after a twelve year relationship that produced two children, Sue Ann (P) brought suit to share equally in the wealth accumulated during the relationship through the joint efforts of both parties.

CONCISE RULE OF LAW: An unmarried cohabitant may assert a contract claim against the other cohabitant so long as the claim is independent of the sexual relationship and is supported by separate consideration.

FACTS: Sue Ann Evans (P) and James Watts (D) lived together for twelve years, holding themselves out to the public as husband and wife. During that time, Sue Ann (P) assumed James's (D) surname and gave birth to two children, who also assumed James's (D) surname. Sue Ann (P) contributed child care and homemaking services and also assisted James (D) in his business, later starting a business of her own. After twelve years, Sue Ann (P) moved from their home. Subsequently, James (D) barred Sue Ann (P) from returning to her business. Sue Ann (P) filed suit, alleging that she and James (D) had a contract to share equally in the wealth accumulated through their joint efforts and that James (D) would be unjustly enriched if he were allowed to retain the benefit of services Sue Ann (P) provided during the relationship.

ISSUE: May an unmarried cohabitant assert a contract claim against the other cohabitant so long as the claim is independent of the sexual relationship and is supported by separate consideration?

HOLDING AND DECISION: (Abrahamson, J.) Yes. An unmarried cohabitant may assert a contract claim against the other cohabitant so long as the claim is independent of the sexual relationship and is supported by separate consideration. Sue Ann (P) has pleaded the facts necessary to state a claim for damages resulting from James's (D) breach of an express or an implied-in-fact contract to share the property accumulated through the efforts of both parties during their relationship. Moreover, if Sue Ann (P) can prove the elements of unjust enrichment to the satisfaction of the circuit court, she will be entitled to demonstrate that a constructive trust should be imposed as a remedy. Finally, Sue Ann (P) has alleged sufficient facts to state a claim for partition of all property accumulated during the relationship.

EDITOR'S ANALYSIS: State courts have taken three different approaches to the problem illustrated in this case. First, in Hewitt v. Hewitt, 394 N.E.2d 1204 (Ill. 1979), the Illinois Supreme Court denied any remedy to unmarried cohabitants. Second, in Marvin v. Marvin, 557 P.2d 106 (Cal. 1976), the California Supreme Court allowed for enforcement of a written or oral agreement between the parties.

Finally, Pickens v. Pickens, 490 So. 2d 872 (Miss. 1986), provided for property distribution between unmarried cohabitants due to the creation of a relationship akin to a partnership.

NOTES:

BOROUGH OF GLASSBORO v. VALLOROSI
N.J. Sup. Ct., 568 A.2d 888 (1990).

NATURE OF CASE: Appeal from a judgment in an action to enjoin group occupancy of a house in an area zoned for single family residences.

FACT SUMMARY: When ten college students occupied a single family residence, the Borough (P) brought suit, alleging that the group did not constitute a "family" as defined in the Borough's (P) zoning ordinance.

CONCISE RULE OF LAW: A group of college students living together may constitute the functional equivalent of a traditional family unit.

FACTS: The Borough (P) adopted a zoning ordinance aimed at preventing groups of unrelated college students from living together in the Borough's (P) residential districts. Vallorosi (D) purchased a house located in the restricted residential zone to provide a college home for her brother Peter and nine of his college friends. All ten students shared the one large kitchen, often ate meals together in small groups, cooked for each other, and generally shared the household chores, grocery shopping, and yard work. A common checking account paid for food and other bills. They shared the use of a telephone. The Borough (P) sought an injunction against the occupancy of the house by the students on the ground that they did not constitute a "family" or its functional equivalent as specified in the ordinance. The trial court found that the occupancy by the ten college students constituted the functional equivalent of a traditional family unit. The Borough (P) appealed.

ISSUE: May a group of college students living together constitute the functional equivalent of a traditional family unit?

HOLDING AND DECISION: (Per curiam) Yes. A group of college students living together may constitute the functional equivalent of a traditional family unit. The uncontradicted testimony reflects a plan by ten sophomore college students to live together for three years under conditions that correspond substantially to the ordinance's requirement of a "stable and permanent living unit." The students ate together, shared household chores, and paid expenses from a common fund. Moreover, they testified to their intention to remain in the house throughout college, and there was no significant evidence of defections up to the time of trial. On these facts, there is no quarrel with the trial court's conclusion that the occupancy at issue here "shows stability, permanency, and can be described as the functional equivalent of a family." Affirmed.

EDITOR'S ANALYSIS: Other ordinances limiting the term "family" to persons related by blood, marriage, or adoption have failed. According to the Vallorosi court, such an ordinance so narrowly delimits the persons who may occupy a single family dwelling as to prohibit numerous potential occupants who pose no threat to the style of family living sought to be preserved. The standard for determining whether a use qualifies as a single housekeeping unit must be functional, and hence is capable of being met by either related or unrelated persons.

[For more information on "family" rights as fundamental, see Casenote Law Outline on Property, Chapter 12, § I, The United States Constitution.]

NOTES:

NOTES

CHAPTER 11
BUSINESS PROPERTY

QUICK REFERENCE RULES OF LAW

1. **Partnerships.** Joint adventurers, like copartners, owe to one another, while the enterprise continues, an undivided loyalty. (Meinhard v. Salmon)

2. **Franchises.** A franchisor who in good faith and for a bona fide reason terminates a franchise for any reason other than the franchisee's substantial breach of its obligations is liable to the franchisee for the loss incurred thereby. (Westfield Centre Services, Inc. v. Cities Service Oil Co.)

3. **Corporations: Stakeholders and Corporate Property.** There is no legally recognizable property right in a job that has been held for something approaching a lifetime. (Local 1330, United Steel Workers of America v. United States Steel Corp.)

NOTES

MEINHARD v. SALMON
N.Y. Ct. App., 164 N.E. 545 (1928).

NATURE OF CASE: Appeal from judgment in an action concerning a joint venture in the lease of certain property.

FACT SUMMARY: When Salmon (D) entered into a new lease shortly before his venture with Meinhard (P) was to end without telling Meinhard (P) about the new lease, Meinhard (P) brought suit to have that lease held in trust as an asset of the venture.

CONCISE RULE OF LAW: Joint adventurers, like copartners, owe to one another, while the enterprise continues, an undivided loyalty.

FACTS: Salmon (D) and Meinhard (P) formed a joint venture for the purpose of leasing certain property for a term of twenty years. Meinhard (P) put up half of the money needed to convert the property from a hotel to use as shops and offices. Salmon (D) was to have sole power to manage, lease, underlet and operate the building. Four months before the end of the lease, Salmon (D) entered into a new agreement, for a maximum of 80 years, with the owner of the reversionary interest in the property. Salmon (D) entered into this agreement individually, without telling Meinhard (P) anything about it. When Meinhard (P) learned of the project, he demanded that the new lease signed by Salmon (D) be held in trust as an asset of the venture. When the demand was refused, Meinhard (P) brought this suit.

ISSUE: Do joint adventurers, like copartners, owe to one another, while the enterprise continues, an undivided loyalty?

HOLDING AND DECISION: (Cardozo, J.) Yes. Joint adventurers, like copartners, owe to one another, while the enterprise continues, an undivided loyalty. Salmon (D) was a managing coadventurer. For him and for those like him, the rule of undivided loyalty is relentless and supreme. The trouble with Salmon's (D) conduct is that he excluded his coadventurer from any chance to compete and from any chance to enjoy the opportunity for benefit that had come to him because of his own diligence. Here, the subject-matter of the new lease was an extension and enlargement of the subject-matter of the old one. A managing coadventurer appropriating the benefit of such a lease without warning to his partner might fairly expect that such conduct would be considered underhanded. Meinhard's (P) equitable interest is to be measured by the value of half of the entire lease, reduced to such an extent as may be necessary to preserve to Salmon (D) the power of control and management.

DISSENT: (Andrews, J.) Here, there was no general partnership, merely a joint venture for a limited object, to end at a fixed time. There was no intent to expand it into a far greater undertaking lasting for many years. The new lease, covering additional property, containing many new and unusual terms and conditions, with a possible duration of 80 years, was more nearly the purchase of the reversion interest than the ordinary renewal with which the authorities are concerned. In distributing the profits of the venture, Salmon (D) has done all he promised to do for Meinhard's (P) undertaking.

EDITOR'S ANALYSIS: Many forms of conduct that would be deemed permissible in a workaday world for those acting at arm's length, are forbidden to those bound by fiduciary ties. A trustee is held to something stricter than the morals of the marketplace. Here, both the majority and dissenting opinions agreed that a partner may not for his own benefit secretly take a renewal of a firm lease to himself. The differing outcome in the two opinions was due to their characterization of the new lease. Where Cardozo saw it as a continuation of the existing lease, Andrews saw it as a good-faith purchase of the reversion interest.

NOTES:

WESTFIELD CENTRE SERVICE, INC. v.
CITIES SERVICE OIL CO.
N.J. Sup. Ct., 432 A.2d 48 (1981).

NOTES:

NATURE OF CASE: Appeal from judgment for franchisee in an action to recover damages for the loss of a franchise.

FACT SUMMARY: When Cities Service (D) notified Westfield Centre (P) that Cities Service (D) intended to sell the gas station property for which Westfield Centre (P) was the franchisee, Westfield Centre (P) objected to the proposed sale, filing suit to enjoin the sale and seeking damages.

CONCISE RULE OF LAW: A franchisor who in good faith and for a bona fide reason terminates a franchise for any reason other than the franchisee's substantial breach of its obligations is liable to the franchisee for the loss incurred thereby.

FACTS: Galligan (P), through Westfield Centre Service, Inc. (P), purchased a gas station that was operated as a franchise of Cities Service (D). The lease term was twelve months, automatically renewable annually, unless either party gave a ninety-day notice of termination. When the agreement was renewed a couple of years later, it included an additional provision allowing Cities Service (D) to terminate the lease upon thirty days' prior written notice. Cities Service (D) later notified Westfield Centre (P) that the station was to be sold, giving Westfield Centre (P) thirty days in which to purchase the property, after which it would be placed for sale on the open market. Westfield Centre (P) objected to the proposed sale, bringing suit for an injunction and for compensatory and punitive damages.

ISSUE: Is a franchisor who, in good faith and for a bona fide reason, terminates a franchise for any reason other than the franchisee's substantial breach of its obligations liable to the franchisee for the loss incurred thereby?

HOLDING AND DECISION: (Schreiber, J.) Yes. A franchisor who, in good faith and for a bona fide reason, terminates a franchise for any reason other than the franchisee's substantial breach of its obligations is liable to the franchisee for the loss incurred thereby. The damages should be measured in terms of the actual or reasonable value of the franchisee's business when the franchisor cuts off the franchise. Reasonable value would be that price upon which the willing parties, buyer and seller, would agree for the sale of the franchisee's business as a going concern. Here, Cities Service (D) had a bona fide economic reason for terminating the franchise, but is still liable to Westfield Centre (P) for the reasonable value of the business less the amount realizable on liquidation.

EDITOR'S ANALYSIS: Disparity in the bargaining power of the parties has led to some unconscionable provisions in franchise agreements. Laws enacted by state legislatures, such as the New Jersey Franchise Practices Act, have addressed the problem of inequality. In applying such statutes, state courts have adopted differing interpretations of the "good cause" language in such statutes.

LOCAL 1330, UNITED STEEL WORKERS OF AMERICA v. UNITED STATES STEEL CORP.

631 F.2d 1264 (6th Cir. 1980).

NATURE OF CASE: Appeal from a judgment in an action seeking to enjoin the closing of a business.

FACT SUMMARY: United Steel Workers of America (P) sought to enjoin U.S. Steel's (D) plan to close two large steel mills that it had operated in Youngstown, Ohio, since the turn of the century.

CONCISE RULE OF LAW: There is no legally recognizable property right in a job that has been held for something approaching a lifetime.

FACTS: U.S. Steel Corp. (D) announced its intention, due to unprofitability, to close two large steel mills that it had operated in Youngstown, Ohio, since the turn of the century. The mills were a dominant factor in the lives of their thousands of employees and their families, and in the life of the city itself. The United Steel Workers of America (P) brought suit, asking the federal courts to order U.S. Steel Corp. (D) to keep the two plants at issue in operation. Alternatively, it sought an injunction to require U.S. Steel (D) to sell the two plants to the Union (P) under a tentative plan of purchase and operation by a community corporation and to restrain the piecemeal sale or dismantling of the plants until such a proposal could be brought to fruition. The district court, after originally restraining the corporation from ceasing operations, held that the plants had become unprofitable, denying all relief. This appeal followed.

ISSUE: Is there a legally recognizable property right in a job that has been held for something approaching a lifetime?

HOLDING AND DECISION: (Edwards, J.) No. There is no legally recognizable property right in a job that has been held for something approaching a lifetime. This court dealt with this problem in Charland v. Norge Division, Borg-Warner Corp., 407 F.2d 1062 (6th Cir. 1969), in which we stated that thus far, federal law has sought to protect the human values called to our attention by means of such legislation as unemployment compensation and social security laws. These statutes afford limited financial protection to the individual worker, but they assume his loss of employment. Formulation of public policy on the great issues involved in plant closings and removals is clearly the responsibility of the legislatures of the states or of the Congress of the United States. There is no basis for judicial relief as to this cause of action. Affirmed.

EDITOR'S ANALYSIS: The problem of plant closing and plant removal from one section of the country to another is by no means new in American history. The former mill towns of New England are monuments to the migration of textile manufacturers to the South, without hindrance from the Congress of the United States, from the legislatures of the states concerned, or from the courts of the land. Here, the Steel Workers (P) failed to point to any authority for their claim that a property right had arisen from the long-established relation between the community and the Corporation (D).

NOTES:

CHAPTER 12
PROPERTY AND SOVEREIGNTY

QUICK REFERENCE RULES OF LAW

1. **Physical Invasions.** A state may constitutionally mandate that a private property owner allow political activity on his property. (PruneYard Shopping Center v. Robins)

   [For more information on the law of takings, see Casenote Law Outline on Property, Chapter 11, § I, Eminent Domain.]

2. **Physical Invasions.** States have broad power to regulate housing conditions in general and the landlord-tenant relationship in particular without paying compensation for all economic injuries that such regulation entails. (Yee v. City of Escondido)

   [For more information on the "just compensation" requirement, see Casenote Law Outline on Property, Chapter 11, § I, Eminent Domain.]

3. **Conceptual Severance: Seizures of Central Strands in the Bundle of Property Rights.** Complete abolition of both the descent and devise of a particular class of property may be a taking. (Hodel v. Irving)

   [For more information on inverse condemnation, see Casenote Law Outline on Property, Chapter 11, § II, Inverse Condemnation.]

4. **Burdens of Citizenship versus Unfair Sacrifices for the Public Good.** The state does not exceed its constitutional powers by deciding upon the destruction of one class of property in order to save another which, in the judgment of the legislature, is of greater value to the public. (Miller v. Schoene)

   [For more information on the power of eminent domain, see Casenote Law Outline on Property, Chapter 11, § I, Eminent Domain.]

5. **Burdens of Citizenship versus Unfair Sacrifices for the Public Good.** The state must compensate a landowner when a regulatory action denies the owner economically viable use of the land, unless the prohibited use constitutes a nuisance. (Lucas v. South Carolina Coastal Council)

   [For more information on regulatory takings, see Casenote Law Outline on Property, Chapter 11, § II, Inverse Condemnation.]

6. **Exactions and Linkage Requirements.** The degree of exactions demanded by government permit conditions on property must be roughly proportionate to the projected impact of a proposed development. (Dolan v. City of Tigard)

   [For more information on the proportionality test, see Casenote Law Outline on Property, Chapter 11, § II, Inverse Condemnation.]

7. **Just Compensation.** When a leasehold is condemned, a lessee with no right of renewal is entitled to receive as compensation the market value of its improvements without regard to the remaining term of the lease. (Almota Farmers Elevator & Warehouse v. United States)

   [For more information on the "just compensation" requirement, see Casenote Law Outline on Property, Chapter 11, § I, Eminent Domain.]

8. **Just Compensation.** An owner is entitled to receive what a willing buyer would pay in cash to a willing seller at the time of the taking. (United States v. 564.54 Acres of Land, More or Less)

   [For more information on the concept of fair market value, see Casenote Law Outline on Property, Chapter 11, § I, Eminent Domain.]

9. **Public Use.** The Public Use Clause of the Fifth Amendment does not proscribe the exercise of eminent domain power where such is reasonably related to a conceivable public purpose. (Hawaii Housing Authority v. Midkiff)

   [For more information on the "public use" requirement, see Casenote Law Outline on Property, Chapter 11, § I, Eminent Domain.]

10. **Public Use.** Condemnation of property pursuant to a public purpose is valid. (Poletown Neighborhood Council v. City of Detroit)

   [For more information on condemnation for a public purpose, see Casenote Law Outline on Property, Chapter 11, § I, Eminent Domain.]

11. **Talking Doctrine.** Where Congress makes a good faith effort to give Native Americans the full value of their land and thus merely transmutes the property from land to money, there is no taking. (United States v. Sioux Nation of Indians)

   [For more information on requirement of a taking, see Casenote Law Outline on Property, Chapter 11, § I, Eminent Domain.]

PRUNEYARD SHOPPING CENTER v. ROBINS
447 U.S. 74 (1980).

NATURE OF CASE: Appeal from decision permitting politically oriented solicitation on private property.

FACT SUMMARY: PruneYard Shopping Center (D) contended that a California decision mandating that it permit political activity on its property violated the Fifth Amendment.

CONCISE RULE OF LAW: A state may constitutionally mandate that a private property owner allow political activity on his property.

FACTS: Robins (P) and others handed out political materials on retail property owned by PruneYard Shopping Center, Inc. (D). The Center (D) removed them from the property. Robins (P) filed suit, contending that he had a constitutional right to distribute his literature there. The California Supreme Court ruled that, under the California constitution, such a right existed. PruneYard (D) appealed, contending that this ruling deprived it of its property rights, in contravention of the Fifth and Fourteenth Amendments.

ISSUE: May a state constitutionally mandate that a private property owner allow political activity on his property?

HOLDING AND DECISION: (Rehnquist, J.) Yes. A state may mandate that a private property owner allow political activity on his property without violating the Fifth and Fourteenth Amendments. It is true that the right to exclude others is one of the inherent elements of property rights, so long as the property's value is not so diminished that the owner has suffered a "taking." Here, there is no evidence that PruneYard (D) has suffered any diminution in property value, so no taking has occurred. Affirmed.

CONCURRENCE: (Blackmun, J.) The federal government may be possessed of authority to define what is property.

CONCURRENCE: (Marshall, J.) The rule adopted by the California Supreme Court should be adopted by this Court as well.

CONCURRENCE: (Powell, J.) The state may not compel a person to affirm a belief he does not hold. A property owner may be faced with speakers who wish to use his premises as a platform for views that he finds morally repugnant. The strong emotions evoked by speech in such situations may virtually compel the proprietor to respond. However, the record gives no indication that the customers of this vast center would be likely to assume that Robins's (P) limited speech activity expressed the views of the Pruneyard (D) or of its owner.

EDITOR'S ANALYSIS: The federal Constitution creates a certain floor, in terms of rights, that states may not go below. States are free to exceed the federal Constitution in terms of rights, if they so choose. The underlying California Supreme Court case here is an example.

That court created a freedom-of-expression right the U.S. Supreme Court does not recognize.

[For more information on the law of takings, see Casenote Law Outline on Property, Chapter 11, § I, Eminent Domain.]

NOTES:

YEE v. CITY OF ESCONDIDO
112 S. Ct. 1522 (1992).

NATURE OF CASE: Appeal from a defense judgment in an action for damages resulting from a regulatory taking.

FACT SUMMARY: The Yees (P), owners of two mobile-home parks, brought this suit for damages alleging that a state law, in conjunction with a local rent control ordinance, deprived them of all use and occupancy of their real property amounting to a physical taking of that property.

CONCISE RULE OF LAW: States have broad power to regulate housing conditions in general and the landlord-tenant relationship in particular without paying compensation for all economic injuries that such regulation entails.

FACTS: The Yees (P) owned two mobile-home parks in Escondido, California. The state enacted a Mobilehome Residency Law, limiting the bases upon which a park owner may terminate a mobile home owner's tenancy. While a rental agreement was in effect, the park owner generally could not require the removal of a mobile home when it was sold. This law was enacted to protect mobile home owners because mobile homes are largely immobile as a practical matter. After Escondido (D) enacted a mobile home rent control ordinance, the Yees (P) brought suit, alleging that the ordinance, in conjunction with the state's Mobilehome Residency Law, deprived them of all use and occupancy of their real property, amounting to a physical occupation of that property. They requested damages, a declaration that the ordinance was unconstitutional, and an injunction barring its enforcement.

ISSUE: Do states have broad power to regulate housing conditions in general and the landlord-tenant relationship in particular without paying compensation for all economic injuries that such regulation entails?

HOLDING AND DECISION: (O'Connor, J.) Yes. States have broad power to regulate housing conditions in general and the landlord-tenant relationship in particular without paying compensation for all economic injuries that such regulation entails. No government has required any physical invasion of the Yees's (P) property. On their face, the state and local laws at issue here merely regulate the Yees's (P) use of their land by regulating the relationship between landlord and tenant. Ordinary rent control often transfers wealth from landlords to tenants by reducing the landlords' income and the tenants' monthly payments. The ordinance does not require the Yees (P) to submit to the physical occupation of their land. Mere regulation of an owner's use of his or her property does not amount to a per se taking.

EDITOR'S ANALYSIS: The Takings Clause of the Fifth Amendment to the U.S. Constitution provides: "[N]or shall private property be taken for public use without just compensation." Where the government authorizes a physical occupation of property, the Takings Clause generally requires compensation. But where the use of property is regulated, compensation is required only if the regulation has unfairly singled out the property owner to bear a burden that should be borne by the public as a whole.

[For more information on the "just compensation" requirement, see Casenote Law Outline on Property, Chapter 11, § I, Eminent Domain.]

NOTES:

HODEL v. IRVING
481 U.S. 704 (1987).

NATURE OF CASE: Appeal from judgment finding unconstitutional a regulation abolishing the descent and devise of certain lands held by Native Americans.

FACT SUMMARY: Irving (P) and two other members of the Oglala Sioux Tribe filed this suit, alleging that § 207 of the Indian Land Consolidation Act, which provided that certain individually held property could escheat to the tribe, resulted in a taking of their property without just compensation.

CONCISE RULE OF LAW: Complete abolition of both the descent and devise of a particular class of property may be a taking.

FACTS: In an attempt to ameliorate the problem of fractionated ownership of Native American lands, Congress passed the Indian Land Consolidation Act of 1983. Section 207 of that Act provided that certain lands would escheat to the tribe under specified conditions. Congress made no provision for the payment of compensation to the owners of such land. Irving (P) and two other members of the Oglala Sioux Tribe filed suit, claiming that § 207 resulted in a taking of property without just compensation in violation of the Fifth Amendment. They were, or represented, heirs or devisees of members of the Tribe who died after the statute was signed into law. Their four decedents died intestate, owning fractional interests subject to the provisions of § 207. But for § 207, their property would have passed to Irving (P) and the others; instead, it went by escheat to the Tribe. This appeal followed a lower court ruling in favor of Irving (P) and the others.

ISSUE: May complete abolition of both the descent and devise of a particular class of property be a taking?

HOLDING AND DECISION: (O'Connor, J.) Yes. Complete abolition of both the descent and devise of a particular class of property may be a taking. The character of the government (D) regulation here is extraordinary, amounting to virtually the abrogation of the right to pass on a certain type of property — the small undivided interest — to one's heirs. Moreover, this statute effectively abolishes both descent and devise of these property interests even when the passing of the property to the heir might result in consolidation of property. Since the escheatable interests are not de minimis, and the availability of inter vivos transfer does not obviate the need for descent and devise, a total abrogation of these rights cannot be upheld. Even the United States (D) concedes that total abrogation of the right to pass property is unprecedented and likely unconstitutional. While there is little doubt that the extreme fractionation of Indian lands is a serious public problem, this regulation goes too far. Accordingly, the judgment of the court of appeals is affirmed.

CONCURRENCE: (Brennan, Jr., J.) Nothing in today's opinion would limit Andrus v. Allard, 444 U.S. 51 (1979), to its facts. The unique negotiations giving rise to the property rights and expectations at issue here make this case the unusual one.

CONCURRENCE: (Scalia, J.) The present statute, insofar as concerns the balance between rights taken and rights left untouched, is indistinguishable from the statute that was at issue in Andrus v. Allard, 444 U.S. 51 (1979). Because that comparison is determinative of whether there has been a taking, in finding a taking today, our decision effectively limits Allard to its facts.

CONCURRENCE: (Stevens, J.) Section 207 deprived decedents of due process of law by failing to provide an adequate "grace period" in which they could arrange for the consolidation of fractional interests in order to avoid abandonment. With respect to the decedents of Irving (P) and the others, "the time allowed is manifestly so insufficient that the statute becomes a denial of justice."

EDITOR'S ANALYSIS: Despite its decision, the Court reaffirmed the continuing vitality of the long line of case recognizing the broad authority of the states, and where appropriate, of the United States to adjust the rules governing the descent and devise of property without implicating the guarantees of the Just Compensation Clause. Andrus v. Allard, 444 U.S. 51 (1979), upheld abrogation of the right to sell endangered eagles' parts as necessary to an environmental protection regulatory scheme. It is interesting to note that Brennan's and Scalia's concurring opinions came to the opposite conclusions as to whether the instant decision limited the decision in Allard to its facts.

[For more information on inverse condemnation, see Casenote Law Outline on Property, Chapter 11, § II, Inverse Condemnation.]

NOTES:

MILLER v. SCHOENE
276 U.S. 272 (1928).

NATURE OF CASE: Appeal from condemnation action.

FACT SUMMARY: Under the authority of a Virginia (P) statute, a state official ordered the plaintiff in error to cut down certain infected cedar trees.

CONCISE RULE OF LAW: The state does not exceed its constitutional powers by deciding upon the destruction of one class of property in order to save another which, in the judgment of the legislature, is of greater value to the public.

FACTS: A Virginia (P) statute provided for the condemnation and destruction of cedar trees which were determined to be infected with cedar rust, a communicable plant disease, and which were located within a certain radius of an apple orchard. The statute allowed compensation of $100 to the owner of the trees to cover removal expense and permitted him to use the timber, but it provided no compensation for loss of the ornamental value of the trees or decrease in real estate value. The plaintiff in error was ordered to remove his cedars under the terms of the statute and appealed the order to the county circuit court. Evidence presented by Virginia (P) showed that cedar rust was communicable between cedars and apple trees and that the commercial value of apple trees was far greater than that of cedars. [The circuit court, the Supreme Court of Appeals, the state entomologist, and the plaintiff in error appealed to the U.S. Supreme Court.]

ISSUE: May a state constitutionally decide upon the destruction of one class of property in order to save another which, in the judgment of the legislature, is of greater value to the public?

HOLDING AND DECISION: (Stone, J.) Yes. The state does not exceed its constitutional powers by deciding upon the destruction of one class of property in order to save another which, in the judgment of the legislature, is of greater value to the public. One of the distinguishing features of the police power as it affects property is the preference of the public interest over the private property interests of the individual. Here, the state was forced to choose between preservation of the cedars and preservation of the nearby apple orchard. Since far greater public interest attached to the preservation of the apple industry, the statute is constitutional.

EDITOR'S ANALYSIS: Although "takings" of private property for public use require just compensation, regulation under the police power does not. A frequent issue arising under the "Taking" Clause is therefore whether the action in fact is a "taking" or is merely an exercise of the police powers. The Court adopted a common approach, balancing public need against private cost. In general, government actions that restrict the use of property which is harmful to others in some way are deemed to be regulatory and do not require compensation. But where the property is needed for some public purpose but is not harmful, there is a "taking" requiring compensation.

[For more information on the power of eminent domain, see Casenote Law Outline on Property, Chapter 11, § I, Eminent Domain.]

NOTES:

LUCAS v. SOUTH CAROLINA COASTAL COUNCIL
112 S.Ct. 2886 (1992).

NATURE OF CASE: Appeal of the denial of a taking claim in action for compensation of property value.

FACT SUMMARY: South Carolina's (D) Beachfront Management Act barred Lucas (P) from erecting homes on two parcels of land near the ocean.

CONCISE RULE OF LAW: The state must compensate a landowner when a regulatory action denies the owner economically viable use of the land, unless the prohibited use constitutes a nuisance.

FACTS: In 1986, Lucas (P) bought two residential lots near the ocean for $975,000. In 1988, South Carolina (D) enacted the Beachfront Management Act, which sought to counteract coastal erosion. The law restricted new development of beachfront areas and barred Lucas (P) from building homes on his lots as he intended. Lucas (P) brought suit contending that the Act was an unconstitutional taking of his property. The trial court ruled that the Act deprived Lucas (P) of any reasonable economic use of the land and was an uncompensated taking. The South Carolina Supreme Court reversed, holding that the regulation was designed to prevent serious public harm and did not constitute a taking. Lucas (P) appealed, and the Supreme Court granted review.

ISSUE: Must the state compensate a landowner when a regulatory action denies an owner economically viable use of the land?

HOLDING AND DECISION: (Scalia, J.) Yes. The state must compensate a landowner when a regulatory action denies an owner economically viable use of his land, unless the prohibited use constitutes a nuisance. Physical intrusions on property must always be compensated. A regulation that denies all economically beneficial and productive uses of land is the equivalent of physical appropriation and must also be compensated under the Takings Clause. The Court has previously acknowledged that regulations that restrict nuisance-like uses of land may provide an exception to the general rule on takings. The court of appeals attempted to distinguish laws that prevented harmful use from those regulations that confer benefits on the public. This distinction should not provide the basis for our determinations because it is impossible to objectively distinguish the two rationales. The better rule is that the government may only restrict uses that are already unlawful under existing nuisance and property laws. South Carolina's (D) Beachfront Management Act deprived Lucas' (P) land of all economically beneficial use and restricted uses which were previously permissible. Therefore, it was an unconstitutional taking. Reversed and remanded.

CONCURRENCE: (Kennedy, J.) The trial court's finding that Lucas' (P) land had been deprived of all beneficial use is highly questionable. Furthermore, the nuisance exception should not be the sole justification for severe restrictions when the state's unique concerns for fragile land systems are involved.

DISSENT: (Blackmun, J.) Lucas (P) may continue to use his land for recreation and camping and retains the right to alienate the land. Therefore, the trial court's ruling is certainly erroneous.

DISSENT: (Stevens, J.) The majority's categorical approach, which attempts to reduce takings to a set formula, does not take into account the complex problems involved in environmental regulation. The determination is properly made by balancing the private and public interests involved.

EDITOR'S ANALYSIS: Justice Souter wrote separately to indicate that he felt the writ of certiorari was improvidently granted because he also thought that the trial court's conclusion as to the value of Lucas' (P) land after the regulation was highly questionable. Souter also indicated that, contrary to Scalia's conclusion, nuisance law should not be the basis of regulatory takings because it focuses on conduct and not on the character of the property.

[For more information on regulatory takings, see Casenote Law Outline on Property, Chapter 11, § II, Inverse Condemnation.]

NOTES:

DOLAN v. CITY OF TIGARD
114 S. Ct. 2309 (1994).

NATURE OF CASE: Appeal from decision on land use permit application.

FACT SUMMARY: The Tigard City Planning Commission (D) imposed conditions on Dolan's (P) permit to redevelop her property.

CONCISE RULE OF LAW: The degree of exactions demanded by government permit conditions on property must be roughly proportionate to the projected impact of a proposed development.

FACTS: Tigard (D) developed a comprehensive land use plan called the Community Development Code (CDC). The CDC included provisions for pedestrian and bicycling pathways in order to cut down on auto traffic, as well as plans to reduce potential flooding. Dolan (P) owned a plumbing and electric supply store which covered 9,700 square feet near a floodplain. Dolan (P) applied to Tigard (D) for a permit to redevelop the site by doubling the size of the store. The City Planning Commission (D) granted the application subject to certain conditions. The Commission (D) required that Dolan (P) dedicate the portion of her property within the floodplain for a storm drainage improvement and that a strip of land adjacent to the floodplain be used as a pedestrian/bicycle pathway. These conditions required the use of approximately 10% of her property. The Commission (D) found that the pathway would reduce the additional traffic the larger store would create and that the anticipated increased storm water flow from the property added to the need to manage the floodplain. Dolan (P) appealed these mandated conditions. The Oregon Supreme Court found that the conditions had an essential nexus to the development and were reasonably related to the impact of the development. Dolan (P) appealed, and the Supreme Court granted review.

ISSUE: Must the degree of exactions demanded by government permit conditions on property be roughly proportionate to the projected impact of a proposed development?

HOLDING AND DECISION: (Rehnquist, C.J.) Yes. The degree of exactions demanded by government permit conditions on property must be roughly proportionate to the projected impact of a proposed development. The Takings Clause of the Fifth Amendment provides that private property shall not be taken for public use without just compensation. However, state and local governments have broad powers to engage in land use planning. Land use regulations do not affect a taking if it substantially advances legitimate state interests and does not deny the owner an economically viable use of his land. The present case differs from land use regulations in that it was an adjudicative decision on an individual parcel of property, and the conditions were not only a limitation on use, but a requirement that a portion of property be deeded to Tigard (D). Thus, courts must look to see if an essential nexus exists between the legitimate state interest asserted and the permit conditions exacted. In the instant case, it is clear that conditions exacted on Dolan (P) have an essential nexus with the legitimate state concerns about flooding and traffic. The standard under the Fifth Amendment for determining whether the degree of exactions demanded bear the required relationship to the projected impact of the development is one of rough proportionality. Requiring Dolan (P) to impose a permanent easement for a pathway on her property would cause her to lose all property rights, despite the interference it might have with her retail store. Therefore, Tigard (D) has not demonstrated this required rough proportionality. Reversed.

DISSENT: (Stevens, J.) The majority ignores the benefits that Dolan (P) would receive as a result of the conditions. Furthermore, the new standard imposed by the Court does not provide local governments with any usable standard by which to judge their actions.

DISSENT: (Souter, J.) The standard used by the majority makes the issues at stake more confusing than necessary. The Court has also placed the burden of producing evidence on Tigard (D), a detour from the usual presumption that a government entity has acted constitutionality.

EDITOR'S ANALYSIS: The issues addressed in this case will likely continue to reach the Supreme Court. The dissents are correct in citing the fact that local governments will have trouble deciding whether their zoning rules and permit conditions are constitutional. Recently, many cities have required that developers of new construction provide low-income housing or child care facilities. The Ninth Circuit upheld such regulations before this case was decided.

[For more information on the proportionality test, see Casenote Law Outline on Property, Chapter 11, § II, Inverse Condemnation.]

NOTES:

ALMOTA FARMERS ELEVATOR & WAREHOUSE CO. v. UNITED STATES
409 U.S. 470 (1973).

NATURE OF CASE: Eminent domain proceeding.

FACT SUMMARY: Almota Farmers (D), long-term lessee of land being condemned, sought compensation based on fair market value of its buildings and equipment in place.

CONCISE RULE OF LAW: When a leasehold is condemned, a lessee with no right of renewal is entitled to receive as compensation the market value of its improvements without regard to the remaining term of the lease.

FACTS: Almota Farmers Elevator (D) leased land adjacent to railroad tracks for many years, constructing a number of buildings and other improvements on the land. With 7° years to run in its current lease, the Government (P) brought eminent domain proceedings to acquire Almota's (D) interest. In district court, the Government (P) maintained that just compensation should be "the fair market value of the legal rights possessed by [Almota] by virtue of the lease as of the date of `taking' and that there should be no compensation for additional value based on the expectation that the lease would be renewed." Almota (D) contended that its compensation should be the fair market value of the leasehold. The crux of the difference lay in the valuation that should be placed on the improvements. The Government (P) would offer compensation only for the loss of use of the improvements over the remaining 7° years of the lease, leaving salvage value only to Almota (D). Almota (D) maintained that it should receive what a buyer would pay for the lease with the improvements since he would expect the lease to be renewed and to have continued use of the improvements in place. The district court found for Almota (D), but the court of appeals reversed.

ISSUE: Upon condemnation of a leasehold, is a lessee with no right of renewal entitled to receive as compensation the market value of its improvements without regard to the remaining term of the lease?

HOLDING AND DECISION: (Stewart, J.) Yes. When a leasehold is condemned, a lessee with no right of renewal is entitled to receive as compensation the market value of its improvements without regard to the remaining term of the lease because of the expectancy that the lease would have been renewed. The Fifth Amendment requires that the owners of property taken for public use should receive just compensation. That is, the owner must be put in the same monetary position he would have been in if the property had not been condemned. That position is determined by "market value," what a willing buyer would pay in cash to a willing seller. By failing to value the improvements over their lifetime, taking into account the possibility of renewal of the lease, the court of appeals did not value the leasehold at market value. The likelihood is that the lease would be renewed and that the improvements would have continued useful life which ought to be compensated. Here, Almota (D) had held the lease over a long period and had every expectation of renewing the lease after the expiration of the current lease. It, therefore, could have sold the lease to a buyer, and it should receive the compensation that that buyer would be willing to pay it. Reversed.

CONCURRENCE: (Powell, J.) The Government (P) must pay the market price for the property interest before the public project is undertaken. Neither the Government (P) nor the other party may take advantage of a change in market price attributable to the project itself.

DISSENT: (Rehnquist, J.) It has been well established that destruction of property value by itself does not create a right to compensation; rather, the right arises only where there is an actual taking. However, there cannot be an actual taking of a mere expectancy, as here, and the Court is wrong to base its valuation of the property interest in part on an expectancy which falls short of a property interest.

EDITOR'S ANALYSIS: This case and United States v. Fuller, 409 U.S. 488 (1973), illustrate some of the problems that have arisen in determining "just compensation" for property taken. The basic rule is that the property owner must be paid the reasonable value of his net loss at the time of the taking and that any gain as a result of the taking itself is irrelevant. Under the Almota decision, certain expectancies not rising to property interests must also be considered.

[For more information on the "just compensation" requirement, see Casenote Law Outline on Property, Chapter 11, § I, Eminent Domain.]

NOTES:

UNITED STATES v. 564.54 ACRES OF LAND, MORE OR LESS
441 U.S. 506 (1979).

NATURE OF CASE: Appeal from judgment in action protesting the offer of compensation in a condemnation proceeding.

FACT SUMMARY: The Southeastern Pennsylvania Synod of the Lutheran Church in America (P) brought suit, protesting the compensation tendered it by the federal government (D) in the condemnation of its property along the Delaware River.

CONCISE RULE OF LAW: An owner is entitled to receive what a willing buyer would pay in cash to a willing seller at the time of the taking.

FACTS: The Southeastern Pennsylvania Synod of the Lutheran Church in America (P) operated three nonprofit summer camps along the Delaware River. The United States (D) initiated a condemnation proceeding to acquire the Synod's (P) land for a public recreational project, offering to pay the fair market value of the property. The Synod (P) rejected the offer, demanding a much greater sum, representing the replacement cost of developing functionally equivalent substitute facilities at a new site. This suit was commenced by the Synod (P). The government (D) appealed the court of appeals' conclusion that the public's loss of the benefit conferred by the camps was relevant to assessing the compensation due a private entity.

ISSUE: Is an owner entitled to receive what a willing buyer would pay in cash to a willing seller at the time of the taking?

HOLDING AND DECISION: (Marshall, J.) Yes. An owner is entitled to receive what a willing buyer would pay in cash to a willing seller at the time of the taking. The concept of fair market value has been chosen to strike a fair balance between the public's need and the claimant's loss upon condemnation of property for a public purpose. Here, the government's (D) expert witness presented evidence concerning eleven recent sales of comparable facilities in the vicinity. Thus, it seems clear that a readily discernible market value existed for the property. No circumstances here require suspension of the normal rules for determining just compensation. The Synod (P) is not entitled to recover for nontransferable values arising from its unique need for the property. Denial of such an award is justified by the necessity for a workable measure of valuation. Allowing the Synod (P) the fair market value of its property is thus consistent with the basic equitable principles of fairness underlying the Just Compensation Clause.

EDITOR'S ANALYSIS: The Court has refused to designate market value as the sole measure of just compensation, noting that there are situations where this standard is inappropriate. Here, the fact that the camps may have benefited the community did not warrant compensating the Synod (P) differently from other private owners. In a subsequent case, United States v. 50 Acres of Land, 469 U.S. 24 (1984), involving a public entity with a legal obligation to replace the facilities lost by the taking, the Court also held that fair market value of the property taken was the correct measure of compensation.

[For more information on the concept of fair market value, see Casenote Law Outline on Property, Chapter 11, § I, Eminent Domain.]

NOTES:

HAWAII HOUSING AUTHORITY v. MIDKIFF
467 U.S. 229 (1984).

NATURE OF CASE: Appeal from a judgment declaring an eminent domain statute unconstitutional.

FACT SUMMARY: The court of appeals held a Hawaiian statute allowing for condemnation of private land for redistribution aimed at creating more fee estates was unconstitutional.

CONCISE RULE OF LAW: The Public Use Clause of the Fifth Amendment does not proscribe the exercise of eminent domain power where such is reasonably related to a conceivable public purpose.

FACTS: The State of Hawaii, through its Housing Authority, sought to redistribute land held in fee simple from a few families to the population in general. Condemnation proceedings were instituted, and Midkiff (P) and other fee holders sued, contending the statute allowing for such eminent domain exercise violated the Just Compensation Clause of the Fifth Amendment. The trial court upheld the statute, while the court of appeals reversed. The Authority (D) petitioned the Supreme Court for a writ of certiorari, contending the statute was reasonably related to a legitimate purpose and was constitutional.

ISSUE: Does the Public Use Clause of the Fifth Amendment proscribe the exercise of eminent domain power where such is reasonably related to a conceivable public purpose?

HOLDING AND DECISION: (O'Connor, J.) No. The Public Use Clause of the Fifth Amendment does not proscribe the exercise of eminent domain power where such is reasonably related to a conceivable public purpose. The purpose of the statute in this case was to allow for more widespread land ownership. This in turn would allow for a more diversified program of land development and add stability to the state's economy. As a result, the statute was clearly related to a legitimate governmental interest, and it therefore was constitutional. Reversed.

EDITOR'S ANALYSIS: The greatest criticism of the result in this case is that it sanctions the taking of private property, albeit for just compensation, in order to benefit another private party. The traditional use of the eminent domain power involves the ultimate use of the land by the condemning governmental entity. However, the police power of the individual state is relied upon to justify the condemnation of property in this and similar cases, and so long as a governmental purpose can be identified, the action will be upheld.

[For more information on the "public use" requirement, see Casenote Law Outline on Property, Chapter 11, § I, Eminent Domain.]

POLETOWN NEIGHBORHOOD
COUNCIL v. CITY OF DETROIT

410 Mich. 616, 304 N.W.2d 455 (1981).

NATURE OF CASE: Appeal from a dismissal of an action to preclude condemnation of land.

FACT SUMMARY: Poletown (P) contended that the city of Detroit (D) could not condemn land for the benefit of a private corporation.

CONCISE RULE OF LAW: Condemnation of property pursuant to a public purpose is valid.

FACTS: Detroit (D) sought to condemn land in order to sell it to G.M. for the construction of an automobile assembly plant. The purpose of the condemnation was to promote industry and provide economic stability. Poletown (P) sued, contending the power of eminent domain could not be exercised for private profit. The trial court dismissed the complaint, and Poletown (P) appealed.

ISSUE: Is condemnation of property pursuant to a public purpose valid?

HOLDING AND DECISION: (Per curiam) Yes. Condemnation of property pursuant to a public purpose is valid. In this case, the paramount objective was to stimulate industry. Even though it ultimately profited the private corporation, the condemnation added to the general welfare. Therefore, such condemnation was valid. Affirmed.

DISSENT: (Ryan, J.) The right to own and occupy land must not be subordinated to private corporate interests unless the use of the land condemned by or for the corporation is invested with public attributes sufficient to fairly deem the corporate activity governmental. Here, individual citizens are forced to suffer great social dislocation to permit a private corporation to construct a plant where it deems it most profitable. With this case, the court has subordinated a constitutional right to private corporate interests.

EDITOR'S ANALYSIS: The overwhelming rationale behind the validity of a condemnation proceeding is its public nature. A taking of private property by a governmental entity must be for a public purpose. If this purpose overrides the private benefit, it is valid. If it does not, it is a taking for private use and is invalid.

[For more information on condemnation for a public purpose, see Casenote Law Outline on Property, Chapter 11, § I, Eminent Domain.]

UNITED STATES v. SIOUX NATION OF INDIANS
448 U.S. 371 (1980).

NATURE OF CASE: Appeal from a judgment awarding just compensation for a taking.

FACT SUMMARY: After the United States (D) and the Sioux Nation (P) signed the Fort Laramie Treaty, pledging that certain land, including the Black Hills, would be used and occupied solely by the Sioux (P), the United States coerced the Sioux (P) into signing a later agreement, ceding the Black Hills and other lands to the United States (D) in exchange for subsistence rations.

CONCISE RULE OF LAW: Where Congress makes a good faith effort to give Native Americans the full value of their land and thus merely transmutes the property from land to money, there is no taking.

FACTS: In 1868, the United States (D) and the Sioux Nation (P) signed the Fort Laramie Treaty, pledging that the Great Sioux Reservation, including the Black Hills, would be set apart for the absolute and undisturbed use and occupation of the Sioux Nation (P). The Treaty provided that any cession of the lands in the reservation would be agreed to by 3/4 of the adult males. In response to rumors that the Black Hills contained gold, prospectors began trespassing on the reservation. The United States (D) later coerced the Sioux (P) into signing a treaty, giving up their right to the Black Hills and other lands in the reservation in exchange for subsistence rations. This agreement was enacted into law in 1877, abrogating the Fort Laramie Treaty. The Sioux Nation (P) regarded this as a breach of the United States's (D) obligation to reserve the Hills in perpetuity for occupation by the Sioux (P). The Court of Claims affirmed a finding by the Indian Claims Commission that the 1877 Act effected a taking of the Black Hills and of rights-of-way across the reservation, but reversed the Commission's determination that the Sioux Nation (P) was also entitled to compensation for the gold that had been taken. The United States (D) appealed.

ISSUE: Where Congress makes a good faith effort to give Native Americans the full value of their land and thus merely transmutes the property from land to money, is there a taking?

HOLDING AND DECISION: (Blackmun, J.) No. Where Congress makes a good faith effort to give Native Americans the full value of their land and thus merely transmutes the property from land to money, there is no taking. The Court of Claims correctly applied the above legal standard. Moreover, the court correctly found that the only item of consideration for the land the government (D) took from the Sioux (P) was the requirement to furnish them with rations until they became self-sufficient. It is immaterial that it ultimately cost the United States (D) $43 million to fulfill that obligation. The critical inquiry is how Congress viewed the obligation it was assuming. There is no basis for believing that Congress anticipated that it would take the Sioux (P) such a lengthy period of time to become self-sufficient. Thus, the 1877 Act effected a taking of tribal property, which had been set aside for the exclusive occupation of the Sioux (P) by the Fort Laramie Treaty of 1868. That taking implied an obligation on the part of the Government (P) to make just compensation to the Sioux Nation (P), and that obligation, including an award of interest, must now, at last, be paid.

DISSENT: (Rehnquist, J.) There were undoubtedly greed, cupidity, and other less-than-admirable tactics employed by the government (D) during the Black Hills episode in the settlement of the West, but the Indians did not lack their share of villainy either. It seems quite unfair to judge by the light of "revisionist" historians or the mores of another era actions that were taken under pressure of time more than a century ago.

EDITOR'S ANALYSIS: The "good faith effort" test applied by the Court in the instant case was first developed by the Court of Claims in its decision in Three Tribes of Fort Berthold Reservation v. United States, 390 F.2d 686 (Ct. Cl. 1968). The Fort Berthold test was designed to reconcile two lines of cases decided by the Court that seemingly were in conflict. The first line, exemplified by Lone Wolf v. Hitchcock, 187 U.S. 553 (1903), recognized that Congress possesses a paramount power over the property of Indians, by reason of its exercise of guardianship over their interests, and that such authority might be implied, even though opposed to the strict letter of a treaty with the Indians. The second line, seen in Shoshone Tribe v. United States, 299 U.S. 476 (1937), concedes Congress' paramount power over Indian property, but holds, nonetheless, that the power does not enable the government to give the tribal lands to others, or to appropriate them to its own purposes, without rendering, or assuming an obligation to render, just compensation. In Shoshone Tribe, Justice Cardozo declared that "Spoliation is not management."

[For more information on requirement of a taking, see Casenote Law Outline on Property, Chapter 11, § I, Eminent Domain.]

NOTES:

CHAPTER 13
PROPERTY IN PEOPLE

QUICK REFERENCE RULES OF LAW

1. **Slavery.** The descendants of Africans who were imported into this country and sold and held as slaves are not citizens of a state within the meaning of the federal constitution, whether or not they are emancipated. (Dred Scott v. Sanford)

2. **Children.** A "surrogacy contract" wherein a woman agrees to have a child and surrender it is void. (In the Matter of Baby M)

3. **American Indian Human Remains.** A burial ground used as a public graveyard prior to the enactment of the cemetery law is not protected under that law as a public cemetery. (Wana the Bear v. Community Construction, Inc.)

DRED SCOTT v. SANFORD
60 U.S. (1 How.) 393 (1857).

NATURE OF CASE: Appeal from a judgment dismissing an action by a slave to assert the title of himself and his family to freedom.

FACT SUMMARY: Scott (P) brought this action, asserting that he and his family, who were held as slaves by Sanford (D), were entitled to freedom.

CONCISE RULE OF LAW: The descendants of Africans who were imported into this country and sold and held as slaves are not citizens of a state within the meaning of the federal constitution, whether or not they are emancipated.

FACTS: Dred Scott (P) and his family were held as slaves by Sanford (D) in the state of Missouri. Scott (P) brought this action, asserting that he and his family were entitled to freedom. Although Scott (P) and his family were held as slaves in Missouri, Sanford (D) was a resident of New York state. Thus, Scott (P) claimed the circuit court had diversity jurisdiction, since the parties were "citizens" of different states. The lower court dismissed the case, and Scott (P) appealed.

ISSUE: Are the descendants of Africans who were imported into this country and sold and held as slaves citizens of a state within the meaning of the federal Constitution, whether or not they are emancipated?

HOLDING AND DECISION: (Taney, C.J.) No. The descendants of Africans who were imported into this country and sold and held as slaves are not citizens of a state within the meaning of the federal Constitution, whether or not they are emancipated. When the Constitution was written, African slaves were considered as an inferior class of beings who had been subjugated by the dominant race and, whether emancipated or not, remained subject to their authority, with no rights or privileges other than the ones those in power chose to grant them. Thus, the words "people of the United States" and "citizens" can not be held to include persons who are descendants of Africans who were imported into this country to be held and sold as slaves. Since they are not citizens, they are not entitled to all the rights, privileges, and immunities guaranteed by the Constitution. One of those rights is the privilege of suing in a U.S. court. It follows, therefore, that Scott (P) is not a citizen of the state of Missouri within the meaning of the Constitution of the United States, and he is not entitled to sue in its courts.

EDITOR'S ANALYSIS: The Court also declared that no state could, by any act or law of its own, introduce a new member into the political community created by the U.S. Constitution. While the language of the Declaration of Independence would seem to embrace the whole human family, the Court found it too clear that the enslaved African race were not intended to be included. For if the language would embrace them, the Court concluded, the conduct of those who framed the Declaration of Independence would have been utterly and flagrantly inconsistent with the principles they asserted, since many of them were themselves slaveowners.

NOTES:

MATTER OF BABY M

N.J. Sup. Ct., 109 N.J. 396, 537 A.2d 1227 (1988).

NATURE OF CASE: Appeal of order determining parentage and child custody.

FACT SUMMARY: Whitehead (D) reneged on an agreement to provide a baby fathered by Stern (P) and give it up to the Sterns (P).

CONCISE RULE OF LAW: A "surrogacy contract" wherein a woman agrees to have a child and surrender it is void.

FACTS: Elizabeth Stern (P) did not wish to give birth due to a possible genetic defect. Nonetheless, the Sterns (P) wanted a baby. They contracted with Whitehead (D) that the latter would be inseminated by William Stern (P), give up the baby, and receive $10,000. Whitehead (D) had the baby, but did not want to give it up. Following a protracted series of maneuverings the Sterns (P) obtained custody. They filed a complaint seeking to have the contract enforced and custody permanently awarded to them. The trial court found the contract valid, awarded custody to the Sterns (P), and cut off Whitehead's (D) parental rights entirely. Whitehead (D) appealed.

ISSUE: Is a "surrogacy contract" wherein a woman agrees to have a child and surrender it void?

HOLDING AND DECISION: (Wilentz, J.) Yes. A "surrogacy contract" wherein a woman agrees to have a child and surrender it is void. A contract of this nature conflicts with at least three categories of statutes: (1) laws prohibiting the use of money in connection with adoptions; (2) laws requiring proof of parental unfitness prior to termination of parental rights; and (3) laws that make surrender of custody and consent to adoption revocable. Further, contracts of this type conflict with nonstatutory, but nonetheless accepted, policy considerations governing child placement. First and foremost of these is that the paramount consideration in deciding where a child shall be placed be the best interests of the child. A contract such as that in question gives no weight to that consideration. Also, such contracts, by favoring the natural father over the natural mother, conflict with the policy that natural parents shall receive equal considerations. Further, it is impossible not to conclude that such contracts constitute baby selling, which public policy strongly disfavors. For these reasons, contracts such as those at issue here are void. [The court went on to decide custody based on a best-interest-of-the-child test, and awarded custody to Mr. Stern (P), but reinstated Whitehead's (D) parental rights, including visitation.]

EDITOR'S ANALYSIS: This was one of the country's most closely watched cases in 1987 and 1988. It was the first major case on the validity of surrogate parenting contracts. What little legislative reaction that had occurred as of the time of this writing tended to codify the court's holding. The court's decision does not prohibit voluntary arrangements performed without consideration (i.e., payment to the natural mother).

WANA THE BEAR v. COMMUNITY CONSTRUCTION, INC.
Cal. Ct. App., 180 Cal. Rptr. 423 (1982).

NATURE OF CASE: Appeal from judgment in action seeking to enjoin development of an area that included a Native American burial ground.

FACT SUMMARY: Wana the Bear (P) filed suit to enjoin continued development, by Community Construction (D), of property containing a burial ground used by the Miwok Indians before they were driven out of the area.

CONCISE RULE OF LAW: A burial ground used as a public graveyard prior to the enactment of the cemetery law is not protected under that law as a public cemetery.

FACTS: While excavating property for development of a residential tract, Community Construction (D) uncovered human remains on the property. Community Construction (D) continued developing the property, disinterring the remains of over 200 human beings in the process. The burial ground had been used by the Miwok Indians until they were driven out of the area between 1850 and 1870. California's applicable cemetery law was enacted in 1872. Wana the Bear (P), descendant of the Bear People Lodge of the Miwok Indians and related to some or all of the persons whose remains lay there, brought suit to enjoin further excavation and other desecration of the property. The lower court found that the burial ground was not a cemetery entitled to protection under the California cemetery law. Wana the Bear (P) appealed.

ISSUE: Is a burial ground used as a public graveyard prior to the enactment of the cemetery law protected under that law as a public cemetery?

HOLDING AND DECISION: (Blease, J.) No. A burial ground used as a public graveyard prior to the enactment of the cemetery law is not protected under that law as a public cemetery. The 1854 cemetery law applied to burial sites created prior to 1872. However, the 1854 law was not incorporated into the 1872 law. The 1872 law contained a prescriptive use condition, vesting title of the graveyard in the city or village using it only when the land was used as a burial ground continuously, without interruption, for five years. In addition, the new law further declared that no part of the code was retroactive unless expressly so declared. The Miwoks were no longer using the burial ground when the new law replaced the 1854 law. Therefore, the burial ground was not made a cemetery by the operation of the 1872 law. The legislative judgment is binding on this court in the absence of a supervening constitutional right, and none has been claimed. Affirmed.

EDITOR'S ANALYSIS: A public cemetery is generally created by one of two methods, dedication or prescriptive use. After the decision in this case, the California legislature enacted legislation providing for the protection of American Indian burial sites. Under the new legislation, when property owners find American Indian remains on their property, they must notify public officials and meet with representatives of the affected tribes to negotiate for reburial of the remains and any other objects found with them.

NOTES:

NOTES

NOTES

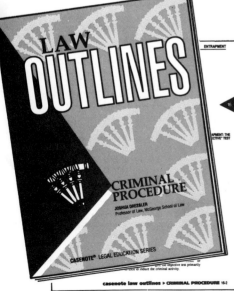